Rouen

Mont St. Michel

St James

Rennes

PARIS

Angers

TOURS
①

VÉZELAY
②

Parthenay   Poitiers

Cluny

Aulnay

Saintes

Limoges

Blaye

Perigueux

Bordeaux

Le PUY
③

Condom   Conques

Saint Sever   Aire   Moissac

Eauze

Montpellier   St Gilles

Ostabat
de Port   Auch   Toulouse   ARLES
④

Roncevaux

Pamplona

tella

ño

THE WAY OF
SAINT JAMES

1 St James on the Sion Cope

THE WAY OF
SAINT JAMES

*or the Pilgrims' Road
to Santiago*

T. A. LAYTON

LONDON   GEORGE ALLEN & UNWIN LTD
Ruskin House   Museum Street

First published in 1976

Printed in Great Britain
in 12 point Plantin type
by Cox & Wyman Ltd.
London, Fakenham and Reading

To
ELEANOR
(again)
with
ALICE
(added)

Contents

Illustrations

Sources: Photographs numbered 2 to 4 were taken by the author; those numbered 5 to 15 were supplied by the Spanish National Tourist Office; the frontispiece was provided by the Victoria and Albert Museum.

Chapter 1

ST JAMES AND THE SHELL
IN ENGLAND

For seven hundred years Christian Spaniards fought endlessly to drive the Arabs from their land. It was more a holy war than one waged against any severe oppression, and they were helped in their campaign by the miraculous discovery of the body of the apostle St James in the extreme north-west of Spain, for he later appeared armour-clad on a charger and helped the Spaniards to win a great battle against the infidel.

Soon he became something more than the patron saint of Spain; he was their spiritual crusader and the battle cry became '*Santiago y cierra España!*' – 'Saint James and close the ranks, Spain!'

But apart from his valour on the battlefield St Jacques, as the French, who did so much for the pilgrimage, called him, was also fulfilling that supreme function expected of any saint who has a church raised in his honour; that he should work miracles.

For with the Dark Ages over, people in Europe wanted to travel and see the sights, and the sights in those days were the great churches which housed holy relics or entire bodies of the saints; in some cases the sanctity of these places and relics was so powerful that the deaf were made to hear and the blind to see. Even if the traveller were fit he benefited. Thus it was that the clergy, who were always wanting money to build more churches and feed the poor, vied with each other in their relic-hunting to get the maximum attendances at their own places of worship.

The first pilgrimage started as a church walk imposed by a priest as an atonement for sin. It was dangerous on account of robbers; it was arduous through having to tramp over mountain passes; and it was extremely uncomfortable with, in the beginning, nowhere proper to halt. But such walks became more and more popular, until the riff-raff thought it profitable to see what pickings they could get from them; then the pilgrims were joined by minstrels, thieves, good-time holiday-makers, and especially confidence tricksters.

The worse your sin the longer your pilgrimage had to be, and the three most remote objectives for an Anglo-Saxon happened to be the three most important in Christendom; they were Jerusalem, Rome, and Santiago in Galicia, the extreme north-western tip of Spain, where St James the Greater was buried.

You will hear in the next chapter how his body was miraculously transported to Spain, but it is important now to take a look around England at places where emblems of the saint can still be seen. These emblems are a scallop shell, a scrip or purse or satchel, a staff, and a big floppy wide-brimmed hat, usually turned up at the front.

The staff is a stout stick such as any country walker might use on a long tramp, but the scrip, or satchel – it takes more different forms than the other emblems – was just a container for food and belongings, and the hat was the sort of thing that a traveller would wear if he wanted protection from the fierce summer sun in the Pyrenees.

By far the most important emblem, however, because it lends itself so well to all forms of decoration, is the scallop shell whose name in French is indeed 'St James' Shell' – *coquille St Jacques*. The reason for the shell's importance at Compostela stems from a curious legend, but the wearing of it in the St James hat was far from a gimmick – it was a proof that the wearer had been to the shrine.

Some have cynically suggested that as some form of token was needed for pilgrims to take back to their native land the shell was chosen because the sea-shore abounded with them, but the legend has it that the horse of the bridegroom at a brilliant marriage procession bolted into the sea – this was at Padrón – at the very moment when the boat carrying St James' body was approaching. When the horse surfaced, to the amazement of all it was seen that the rider was covered from head to foot with scallop shells, whereupon one of the disciples took one of them, scooped up the sea water and baptised the bridegroom.

You will find representations of the shell on household silver, china plates, family crests, the coats of arms of many towns, on badges, in pictures, but above all on statues, rood screens, reredos and stained glass in cathedrals and churches. It also appears on hundreds of coats of arms in *Burke's Peerage and Landed Gentry*, supposedly to signify that the family had been to Compostela, but my researches show that this was hardly ever the case.

Although there would have been a trickle of pilgrims to Santiago from the ninth century onwards, that trickle did not become a flood until the twelfth century, which was the 'Golden Age of Christianity'. By then it was world famous. Pope Calixtus II in his *Book of Saint James*,[1] writing around AD 1150 in what was really a propaganda guide for those who set out from Cluny, writes:

'They come, they come from all climates and nations of the world and even further away, French, Normans, Scots, Irish, Welsh, Teutons, Gascons, those from Navarre, Basques, Provincials, Anglo-Saxons, Britons, those from Cornwall, Flamands, Frisians, Italians, those from Poitiers, Danes, Norwegians, Russians, Sicilians, Asians, Indians, Cretans, Jerusalemers, Antiochans, Arabs, Moors, Lybians, and many others of all tongues, who come in companies or phalanxes and they all sing in unison to the Apostle. One cannot contemplate without marvelling the spectacle of the cohorts of pilgrims walking around the altar of this venerable saint. In one corner will be found Teutons, in another the French, in another Italians, all with lighted candles in their hands in such a way that the cathedral is lit up as resplendently as on one of the lightest of summer days.

'And they keep vigil and chant songs to the accompaniment of a multitude of musical instruments; lyres, zithers, tympans,[2] flutes, fifes, trumpets, harps, violas, bagpipes and other diverse classes of musical instruments. Here some will be lamenting their sins, others will be giving alms to the blind, while others will be reading psalms. Here will be heard all kinds of languages and the various voices and songs of strangers.'

Of course, when anyone had been on such a momentous walk as this it was only natural that he should want to have a written record of his adventures and give some useful advice to future

---

[1] Although the book was actually written, it was in fact falsely attributed to Calixtus II for propaganda reasons.

[2] I do not think they would have used drums or tamberines in the Cathedral but (in another sense of this word) it would more likely have been an ancient Irish stringed instrument played with a bow – a tiompan.

travellers. The two most important works of the fifteenth century are *Purchas His Pilgrims* and a Latin text by William Wey. This first is a quaint poem (author unknown) in rhyming couplets, published in 1625, and in the Cotton Collection in the British Museum.

That part referring to the journey to Compostela alone consists of one hundred rhyming couplets. It is important to mention here that although it was printed and published in the early seventeenth century it describes a period over two hundred years earlier, when it was actually written. Spanish scholars have placed its date between 1370 and 1450, mainly on account of the mention of a Navarese coin minted during the reign of Carlos II.

The work opens with these words:

'Here beginnith the way which is marked and made wit Mont Joies from the Lond of Engelond unto Sent Jamiz in Galis and from thennez to Rome and from thennez to Jerusalem, and the manner of her governance and namez of her silver that they use be all of that waie.'

Purchas is not very accurate, but he takes a great interest in the exchange rate. What follows is an abridgement:

'In the name of the Father who sits on the throne of Jesus and the Holy Ghost, I want to tell you how I travelled to Saint James. First I went to Plymouth and crossed to Brittany, where I rested two days, then on to Bordeaux, a fine city where I rested two days. Then on to Saint Jean Pied de Port, the first definite town of Navarre. Here men pay a tribute according to how much gold they have. Then to Roncevalles, a dark stretch where food is most necessary and my mouth became parched. Then on to Pamplona, Navarre's chief city and then on to Logrono, and then on to Santo Domingo. Here the Jews are the overlords. Next is Puente la Reina, which is in the realm of the King of Spain. Next I went on to León, passing several pretty towns, but here you must pay for your passage or you will not get any further. In this region women do not wear woollen clothing but are dressed all in leather. Here the wine is as thick as blood, which certainly makes men lustful; and there is no bedding nor are there tables to eat on. Here they all sit around on the floor and eat in company as they do in Ireland.

'From León I went over the moor to Astorga, after which come the great mountains and we got to Villafranca (del Bierzo), a lovely country where there are vines and raspberries.[1]

'Then on to Lugo, after which there are many villages until we come to Mont Joie, where there are four pillars of stone set in a very stately way.

'Then one sees the great cathedral, which has not many windows, and where there are seven cardinals to grant pardons to pilgrims.'

The other English traveller of the same period did not start from Bristol but from the almost equally important pilgrim departure port of Weymouth. Setting off on 17 May 1456 with a licence from King Henry the Sixth, William Wey, fellow of Eton College, also recorded his experiences, but in Latin. Wey was nothing if not observant, for he tells us that he went out with a convoy of six ships (one was from Lymington) and that the sea journey to Corunna (Grwne) took eight days. He had, of course, as he especially mentions, obtained a licence from his 'king and founder', Henry VI.

He was duly impressed with the splendour of the ceremonies at the cathedral and with the mitred cardinals, and he gave a summary of a sermon he heard, and reported in addition two miracles performed by St James. But he was not above giving advice to future pilgrims, such as to take 'a lytel cawdron', a frying pan, dishes, cups, and other such necessities.

As the flood of pilgrims from England grew so did those returning wish to have in their churches mementos of their wonderful journey, and they can be seen all over the country.

Winscombe town in Somerset, possibly from shame at its ugliness, moved away down the valley from the beautiful church which massively dominates the eye from whatever direction you come. Built in the fourteenth to fifteenth century, it is certain that the striking position of the site was no accident. The Winscombe valley is L-shaped; so that all the parishioners who were scattered in farmsteads and hamlets all around the valley should be continuously reminded of their Sunday duty, the church builder selected the one spot, a small ledge half-way up the north face of Wavering Down, where his handiwork could be seen from a surprising number of viewpoints. I knew that the church was of exceptional interest for my purpose, so I wrote to the vicar, the Reverend Bernard Salmon, who replied:

.   .   .   .   .

[1] *The raspis groeth ther in the waie.*

'Saint James' Church, Winscombe has more than one representation of her patron saint. Most of these are medieval.

'One you mention is in the glass in the south aisle. The fifteenth-century glass was sympathetically restored in the nineteenth century, but there are also certain pieces missing.

'Saint James carried a staff in his left hand and in his right (which is missing and whose position is not clear) a book, though I suspect that, too, is out of position. He is barefoot and wears a blue chasuble.

'The other ancient figure is in stone. The features are weathered, since he stands in a niche on the east face of the tower above roof level. I take it that this would be contemporary with the tower (built between 1380 and 1440), and if you wanted to get a closer look at the latter it would have to be from the roof. But it so happens that this summer the tower will be partly clad in scaffolding for repairs which will afford a unique view of the carving.'

The scaffolding was not yet up and I had arrived unannounced, but I eventually found a spiral staircase and negotiated a heavy iron trap-door with an exceedingly rusty iron bolt. I finally stepped out in the blazing sunshine upon the lead-covered roof of the church; and there on the tower, some fifteen feet up, was the statue of the saint in excellent condition.

Alas! The roof was not flat, for along the centre ran another steeply angled roof which housed the nave of the church below. The sun was brilliantly in the right place and I had two cameras slung around my waist, but the slope was too dangerously steep in spite of my rubber-soled shoes. So I ran half-way up, steadied myself with my left hand and clicked with my right, fell deliberately and slid down.

My next trip was to East Anglia. There cannot be many roads in England which half-circle a city town with houses numbered up to five hundred, but such is Unthank in Norwich and here I put up at a modestly clean bed and breakfast hotel prior to visiting Dennis King, owner of the stained-glass works which bears his name.

I picked him up near the Romany Rye Arms at his house in George Borrow Road, named after another famous traveller in Spain, and we were soon in his glass works in the centre of Norwich. From father to son for half a century the Kings have loved stained glass and Dennis King was able to plan my minor pilgrimage in a circuit so that I did not cover my tracks twice. 'But don't call at the Long Melford or North Tuddenham churches,' he said, 'since both of the Saint James windows are in my workshop for repair.'

He took me up to his workshop, where there were a large number of glass panelled tables, and flicked on a light which brilliantly lit the stained glass lying upon them. I marvelled at the mellowness of the blues and yellows and the thought that they had remained unbroken for half a thousand years.

Ranworth was my first place of call, to visit Canon Hugh Blackburne, the Bishop's Chaplain for the Broads. The whole of this part of Norfolk is famous for its painted screens, but a report of the Society of Antiquaries with reference to the Ranworth rood screen states that of the forty or so in Norfolk this one is taken as a whole to be the most perfect, though in certain minor details the paintings on others are finer. The reason for its uniqueness lies in the fact that the screen is built across the entire width of the church and, rarer still, it has the parclose[1] wings which enclose the two side altars restored to their original position.

Canon Blackburne pointed out to me that, just as the Victorians in their stupid craze for decency had the legs of their pianos enclosed in little trousers, so did the Puritans try to paint out all the fleshy parts of any saintly portrait whenever they saw something which offended them.

These daubs of paint were put on the emblems as well as the flesh and feet of the saints, but at Ranworth – the screen was painted by more than one artist – the experts think that the paint over the original must have been quickly removed by well-wishers; had it been allowed to dry it would have been ineradicable. Also, a blessing in disguise, the whole screen was whitewashed at a later date and this may have protected the original paint in the late eighteenth century.

Anyway St James is there in the third panel from the left, facing the altar with both hands – one with the scallop[2] painted out, though his staff, purse and hat are clearly visible.

Turning north towards Cromer I next visited Edingthorpe church. A great number of these very old churches in Norfolk and Suffolk are well away from the present villages, but this one was exceptionally isolated, being not only along a tiny cart track but then for several hundred yards along a path through a barley field,

[1] A screen enclosing an altar.
[2] The scallop was also daubed out because this was a living thing.

where a man transported thither by a tricycle was cutting away with a scythe. Here, on a rood screen, was a very good St James with a scallop, but there was no one to talk to, so I went on to Beeston Regis near Sheringham to inspect the magnificent – I thought it almost as good as Ranworth's – rood screen at All Saints' Church, and again St James was third from the left.[1]

This church, with its late eleventh-century or early twelfth-century square tower, is in one of the most beautiful settings imaginable, for it is placed in splendid isolation in an immense high field, overlooking the sea.

To my west now was Walsingham, home of one of the great pilgrimages of the Middle Ages, resuscitated in the 1930s; it is only a mile away from Houghton St Giles – the hermit of Languedoc (d. 541) who protected a hunted hind – where the Reverend Alan Roe had told me that I must collect the key from him, as the church was kept locked. I did and the St James on the screen was well worth the visit, for this time he was, though still with staff, wallet and scallop, with brother St John the Evangelist and his mother Mary Salome. The scenery around here is particularly lovely, as was the setting of the church, so I made a slight detour to look at the much publicised tiny and ancient Slipper Chapel from whence pilgrims, taking off their shoes, walked barefoot to the Walsingham shrine.

Satisfied with my day – and seeing a good St James on a panel at the Church Museum at St Peter Hungate, Norwich – I went back for a good dinner at the Maid's Head and thence to bed. The next morning I turned my wheels due south and, bowling over that most exceptionally uninhabited part of England, Thetford Forest, I soon got to Bury St Edmunds.

There are roughly four hundred churches in England consecrated to St James and of these three-quarters were built before the seventeenth century and would therefore have connections with the cult of St James at Compostela. Of these the most important now functioning is the cathedral at Bury St Edmunds, built between 1510 and 1530. One thing is beyond all doubt: the connections here with the cult of St James in Spain are certain.

The man responsible for building the first church was a nephew of the great St Anselm, the devout and perhaps rather ostentatious Bishop Anselm (1121–48), who was sufficiently devoted to St James that he planned to make the journey to his shrine. It is fair

[1] Is that his traditional position?

to conjecture that he was going as a genuine penitent because, when he found himself unable, probably through ill health, to make the journey he petitioned the Pope to allow him to build and dedicate a church to St James and get exactly the same absolution as he would have done if he had gone to Compostela.

There remains almost nothing to be seen of Anselm's church except the stone shafts which were built into the outer side of the north wall of the present building, but these are quite clearly visible. The nave of the present church was started about 1502 by one of the great church builders of the time, John Wastell, who lived most of his life in Bury St Edmunds. The church was still building when he died in 1515 aged fifty-five; it must have looked a fine church, even half-finished, because King Edward VI after the Reformation gave two hundred pounds towards its completion.

Bury St Edmunds is a town with a strong tourist attraction, but it has not allowed itself to be spoilt by the fact that it houses one of the greatest medieval abbeys of England. The best hotel is The Angel, an enormous establishment on one side of the great central square and overlooking the gigantic Great Gate of the Abbey, which was built between 1327 and 1346.

Dickens mentions The Angel in *Pickwick Papers* and so there is, of course, a Pickwick Snack Bar. But I settled, after being shown a good bedroom, for the restaurant and when congratulating the head waiter on the choices on the menu I was told that this was the first day under a new proprietor. Some of the dishes were imaginative without conceding to sensationalism, and they were well cooked:

Mushrooms stuffed with ham and prawn mixture dipped in batter, fried and served with a sweet sour sauce.

Smoked eel in cream and batter sauce with paprika potatoes.

I had the mushrooms followed by roast young guinea fowl with chestnut stuffing and felt so well after it that I asked the Provost, the Very Reverend John Waddington, if I could call that evening instead of the next morning.

Minutes later, over a 'Fundador', I was hearing more about the other buildings in the abbey grounds. They were great church builders these monks of St Edmund's monastery, for in addition to James' church they built those of St Margaret, of which only a few traces remain, and St Mary which, now the parish church, still stands so beautifully beside St James. Thereby hangs one rather ironic tale, for at the time of the Dissolution, had the monks not provided these three extra beautiful churches for the people, the great Abbey church might well have been spared.

As for St Mary's, we must remember that the church which Anselm built for love of the Apostle was only raised to cathedral status in 1914, after the new diocese of Ipswich and St Edmundsbury had been created in 1913, and that as St Mary's was considered far more beautiful there was much bitterness when finally the male saint won the day.

Verger Coomber took me round the cathedral the next morning and first showed me the huge Victorian stained glass St James which, with its crude red hat and over-sized scallop shell therein and fancy scrip, presents rather a vulgar portrayal. On the outside of the cathedral are carvings of the shell and wallet; they are only about two feet from the ground and, as I crouched painfully to photograph them, Mr Coomber said:

'You wouldn't have had to bend down like that when the monks were carving them, for they would have been over your head. You see, the road was then seven feet lower than it is now and in times of flood people had to come to the church on stilts.'

Then, quite a realist, Mr Coomber continued:

'Yes, the monks carved a lot of emblems on this front where there were plenty of passers by, but you won't see a single one on the longer side, which was not seen by the public.'

In London the most important remembrance of St James is the Court of St James, which derives its name from the fact that the Tudor palace, then just outside old London, was built upon a leper house consecrated to the saint.

There is also the ugly church of St James Garlick Hythe in the vintry ward of the City, which has a great scallop shell on the front, and there is also an equally ugly large statue on the St James in the Catholic church of his name built on the former site of the old Spanish Embassy in Spanish Place.

In the Victoria and Albert Museum there is a representation of him, along with the other saints, on the famous fifteenth-century Syon cope.[1] More interesting are the statues of the saint in the collection. These were carved out of alabaster or gypsum from mines at Chellaston in Derby and Tutbury in Staffordshire from 1420 to 1520; such carvings were quite a thriving 'cottage industry'.

---

[1] A vestment of silk made of a semi-circular piece of cloth worn in outdoor processions.

Every conceivable religious scene is portrayed, but in the showcase of the apostles it is noteworthy that St James has three statues while the others have only one each. And apart from the usual things connected with him one can see whelks – not scallop shells – in a line down the centre of his garment. But there is also a surprise: St Roch is there among the top brass with a scallop shell in his hat.

Although in the early days of the pilgrimage it was an actual scallop shell which the pilgrim fixed to his hat, as the centuries passed and the organisation became more sophisticated, reproduction badges were made in various metals and one rare example is to be seen in the London Museum.

I have mentioned that this was an age of relic hunting but may not have stressed sufficiently how important it was to have really good relics; one of the greatest to come to Britain was that which eventually found its way to Reading Abbey. The Abbey remains are in the Forebery Gardens and, unlike the ruins of Bury St Edmunds, those of the former mighty abbey church and monastery at Reading are sufficiently reduced and so tucked away as to attract no tourists whatever. They are, moreover, somewhat forbiddingly sited, for they abut upon Reading gaol.

The Abbey was founded on 18 June 1121 by King Henry I and the former magnificent romanesque church with its three naves was consecrated by Thomas à Beckett in 1164, during the reign of Henry II. According to various medieval chronicles, Princess Matilda, daughter of Henry I and wife of Emperor Henry V of Germany and the Rhine, finding herself a widow at twenty-three returned to England with her father, bringing with her two exceptional treasures: a hand of St James and the Imperial Crown. The King kept the latter for himself but presented the most holy relic to his monks at Reading, in which church he was planning to be laid to rest.[1] The Royal Charter making the gift states:

'Henry, King of England and Duke of Normandy to the Abbot and community of Reading greetings. Be it known that the glorious hand of the Blessed Saint James which Empress Matilda my daughter gave to me when she returned from Germany, I now give, following your request, to you and deed it for all time to the church

---

[1] Several writers state that the Abbey was founded to house the hand, but Matilda did not return to England with it until September 1126, five years after the foundation.

at Reading. I now demand that you receive it with all veneration and that you and your successors at this church look after it with the full degree of reverence that such an important relic of so great an Apostle demands.'

As might be expected, this put Reading Abbey right on the map. Soon the miracles started to occur which caused kings and bishops to be buried in the church, and this in turn caused further miracles; St James of Reading quickly became an English sanctuary as important as St Thomas of Canterbury or St Hugh of Lincoln.

As for the hand, thereby hangs a tale. Although Henry VIII and his Spanish wife Catherine of Aragon often visited the monastery in the early days of their marriage – Catherine called it her 'personal abbey' – and although Abbot Hugh Farringdon and the King were such good friends that they exchanged many a present, this did not prevent the former from being accused of high treason and executed and the rich Abbey from being plundered in 1539. But the Royal Commissioners did produce an inventory of its holy relics, including, to begin with, two fragments of the Holy Cross, the hand of Saint James, the cranium of Saint Philip, a bone of Mary Magdalene, and a hand of Saint Anastasius.[1] This last relic was the cause of one of the three Reading martyrs (the other two were Abbot Farringdon and Blessed John Eynon) being executed outside the gateway of Reading Abbey in 1539.

John Rugg, former prebendary of Chichester who was living in retirement at Reading Abbey, obviously thought that the hand of this saint was too holy to be given up to the royal plunderers and equally obviously he was caught with it red-handed. Thus it was that the most serious charge against him was that he had preserved the relic, 'knowing that His Majesty had sent visitors to the Abbey to put down such idolatry'.

We now have two hands, one of St James and one of St Anastasius, and the story continues. I have mentioned that Reading gaol lies adjacent to the ruins of the Abbey; in fact, one day in October 1786, when workmen were excavating for the foundations of the prison, they dug up an iron chest which was near to where the High Altar of the Abbey church used to be. They were probably more than surprised when they opened it for they found that the chest contained an embalmed hand which local experts, taking

[1] Martyr decapitated in Persia in AD 628, his remains being brought back to Constantinople during one of the crusades and from there taken to Rome.

2a Mont St Michel – where the pilgrims started from in France

2b A *palloza* or pre-Roman hut at Cebrero

3a   The ancient church at Cebrero

3b   The fortified church at Portomarin

time to the tune of half a century, pronounced to be that of a woman, and probably of Queen Adelisa the second wife of Henry I, who was buried in the Abbey with her husband. But other anti-quarians declared that it was a man's hand and affirmed that it must be that of St James. Correspondence was then started between Reading and Compostela; next a visit was made, and then in 1879 the tomb of the apostle was opened and the skeletons of James and two of his disciples appeared which, by a Papal bull of 1 November 1884 called *Omnipotens Deus,* declared the relics genuine. Unfortunately these were bones, whereas the embalmed hand was flesh, though one of the saint's arms lacked a hand.

But the reason why the hand – the right one – was not imme-diately transferred to Westminster Cathedral is that there is no record in the archives at Compostela that such a valuable relic was ever parted with, and this also has caused historians over the cen-turies to wonder how Matilda's Emperor husband came to possess the Apostle's hand, though it has been explained that it was the practice of European princes in the Middle Ages to exchange relics amongst themselves.

As to the hand itself, after a sojourn in Scotland it finally landed up in St Peter's Catholic Church at Marlow in Buckinghamshire, where it remains today, though the latest thought on the matter is that it is the hand of St Anastasius.

After Reading I took a careful look at the list I had compiled of sixty-five villages in Southern England and Yorkshire where repre-sentations of St James on stained glass, sculpted screens and so forth, could definitely be seen. Thus I went on to a church at South Leigh in Oxfordshire which, like that at Winscombe, is dedicated to the saint. Again, as at Winscombe, the church has been built on a small ridge above the surrounding farmland. The name Leigh is derived from Lege, an obsolete term meaning a glade in a forest. I had already written to the vicar, and the Reverend Hodgson had replied that he had been unable to find in the church the stained glass St James I thought was there, but in the vicarage garden there was a statue of a saint with a sword, which might be St James, since the church is dedicated to him.

When I got there I was warmly welcomed by the vicar, who took me to the statue in the rose bed, which was – alas! – of St Michael. But all was not over, for the little Japanese telescope I had bought came into its own at last. It had become increasingly clear that small sections of stained glass high up in church windows were not going to be easy to look at. I had on one occasion used a step ladder, but had given this up when a rather simple cleaner at Wisbech muttered dark threats about calling in the police, which so unnerved me that I nearly fell off. A telescope was the answer, but until now it had merely made much clearer what I already knew existed. At South Leigh people come from afar to look at something, unconnected with the patron saint, which is superb. It would have been churlish, therefore, not to have followed Mr Hodgson's pointed arm as he indicated certain important features of the enormous fourteenth- and fifteenth-century mural paintings which had been covered up by several coats of whitewash until they were found during restoration in 1872.

The *pièce de résistance* is on the south wall of the nave and is over twelve feet high. The theme is the Weighing of the Soul. In the centre is Archangel Michael with the scales; in one panel an evil spirit issues from the mouth of a dragon, trying to tilt the scales downwards and send the kneeling soul to perdition. The evil spirit appears to be winning, but no! The Blessed Virgin Mary is dropping beads from her rosary into the other side of the scales and all is well.

But I was still fairly sure that there was a fragment of stained glass representing St James somewhere in this church in South Leigh, which raised the problem of the difficulties that church restorers of very old stained glass have had to encounter. The trend over the past two hundred years has been to gather together all the very old fragments of stained glass and reposition them, all jumbled together, in any one window of the church. One's first reaction is to regard such a practice as absurd. But what else could or can be done? Not to remove them would mean that the wonderful old fragments would eventually fall to the ground and be broken. To remove and repair one or two segments of old glass and put them back means denying a whole modern stained-glass figure, and if a patron rich enough to endow one is in the offing it seems a pity to let the opportunity slip. Alternatively if you have half the body of a saintly figure you can build up the rest with modern glass; this is not satisfactory. At South Leigh, then, the fragments had all been assembled in the vestry but rather high up. It was a dull day; the pieces could not be distinguished with the naked eye. But with the telescope I could espy there in blue about half of a floppy hat with a white scallop shell placed right at the centre of the up-turned brim.

Lastly, still in Oxfordshire, I went to St Mary's Bampton Proper, where on buying the vicar's notes I read that the Reverend Selwyn Taborn regretted that Mrs Stroud's health prevented her from cleaning the church for the time being.

He certainly had a treasure, for the church is not only of superlative beauty and in a beautiful setting, but the inside is so magnificently polished that it would surely be voted 'Church of the Year' if ever such a competition were started. Mrs Stroud obviously puts much effort into polishing the red floor tiles until they sparkle, but I suspect that when she gives a light flick of a turkey feather broom to the most interesting thing in the church she does not realise what a rarity it is. This is a Gothic retable or reredos and one of the very, very few of its type in England. It is in stone and consists of a horizontal line of niches – the back is painted blue – and they are occupied by Our Lord and the twelve Apostles. The third from the left (as usual) is St James, with – the only one to wear one – a high hat, pilgrim's staff and large pouch.

Chapter 2

THE GOLDEN LEGEND

The first of the Apostles to suffer martyrdom by beheading, at the orders of King Herod Agrippa I and to please the Jews, was St James the Greater, future patron saint of Spain, around AD 44. The Gospels and the Acts of the Apostles say that he was the elder brother of St John Evangelist, that his mother was Salome – she who asked Christ if her two sons could sit on his right and left hands in his Kingdom – and his father Zebedee, a fisherman, both probably of good family, living probably at Bethsaida. The two young men were working for their father and were one day in the family ship with Zebedee on the shore of the lake of Genasareth when Jesus passed – he had just enrolled Peter and Andrew and promised to make them fishers of men. So the two brothers promptly left their father and joined Jesus, who gave them the surname Boanerges, or sons of thunder, on account of their impetuous spirits and fiery tempers.

This James was one of Christ's favourite disciples and he, along with Peter and John, were the sole spectators of the transfiguration.

That is all the biblical history. Butler, in his great *Lives of the Saints,* says that we have no authentic account of where St James preached and spread the gospel, although according to Spanish tradition he made an evangelising visit to that country, but the earliest known reference to this is only in the latter part of the seventh century, and even that was from an oriental and not a Spanish source.

Incredulous historians over the past centuries have doubted that it was physically possible for St James ever to have got to Spain, and what is surprising is that the learned St Isidore of

Seville (seventh century) twice makes mention of the Apostle *without* commenting that he had any particular affinity with Spain.

Then we have the almost damning negative evidence of St Julian, Archbishop of Toledo. When he died in Spain at the end of the seventh century he was the most important person in that country, he was acknowledged to be of outstanding ability and was a voluminous writer, one book being important enough, so he considered, to be dedicated to the King. In this work he mentions St James but says nothing about his having any connection with Spain. But does it really matter how much truth there is in a legend? If everyone had been as sceptical as this there would now be no glorious, mellow and majestic cathedral at Santiago de Compostela, and civilisation would be just that much poorer.

The story that grew up about St James came from many sources, but the best account comes from Blessed Jacques of Voraigne (now Varazze near Genoa), Archbishop of Genoa, born about the year 1230, who wrote the most popular stories of the saints in the Middle Ages. Voraigne was a man of exceptional ability and one of the youngest priests ever to be consecrated a bishop. Controlling as he did the vast revenues of his rich see, he became a wealthy man, though most of his money went to charity. But it is as a writer that he is chiefly remembered, and by far his most famous work was his *Liber Sanctorum*, now universally known as *The Golden Legend*. Caxton printed the first English edition at Westminster in 1483, and by 1500 there were known to be over seventy editions in Latin, eight in Italian, five in French and three each in English and Czech. It was the first best-seller ever printed.

Caxton's English is easy to read, but the spelling is so outrageous that the stories take time to 'translate', and so hold the modern reader up. 'Fals', 'moeve', and 'devylles' for false, move and devils respectively; 'pite', 'delyverer', 'gyve' and 'hool' for pity, deliverer, give and whole; 'recyve', 'bullis', 'hye', and 'sylver' for receive, bulls, high and silver. All very charming but time-consuming; in what follows, therefore, I have kept the style but modernised the spelling and slightly abridging the text.

OF SAINT JAMES THE MORE

'James the Apostle after the ascension was sent to Spain to sow there the words of Christ. But when he was there he profited but little for he converted into Christ's law but nine disciples of whom he left two there for to preach the word of God and took the other seven with him and returned again to Jerusalem. Here he converted only one man, after which there was an enchanter named Hermogenes with the Pharisees who sent his disciple Philetus to James to overcome him before all men, to prove that his preaching was false. But the apostle overcame him and did many miracles before him. Philetus then returned to Hermogenes and proved the doctrine of James to be true, and recounted to him his miracles. Philetus said he would like to be his disciple and councilled Hermogenes to do likewise.

'Then Hermogenes was wroth and by his craft and enchantments made Philetus in such wise that he might not move and said: "Now we shall see if thy James may save thee."

'Then Philetus sent his child to Saint James to let him have knowledge of this. Then Saint James sent to him his sudary[1] or kerchief and said: "Say to him that Our Lord redresseth them that are hurt and unbindeth them that are impressed."

'And as soon as he said so and touched the sudary he was unbounden and freed from all the enchanting of Hermogenes and he went joyfully to Saint James.

'Then Hermogenes was angry and called many devils and commanded them to bring him Saint James and Philetus to avenge himself on them.

'Then the devils came before Saint James and cried: "James the Apostle have pity on us!"

'To them James said: "Wherefore come ye to me?"

'And they said: "Hermogenes hath sent us to thee and to Philetus to bring you to him and the angels of God hath bound us with chains of fire and torment us."

'And James said: "The angels of God shall unbind you. Go ye to Hermogenes and bring him to me bound but hurt him not."

'Then they went and took Hermogenes and bound him and brought him so bound to Saint James.

'And the devils said to Hermogenes: "Thou sent us thither where we were strongly tormented and grievously bound."

'They also said to Saint James: "Give us power against him that we may avenge our wrongs."

---

[1] A napkin to wipe tears or sweat from the face; such cloths are especially venerated as the relic of a saint.

'But James turned to Philetus and said: "To the end that you do good for evil like as Christ bade us unbind him."

'Then Hermogenes was all confused and he went and brought the apostle all his books of his false craft for burning.

'But Saint James, because the odour of the burning might do evil to some fools,[1] made them to be cast into the sea.

'Then Hermogenes holding his feet said: "Oh deliverer of souls receive me as a penitent."

'And he began to be in the dread of our God.

'And when the Jews saw Hermogenes converted they were all moved of envy and they went unto Saint James and blamed him because he preached Jesus Christ crucified.

'Abiathar, who was the bishop that year, moved the people against him and then they put a cord round his back and brought him to Herod Agrippa. And when he was condemned to be beheaded a man with the palsy cried to him and the apostle gave him health and he was whole.

'Then the scribe named Josias who put the cord around his neck, seeing the miracle, fell down at his feet and demanded forgiveness and asked that he might be christened. But when Abiathar saw that, he commanded that Josias be smote on the mouth with fists and he sent a messenger to get consent for Josias to be beheaded with Saint James. And then Saint James desired a pot full of water, and therewith he baptised Josias, and anon both were beheaded and suffered martyrdom.

'Then his disciples took the body away by night for fear of the Jews and brought it to a ship and committed it unto the will of Our Lord and they all went in the ship without sail or rudder. And by the conduct of the angel of the Lord they arrived in Galicia in the kingdom[2] of Lupa.

'There was in Spain a queen which had the name and also by deserving of her life Lupa, which is as much as to say in English as a she-woolf.

'Then the disciples of Saint James took out his body and laid it upon a great stone. And anon the stone received the body into it as it had been soft wax.

'Then the disciples went to Lupa the queen and said to her: "Our Lord Jesus Christ hath sent to thee the body of his disciple

---

[1] i.e. that the smoke and flames might draw exaggerated attention.

[2] Royaume in Caxton's English text.

so that him though wouldest now receive alive thou shall receive dead."

'And they recited how they were come without any rudder to the ship and required a convenient place for his burial.

'And when the queen heard this she sent them unto a right cruel man of treachery and guile, who some say was the King of Spain, to get his consent for this matter. But he took them and put them in prison. And when he was at dinner the angel of the Lord opened the prison and let them escape.

'And when the King knew this he sent hastily knights to overtake them; but as these knights passed over a bridge, it broke and they fell in the water and were drowned. So when Lupa heard this she was much sorrowful, and when they came again to her, they did unfold to her of the agreement of the King.

'She answered: "Take the oxen I have in yonder mountain and yoke them to my cart or chariot and bring ye then the body of your master and build for him such place as you will."

'And this she said to them in guile and mocking for she knew well that they were not oxen but wild bulls, and supposed that they would never join them to her chariot, and even if they were so joined they would run hither and thither and would break the chariot and throw down the body and slay them.

'But there is no wisdom against God.

'And they that knew nothing of the evil courage [disposition] of the Queen went up to the mountain and found there a dragon casting fire at them and running towards them. And they made a sign of the cross and he broke in two pieces.

'Then they made the sign of the cross on the bulls and anon they were as meek as lambs. Then they took them and yoked them to the chariot and took the body of Saint James and the stone they had laid it on and placed it on the chariot and the wild bulls without the governing of anybody took it forthwith into the middle of the palace of Queen Lupa.

'And when she saw this she was abashed and believed and was christened and delivered to them all that they demanded and she deeded her palace into a church and endowed it greatly and ended her life in good works.'

Though Jacques de Voraigne has several stories – including one of a man being told by the devil to cut off his own genitals – of miracles wrought by St James, especially for those going on his pilgrimage,

St James as the Moor slayer on the church at León

4b   Christ in Majesty on the Church at Carrión de los Condes

5 Hermitage at Roncevalles

that is all he has to say about how the saint arrived and what happened to him in Spain.

Another ancient tradition has it that after the first Pentecost (the seventh Sunday after Easter) St James was given Spain as his place of mission and that he set forth for Andalucia probably in AD 39 but possibly 38 or 40. From Andalucia he went via Merida – of great importance in Roman-occupied times and even today a town with more Roman remains than any other save Tarragona – to a place then called Iria Flavia on the river Sar, quite near where it joins the river Ulla and about nine miles from the coast of Galicia. It is now called Padrón, a very important place in the history of the pilgrimage.

He does not get credit for any conversions, but he is supposed to have founded bishoprics in León and Astorga and one of his disciples, Pedro Rates, became Bishop of Braga (now in Portugal) and as such became the first bishop on the Iberian peninsula.

After this the saint wended his way along the then flourishing Roman road through Palencia, Osma, Numantis (splendid Roman ruins are to be seen there today) and on to Caesar Augusta, today known as Saragossa. Here it was that another legendary miracle connected with St James, though having no connection with Compostela, took place.

In this ancient city the Apostle only made eight converts; apart from this he was extremely depressed at the sight of the enslaved population and all in all he felt that his mission, so the legend goes, had been in vain. Things had to go on, however, and it was the custom to assemble his tiny party of Christians to play at night in some quiet place where they could be undisturbed.

Thus, at about midnight on a certain first of January they were praying quite close to the river Ebro when James heard angelic voices singing *Ave Maria Gratia Plena*, as though they were beginning matins. Kneeling in amazement, he saw that a multitude of angels was bringing the Virgin Mary to visit him in her mortal flesh. She was standing on a marble pillar, and when the angels had finished singing she said, 'This is the appointed place, James my son, in which I am honoured. Behold this pillar on which I stand. Jesus Christ has sent it by means of angels. Here build a church in my honour and there shall never cease to be Christians in Saragossa.'

This gave St James great joy. He built a church to enclose the sacred pillar and it was the first church in the world to be dedicated to the Virgin Mary. Before he left for Jerusalem and his martyrdom, the Apostle consecrated Athanasius as first bishop there, while Theodore, another disciple, was ordained as priest.

From other sources there are one or two very slight variations to the 'Golden Legend', stopping just short of telling us what happened to St James' body after it had been taken to Queen Lupa's palace and she had been converted. We learn that the Jews hated the saint so much that they actually threw the head and body into a field and that the person to whom the Queen sent the disciples in Galacia was not King of Spain but a Roman official.

The legend says that the disciples accompanied James in a boat, but another version has it that after his death the Apostles put the body on a barque and at that moment a prodigious wind arose and whisked the corpse right up into the rays of the sun and transported it towards the west. Utterly confounded, the disciples were frightened of losing their treasure and, devoured with curiosity, set off in a westerly direction, finding the body in the kingdom of Queen Lupa; it was she who had caused the corpse to be lifted from the barque and deposited on a great stone, which received the body in the way we have already heard.

We now come to the most important part of the legend, not mentioned by Jacques de Voraigne, which makes as neat an ending as you can wish for and makes a convenient starting point after the seven centuries of silence much commented upon.

Before leaving the mountain called Ilianus or Ilicino the disciples named it Pico Sacro, now the Sacred Mount,[1] and went down to the palace where the Queen was converted. After this the tamed bulls were allowed to wander off, or rather to lead the disciples, and going north-west after three leagues they halted (in a field given to them to build a mausoleum, adds one tradition) at a place where there may have been a ruin of some kind that could be made to serve as a crypt. They called the spot (later to become Santiago de Compostela) *liberium donum* or *libre-don* in memory of a free gift. Here they deposited the saint in a marble sarcophagus (one version is that they may have found something suitable for this purpose lying around) and then built an altar and a tiny chapel

---

[1] Some ten minutes south-east of Compostela.

above it. Then two of the disciples – a variation is that they were Athanasius and Theodore, after their work in Saragossa was done – kept watch over the saint's sepulchre until they died, where they are entombed beside their hero, while the rest of the disciples dispersed or returned to Palestine.

And after that the silence is complete for seven hundred years.

Chapter 3

SPAIN IN THE CENTURIES OF SILENCE

The unanimity with which all writers on the history of the pilgrimage have commented upon the seven centuries and more of silence concerning the very existence of St James in Spain makes me think that an outline sketch of the history of the Iberian peninsula up to the year 800 would at this point be welcome.

The three towns which I regard as most significant in the very early history of Spain are Cadiz, Sagunto and Cartagena. Cadiz is the Gadir (fortress) of the Phoenecians who founded it in 1100 BC. About 500 BC the Carthaginians occupied the town and from thence overran the entire southern part of the Iberian peninsula. In 200 BC Cadiz fell to the Roman legions and the African army was after seven hundred years forced back across the Straits, Cadiz was the last place to succumb.

Sagunto, which still has perhaps the best preserved Roman theatre in Spain, was called Saguntum and when Hannibal attacked it in 219 BC he sparked off the second Punic war, since Rome claimed that this heavily fortified town was under her protection.

Cartagena is with El Ferroll the most important naval base of Spain; far from beautiful, it has perhaps a worse selection of hotels than any other city in the country with as many as 150,000 inhabitants. Called Carthago Nova (New Carthage), it was founded by Hasdrubal, brother of Hannibal, as a strategic centre of Punic power and was brilliantly assaulted and captured by the younger Scipio in 209.

During this time the native inhabitants, seeing their own land used as a battlefield by two foreign powers, had fought indifferently on whichever side pleased them and indeed frequently changed sides as the fortunes of war favoured one general or the other. Little did they realise that the Romans thought of them as a vanquished foe and so started on a programme of romanising them with such thoroughness that Roman Spain can be said to have begun at this point.

Let us now see Spain with Roman eyes as they speedily took over the peninsula; our best source is the writings of Strabo of the first century B C. The Iberians as a whole, he considered, were war-like in disposition. They fought lightly, armed 'rather like bandits' with javelin, sword and sling. As horses were plentiful, foot soldiers and horse commonly fought together and their bravery in battle was surprising. And surprising, too, was their tenacious devotion to their leader, for whom they would gladly lay down their lives. Strabo held the theory that it was the fierce independence of the independent tribes which led to their downfall. He attributed the collapse of Greece to its division into small states, so that their local pride inhibited them from becoming united when an external enemy threatened. In the same way the fierce independence of the Iberian tribes, making their relationship one of continuous alarm, left them so nerve-racked that they lacked the ability to make common cause against a common threat, 'so the Romans conquered the tribes one by one and, although it took a long time, two hundred years or more, at length they had the country wholly under their feet'. The process of subjugation, however, was much quicker in the extreme east and south because the natives had experienced many generations of invasion and had conditioned themselves to a foreign overlordship and especially to the civilisation it brought with it, resulting in a better living standard.

But it seems to have taken the Iberians some years to realise that the Romans were in their land for good and so it was more than ten years after the fall of Carthage in 197 B C before the first serious wave of revolt took place. At one time it seemed that all might be lost to the Romans; further legions had to be drafted in and by 179 B C over 160,000 troops had been used to conquer 'this horrific and bellicose province'.

It was at this period that the *guerilla*, a uniquely peninsula term for a strategy, became recognised. The tribes, as has been said, lacked the cohesion needed for a big war but the favourable terrain of many parts of the country made it ideal for the 'little wars' and these proved most costly to the orthodox commanders.

All wars throw up a few great heroes and the greatest of all was at this time Viriatus. Though he was only a shepherd from the wilds of what was then known as Lusitania (present Portugal plus a large triangular part of Estremadura, bounded by Salamanca, Madrid and Merida) he was a born leader of men. For eight years, fighting honourably and chivalrously in contradistinction to Roman treachery and barbarity, he so harassed the Roman troops that at one time they actually rebelled. Viriatus' first success was in the Sierra Ronda, when some four thousand Romans were ambushed and put to the sword. Encouraged by this success, the Lusitanians marched in the next campaigning season into the La Mancha territory, into the centre of the Carpetani tribe and, claiming five thousand victims, advanced over the Guardarrama mountains to Segovia.

Viriatus' name is always coupled with the siege and ferocious bravery associated with the defence of the pre-Roman camp of Numantia. This place I warmly recommend – to those who travel by car – to visit. It lies near the banks of the river Douro and five miles from the town of Sonica in the province of that name. The ruins lie on high ground and an obelisk has been raised to commemorate the final siege gallantly endured in 133 B C. Modern maps show Numantia as a Roman ruin, but they are actually *pre*-Roman, as evidenced by the dramatic happenings there.

Around 143 B C the Roman commander Metellus had crushed all native opposition south of the Ebro but was obliged to leave the assault upon Numantia to his successor Scipio Aemelianus, who in two years was unable to make any headway, though his forces of 30,000 men outnumbered the defenders by well over three to one. In the end he negotiated a sort of peace with the Numantians, who for the third time in twelve years got the worst of the deal through Roman trickery.

Thereafter Roman morale fell into a severe decline and both veteran soldiers and recruits began so to dread the name of Numantia that frequently they rebelled on being ordered there. The inevitable end came when Scipio (Africanus), hero of the assault on Carthage twelve years previously, returned – public clamour in Rome was the cause – to Spain with an army of 60,000 men.

Historians think that they must have been a pretty poor bunch of soldiers since Scipio decided to take – and this was his prime reason for coming to the peninsula – Numantia by siege rather than assault. In the late summer of 134 B C he marched up the river

Ebro and arrived outside the fortified camp in October just in time to stop the Numantians getting in their grain. In 133 BC it was all over; the besieged men made a useless effort to get honourable terms and most of the four thousand men slew themselves rather than grant the conquerors their triumph. Without waiting for permission from Rome, Scipio made as good a job as he had at Carthage of razing Numantia to the ground and the first phase of the Roman subjugation of Spain was accomplished. With this defeat of her attempt to throw off the Roman yoke, Spain now passed into tranquil anonymity for just upon a century.

Then came the 'New Spanish Era'; until the late Middle Ages early historians and Iberian scribes were agreed that this was in 38 BC, the year that Augustus (even before he became Emperor) mounted a devastating attack on corruption and administrative abuses in the peninsula. To pave the way for far-reaching fiscal reforms Augustus made salaried officials of all the Spanish provincial governors. But it was a new general tax which needed certain measures of social reorganisation that historians considered the most important reform of all; it took place in the above-mentioned year.

The peace brought to the country by Augustus caused a decisive mingling of Roman and Iberian blood and it was not long before a colony had been founded at Carteia (El Rocadillo near Algeciras) solely for people of mixed parentage. And Latin, the language of the conqueror, soon became the speech of the populace. Certainly it was not classical Latin and it contained many a local word which made the Romans laugh, but it was still Latin; the native tongue had been forgotten.

Under Emperor Flavius (AD 59–96) Spain went through a period of economic growth which would be hailed today as a miracle. Gold, which hitherto had come only from Galacia, was now coming from the rivers Tagus and Douro; silver still came in great quantities from Cartagena and fresh deposits of iron ore were discovered on the east coast of Dianium (Denia)[1] to supplement the older ones of Cantabria.

But surely worth recording is that the silver age of Latin literature was dominated by peninsula names and that Lucan and the

---

[1] Rose Macaulay, in her great book *Fabled Shore*, says she would have been happy to have ended her days in Denia. It certainly is a charming town and lies between Valencia and Alicante.

two Senecas were born in Cordoba, which had been founded in AD 151 as a Roman colony and soon became the focus of the peninsula's intellectual life.

Then there was Trajan, one of the great Roman emperors: he was born in Italica near Seville in the year 98; two other emperors who achieved greatness, Hadrian (117–38) and Theodosius (378–95), were also Spanish born.

But while St James slept in his sepulchre in Galicia, Rome's power to defend herself against tribes from the north was becoming less and less effective. With an empire in decay, with frontiers straddled across Europe, it was impossible to top the so-called 'barbarians', and the date when those tribes which I have previously mentioned invaded Spain and established their settlements was AD 409.

We now have almost exactly four more centuries to cover before St James was discovered and it is time to discuss the rise of the Christian–Catholics in the peninsula and to assess what bearing the much-aligned Visigoths had on its permanence.

The second and third centuries saw the rise of scores of Christian communities; because their teaching did not approve of the methods of tax collection of the rapacious Roman Emperors, they suffered cruel repression and martyrdom, especially under Diocletian. But Constantine became converted to Christianity and so for a variety of political and personal reasons he announced (the edict of Milan) a new policy of religious toleration. All Roman citizens throughout the Empire could henceforth worship as they pleased and Christians of the new faith could even hold property.

About half a century later the last emperor to rule over an undivided Roman world, Theodosius, made Christianity the official religion. This recognition gave a tremendous stimulus to the organisation of the Church, and each provincial capital throughout the Empire became the seat of a bishopric with the Bishop of Rome as titular head or pope.

And among the very earliest of these popes was St Damasus (834), a Spaniard famous for his 'care for relics and resting places of martyrs and for his work in the draining and opening out and adornment of the sacred catacombs', says Butler in his *Lives of the Saints*, 'and the inscriptions he set thereon'.

Three of the early councils that met to discuss and organise the Christian Church were held in Spain. The first was at Illiberis

(Elvira[1] near Granada) in 313, when it was decided that the clergy should not marry and marriage with non-Christians was prohibited. The second was at Saragossa in 380, and the third at Toledo in 400.

But in Spain, far more than in any other province of the Roman Empire, the Church became an instrument of state policy, and compulsory orthodoxy, coupled with the fiercest intolerance of heresy, was a basis for state unity. It was during this formative century that seeds were sown, sub-consciously, of the almost blind readiness if need be to do battle for the Christian faith, not only in their own country but in other countries as well.

It was certainly during this century that the ultimate idea of a 'Catholic Majesty' took its roots.

It should be explained here how it happened that the Vandals (from whom we derive the name Andalucia), Alans and Suevi, who thought admittedly warlike were only wild tribes, were able to overrun Spain so easily. Historians are unanimous in the opinion that it resulted from the over-indulgence of both the emperors and the Roman people. Writing nearly a century ago, Stanley Lane-Poole, in his book *The Moors in Spain*,[2] says 'like many warlike peoples the Romans, when the work was accomplished and the world was at their feet, rested contentedly from their labours and abandoned themselves to pleasure'. And he continues:

'In Spain the richer classes were given over to luxury and sensuality; they lived only for eating and gambling. The mass of the people were either slaves or worse, labourers legally bound to the soil they cultivated. Between the rich and the poor was a middle class who were perhaps even worse off; for on their shoulders lay all the burden of supporting the state; they paid the taxes, performed the civil and military functions and supplied the money which the rich squandered on their luxuries.'

The comment that the burghers were worse off than slaves sounds a little exaggerated, but it is the stark truth.

As I have said, the Romanisation of Spain started by Augustus and pursued for a hundred years was brilliant in conception, for

---

[1] The estates of the Duke of Wellington are here.
[2] And the following is *his* footnote: 'The word Moor is conveniently used to signify Arabs and other Mohammedans in Spain, but properly it should only be applied to Berbers of North Africa and Spain.'

by giving the Spaniard the feeling that he 'belogned' instead of having the legions drawn off from the northern frontiers to subdue them, these very Spaniards could now be trusted to become soldiers for Rome. Then there were further inducements, grants of land, reductions in tribute, more justice, culminating in 74, when Vespasian enfranchised all the remaining towns in Spain and granted a charter of full Roman citizenship to chief magistrates – it is important to remember that they were freely elected annually – and their families in return for governing the town.

But gradually the greed of the second- and third-century Roman Emperors turned Roman 'citizenship' in the Spanish view from a coveted position to one that was dreaded. Election to the council soon became something to be avoided at all costs and so when fewer and fewer people came forward it was found necessary to make the post of magistrate hereditary. Then the degree of exaction became so awful that men abandoned their estates and even free men sold themselves into slavery.

Thus when the Teutonic tribes came, life in Spain was so miserable it did not matter much who were the rulers. And thus the Visigoths came, the Western Goths as distinguished from the Ostrogoths or Eastern Goths, who conquered and occupied Italy.

At this point it is necessary to state that the Visigoths were not the same as the Vandals; they were a cultured race. They had lived cheek by jowl with the Romans on the latter's northern frontier for centuries and for many years they were allies, even if uneasy ones, of Rome. And a condition of their partnership was that the Visigoths should embrace the Christian religion. They did so with such fervour that they possessed the Bible in their own language. It is noteworthy, however, that the Visigoths came to Spain differently from the Romans, for they arrived not as armies but as communities with their cattle, children and wives.

They were conquerors nevertheless, and it was indeed an extraordinary situation; the Hispano–Romans outnumbered the Visigoths by more than ten to one but they made no effort to win back the country which the invaders left to them in peace so long as their tributes were paid. Indeed, in 411 the Goths were accepted as *foederati* by the Hispano–Romans, receiving two-thirds of the territory.

The greatest king of the Visigoth period was Leovigild (568–86) and it was under him that Spain became united again and was for the first time ruled by a monarch instead of being a number of separate provinces of an Empire ruled from a distance.

This is the period of Spanish history least known and the least written about, but the extraordinary thing is that it was during the seventy-two years from the beginning of Leovigild's reign to the death of the great St Isidore of Seville in 636 that the fusion of state monarchy and the Roman Catholic religion took place which has lasted to modern times. Incidentally Leovigild was the first Gothic King to permit marriages between Goths and Hispano–Romans.

Until Leovigild's time the Visigoth king had been chosen from among the nobles as the best man to lead them into battle. But Leovigild (he was the first Visigothic king to try and give the monarchy some sort of dignity and to wear suitably regal clothes and a crown), aiming at an ordered stable society, changed this in favour of the hereditary concept. The plan did not work; the theory was all right, but the nobles, though they gave the idea token approval, were not ready for such advanced thinking. Indeed of the thirty-five Spanish Visigothic kings, nearly half died by assassination.

It was during the reign of Leovigild that Hermenegild comes dramatically on to the scene and it was through his actions that the Roman Catholic religion finally became stabilised in the peninsula. Canonised exactly a thousand years after his death, at the instance of Philip II, Hermenegild was the elder son of Leovigild, who, making the only political mistake of his life, had married the young man to Ingunda, the daughter of Sigbert I of Austria. The girl was an extremely devout *orthodox* (my italics) Catholic and soon, with the help of St Leonard, converted Hermenegild to the true faith.

A brief explanation is now necessary of the two Catholic religions of that time since otherwise the story would be incomplete. Bishop Arius (d. 336), the most obstinate old man that can ever have waved a crozier, started a heresy eventually called Arianism, which the Oxford English Dictionary says 'denied that Jesus was consubstantive or of the same essence as God' and adds that 'it split the Catholic church for a hundred years'. To put things a little more bluntly the Arians denied that the Son was begotten of God, but was merely the highest of created beings. The orthodox Catholics thought otherwise and their orthodoxy was established at perhaps the most important synod of all time, that of Nicaea in 325.

The Visigoths had been converted to Christianity, but to Arian

Christianity, by the Romans some two hundred years before, and it is now thought that they did so solely to gain their own political ends. In Spain the situation was reversed, for it was patently obvious that if they wanted to secure a real grip on the country they should allow themselves to be converted back to orthodox Catholicism.

At this time Toledo, that incredible natural fortress bounded on three sides by precipitous rock cliffs falling to the river Tagus, was the capital of the country, and one of the provinces, still the original delineation of Roman times, was Baetica (most of deep southern Spain), to which Leovigild sent his son as governor.

One is tempted to a fanciful surmise that the father knew what was going to happen, for when away from parental control Hermenegild raised the province against the Arian heresy of Toledo and there were five years of fighting before he sued for peace. In spite of the fact that Hermenegild had even proclaimed himself king in Seville and had even had coins minted ('Life to the King from God' they said), Leovigild did not immediately have him put to death when he returned as captive to Toledo. Indeed, a genuine reconciliation took place. But the old king wanted his son to revert to Arianism and this Hermenegild refused to do, and so in 585 in Tarragona he was killed – by one blow of an axe by his jailer a Goth called Sisibert.

One of the puzzles of Spanish history is whether Leovigild secretly took revenge on Arianism before he died. Both Pope Gregory the Great and an even greater Gregory, he of Tours, state that this was what had been reported to them and a telling point is that towards the end of his reign, after Hermenegild's death, there are no reports of any measures having been taken against the other sect. Modern historians, however, all take the view that Leovigild was not converted, and that he had himself was not secretly baptised around the time that his second son returned to orthodox Catholicism, even though Gregory expressly says that the reason he did not proclaim his conversion publicly was the fear that his people would revolt if it became known that he had abandoned Arianism.

What, however, is fact is that his son King Reccared was converted in February 587 and almost certainly that Leovigild had 'commended him to Saint Leander', who carried out the job.

It was with real cunning that Reccared moved before he made

his conversion public, for he called no less than three 'market research' preliminary meetings before the famous third Council of Toledo was assembled. At one of these he summoned a joint meeting of Arian and Catholic bishops to find out what was the true faith and then a debate was started at which Reccared, pointing out that no miracle of healing had been performed by Arians, emphasised this by asserting that during his father's reign an Arian bishop had failed in his guarantee to cure a blind man.

The preliminary softening-up worked wonders, for when the Third Council opened Reccared swept all before him and the culminating point was reached when eight of the bishops who had defected from Arianism anathematised the heresy in twenty-three articles, especially those who asserted that the Son and the Holy Spirit progressed from the Father, and those who assigned to the Son a beginning in time.

When the King and his Queen Bado signed the final document all the bishops burst quite spontaneously, so it is said, into vociferous applause and chanted slogans in praise of God and King.

Reccared then made a second speech, setting out rules for tightening up church procedure. The most important of these, which he frankly admitted was aimed at seeing that everyone knew the new creed and could not plead ignorance of it, was that it should be recited out loud in unison before the Lord's Prayer after communion was celebrated.

Seventy-two bishops signed the document recording the Council's proceedings, and the leading light of the whole affair, Saint Leander, made a speech in which he did not (nor did Reccared) once mention poor Hermenegild's tragic contribution. Arianism in Spain died almost overnight.

With the end of the Third Council of Toledo, when the Roman Catholic religion became the one and only faith in Spain, 124 years was to elapse before the second most important event of Spanish history took place. This momentous and unhappy date is 711, when the Moors invaded the Peninsula.

Reccared died in 601 and from then on a succession of kings fought and were assassinated with bewildering frequency, but at the same time the Councils of Toledo continued and before the Visigothic kingdom disappeared had reached eighteen in number, every one of which made laws which gave the Church and its bishops a still greater hold on the lives of the people. I have already said that the Hispano–Romans governed themselves by their own laws and the Visigoths governed themselves by theirs, but it is to the credit of these last Visigothic kings that they made every effort to bring the two sets of laws together, until in 654 or thereabouts the two were fused as one and drafted into Latin, the *Forum Judicum* (*Fuero Juzgo* in Spanish).

At the turn of the seventh century King Egica had been on the throne for thirteen years and on 15 November he anointed his son Witiza as joint king with himself. Witiza died in 710 and the nobles, who were by now tired of sons succeeding their fathers, placed King Roderic on the throne.

A year later the Arabs landed in Spain and with this landing, which is such a turning point in Spanish history, it is necessary to discuss the most important and most *vraisemblable* of Spanish legends.

What is the difference between a legend in which a marble column flies miraculously through the air or a fiery dragon is destroyed by the sign of the cross, and one in which some incidents are historical fact and the rest contains nothing which *could not* have happened? Writing in 1887, Stanley Lane-Poole tells the story of Count Julian's treachery in some detail and adds a footnote, 'I reproduce this celebrated legend of Florinda without vouching for its truth because it plays too prominent a part in Spanish history to be ignored; and if her part be fictitious her father's treachery is at least certain.' Writing in 1897, H. E. Watts says, 'The story of Florinda, which fills so prominent a part in Spanish romance, is now rejected by all sober historians.'

The legend part of history is as follows. It was the Gothic custom that the families of the nobility went to receive education in the royal household, and Count Julian of Ceuta sent his daughter Florinda – or Cava as the Moslems called her – to King Roderic's court at Toledo, and this king (there is much detail about seeing her undressed by mistake) ravished her. The dishonour was the greater because Julian's wife was in fact a daughter of Witiza. Julian swore revenge and came to Roderic, who remorseful and hoping that Florinda had not informed against him, gave a lot of secret service advice about the military situation in Spain and even sent Julian his best horses; he also sent his own armies south to be ready against the expected rebel invaders. Julian took his daughter with him and Roderic made a parting request for some special hawks for hunting. Julian replied that he would bring Roderic such hawks as he had never seen before; with this he returned to Ceuta. What now follows is fact.

Across the straits in North Africa the Arabs were overrunning what is now Morocco, save at Ceuta, where Count Julian held them off. Soon, however, he came to terms with Musa the Arab leader and filled this general's ears with stories of the riches of Spain and how easy it would be to conquer. Musa, however, was cautious, but he eventually accepted Julian's offer of four ships and sent a small body of 500 men under one Tariff to make, in 710, a raid on the coast of Andalucia at a place now called Tarifa. This foray was successful and so the following year Musa sent an Arab leader, Tarik, with 12,000 men, not Arabs but mainly Berbers, and they landed at a place called the Lion's Rock, though it has ever since borne the name of the leader of the army, Gebel Tarik – Gibraltar.

King Roderic was up in the Pyrenees at this time, trying to put down yet another revolt, but he hurried south and with an army of 90,000 men he was routed in a seven-day encounter by the 12,000 'soldiers of Islam' at a spot near Jerez-de-la-Frontera (the home of sherry) on the banks of the Guadalete, a corruption of *wad-el-leded*, the river of delight.

In spite of the most detailed explanations of the military weakness of the Visigoths, historians still express surprise at the speed with which the Arabs overran Spain: a mere two years, as compared with the two centuries of hard campaigning the Romans had endured. The Saracens,[1] too, stood amazed at the completeness of their triumph: 'O Commander of the faithful, these are not common victories; they are like the meeting of the nations on the Day of Judgement.' Thus wrote Musa, Governor of Africa, to the Caliph Welid, describing the victory at Jerez.

Actually Tarik had exceeded his instructions and Musa, wishing to take a share in the glory, crossed the straits in the summer of 712 and, after reducing Carmona, Seville and Mérida, joined Tarik in Toledo. The meeting between the conquerors was far from amicable, for Musa struck Tarik with his whip, reprimanded him for exceeding his instructions and cast him into prison. However, when this act of jealously came to the ears of the Caliph, Musa was summoned to Damascus and Tarik restored to his command in Spain.

In this account of the fall of the Visigoths we have been dealing

[1] Saracen actually means 'from the west.'

only with kings, princes, nobles, generals and commanders. It is now time to consider the position of the rank and file. Both sides had one feature in common: although of mixed race each side had one religion. The new conquerors were Moors, Berbers, Syrians and Arabs, but all were Moslems. The vanquished were Roman–Spanish and Goths, but all were fervent Christians.

It would be interesting to know what went on in the minds of the masses, as distinct from the nobility, when they found that the followers of Mohamed were to be their new masters. We might think that they would have been in terror lest they should be massacred, but past history would doubtless have come down to them by word of mouth and told them that the Visigoths, when they overran the country three hundred years earlier, had been kind; why, therefore, should these new conquerors not be equally kind?

With religious tolerance it must surely have been the same. When we ponder upon the crass intolerance which went on during the Spanish Inquisition and in England under Mary Queen of Scots, we stand amazed that the Arabs should have allowed the Hispano–Romans to continue their own way of worship so unmolested. Word had obviously spread from over the Straits of the tolerance of the Moslems, and it became a matter of indifference to most ordinary people whether they were to be ruled by Goth or Arab. Further, many Visigothic strongholds were garrisoned by Jews, who happily opened the gates to their Moslem deliverers.

With the nobility things were different; they had been so indoctrinated (and if that word conveys a scintilla of disapproval or anti-religious prejudice, it is not meant) with the Roman Catholic religion that they must have felt that for any infidel to be on the soil of Spain was an insult to Christ. That is why a few of them beat a retreat to the Cantabrian mountains and Galicia and prepared for the *reconquista* (such an important word in Spanish history!) which would take 774 years.[1]

Actually the Arabs found their conquests too easy and instead of first subduing all the Christian Visigoths in Spain, they surged northwards until they reached a point between Poitiers and Tours where one of the fifteen most decisive battles of the world took place, and the Moors were so badly crushed by Charles, hence-

---

[1] Some might add a further seventy-eight years to this, for it was not until 1570 that Don Juan of Austria put down the final Moorish rebellion in the Alpujarras mountains.

iew of Logroño: Plaza de Espolon

7 St James at the Hermitage at Valdefuentes

forth called 'the Hammerer', that they never again crossed the
Pyrenees but – and this is important – concentrated on finishing
the subjection of Spain instead.

One of the mysteries of the Arab conquest and subsequent rule
of most of the peninsula is where these men acquired their talent
for administration. After all, they had come almost direct from
the Arabian deserts and their sensationally rapid succession of
victories had left them little leisure to acquire the art of managing
foreign nations. Some writers have pointed out that many of their
counsellors were Greeks and Spaniards, but this is scarcely valid
since these same counsellors had not been very successful elsewhere.

Be that as it may, the next seventy years saw what can best be
described as the cultural miracle of Arab Spain. Cordoba became
the capital of al-Andalus and descriptions of the incredibly good
civilised life led there are unending. The culminating glory was
the building of a fabulous city of 'pleasaunce' just outside Cordoba,
Medina Azahara. It is now being renovated and brought back to
life for tourists and is a marvellous sight. The luxury government
parador in Cordoba is incidentally named after this former Arab
palace.

The Arabs did not have things all their own way, however, for
they were warring too frequently and too fiercely for that.

In the latter part of the eighth century the kingdom governed
from Cordoba was bounded (but very roughly, because there were
continuous skirmishes on the frontiers) by Pamplona, Soria,
Medinaceli, Guadalajara, Madrid, Talavera and Badajoz. To the
north-west were the as yet nebulous districts and kingdoms-to-be,
from west to east along the coast: Galicia, Asturias, Cantabria,
Navarra and inland, bordering on what is now Portugal, León.
The chief towns or headquarters to be were: in Galicia, Lugo; in
Asturias, Oviedo; in Cantabria, Santander; in Navarre, Pamplona;
and in León, León.

These strips of land, only a fraction of the whole Iberian Peninsula, were the areas to which the Christian Goths fled, and the
numbers were too small and the terrain too cold and mountainous
for the Arabs to think it worth while to follow. If they had – instead
of wandering on up to Poitiers – Spain would be an Arab land
today.

Instead of sending an army to this remote corner they sent a
skirmishing party and there they met what Arab historians call 'the

contemptible Goth' and whom the Spaniards revere as their first
Christian king, except that semi-legendary Pelayo or Pelagius was
probably a chieftain at the court of King Roderic (nothing more
was heard of him after the battle of Guadalete). But at all events,
issuing from a cave at Covadonga near Oviedo, and one of the most
beautiful mountain sites in Spain, and with only a handful of nobles
the Christians gave the Moors a terrible beating. Henceforward,
the year 718 has always been regarded as the beginning of the reconquest.

From then on the Christian Goths took heart and for the next
century, while the Arabs were quarrelling among themselves or
alternately indulging in peacefully cultural pursuits, the former
inhabitants of the Iberian Peninsula were advancing, albeit slowly,
down from the north. What they needed was a portent, a miraculous something to help them, and they found it in north-west
Spain.

We left the warrior saint in his sepulchre in the land of the
converted Queen Lupa and there he rested in utter silence
until he was re-discovered by one of the many hermits who
inhabited the outer wilds of Galicia, men who lived on nothing
but what they could get by tilling the land, and honey from wild
bees.

One of these famed as more godly than the rest was Pelayo –
nothing whatever to do with the above-mentioned Pelagius – who
one night during his meditations was astonished to see a big star
shining particularly low over a densely wooded spot near the river
Sar and only some ten miles from Bishop Theodomius' seat at
Iria Flavia, now Padron. When the Bishop was told this he instructed the hermit to hold three days of fasting and prayer and
sent labourers to clear the wood, where they found a small shrine.
Theodomius told the good news to Alfonso II ('the Chaste'), who
with the nobles of his court at Oviedo immediately set out for
Galicia.

This king, of course, like all good public relations experts,
quickly realised the tremendous significance of the discovery. The
Moslems drew their moral strength from having relics of the
Prophet in the great Cordoba Mosque; now Spain could have a
warrior saint, and so a church was at once built over the place
where the shrine had been discovered. Immediately a number of
miracles began to take place. Alfonso also told Pope Leo III the

good news and at once the first trickle of pilgrims began, until it had swollen to the third most important pilgrimage of Christendom.

Early chronicles say that a wall was built around the town which was planned there, but that did not stop the mighty Almanzor from sacking the town about a hundred years later and taking away the bells to use in his mosque.

Chapter 4

THE STARTING POINTS
IN FRANCE

The tightness of the grip that Aimery Picaud of Parthenay le Vieux near Poitiers and his early twelfth-century guide has had on the construction, planning and form of every writer about the pilgrimage – certainly in English, French and Spanish – in the past hundred years has been extraordinary. My resolve, in the ten years during which I have contemplated this book, to be 'different' soon withered when I started to write. The only possible difference would have been a very minor route through France, along which only a handful of pilgrims over the centuries would have trudged, and to have given prominence to lesser buildings along that route.

But I could not have kept it up for long; the shameful feeling of hoodwinking the reader and of being forced to make deviations back to the accepted route to describe the monasteries thereon would soon have brought me to earth.

Picaud, then, has four starting places in France and these are Tours (from which we follow the route in detail later), Vézelay due east, Le Puy down south and farther south still Saint Giles du Gard, or Arles.

Incidentally most cartographers give Paris as their 'official' starting point of the Tours route, but Picaud does not mention it as such, though eventually it became the busiest starting point of all.

Vézelay, the second gathering point, has a population of five hundred, and a good hotel called the Poste et Lion, with a restaurant where you can have a fricassée of chicken in old

Burgundy, snails in chablis or a dodine[1] of jellied duck with truffles.

The tiny village is entrancing; you march up a long narrow street – too full of souvenir shops – and arrive at a great square where stand the remains of the monastic buildings, and what remains is enough.

The place was founded, helped by a few miracles, by Gérard of Roussillon and his wife Berthe in the ninth century, and around 1000 it was discovered that within the shrine were the true relics of St Mary Magdalene. This was the beginning of the trouble, for as the miracles started to flow so did the large number of pilgrims to the abbey. With them came votive offerings and in many cases gifts of rich lands. The Abbey became rich by the traffic in the bones and other relics of saints and a holy population came to settle on the narrow ridge outside the walls of the huge edifice.

Then started the old story of pride and then came a fall. Soon Vézelay began to make enemies, and the Abbey of Cluny anyhow had no liking for its rival. The abbots were so powerful that they acted more or less as vice-regents of the Popes and were used to having the last word in matters of ecclesiastical preferment. Vézelay, however, maintained her claim to be exempt from all authority save of the papacy itself and was continually resisting Cluny's interference.

But the Counts of the house of Nevers (men of high rank and with considerable influence in the Councils of France) were the arch enemies, nor can one entirely blame them for their ill-will. They viewed with envy and anger a rich body owning fat lands within their domain, who themselves exercised feudal rights to the full, yet refused in return to render any feudal dues.

Vézelay's period of supremacy and fame was during the whole of the eleventh and the best part of the twelfth centuries and its connections with England were at that time considerable. Thomas à Becket went there in 1164 when he was declared a traitor and driven from England; to the abbey in Holy Week of 1146 went Eleanor of Aquitaine, the future Queen of England when she married King Henry Plantagenet. And from there in 1190 Richard I the Lion Hearted set off on his fatal journey to the Holy Land. During the thirteenth century its fortunes declined rapidly and

---

[1] *Dodiner* is to rock a sifting machine, but the word is not in the Larousse Gastronomique, Soyer or Escoffier. It also means to parboil or to cook gently, *Faire dodo* is 'to go bye-bye'.

the *coupe de grâce* came from Pope Boniface VIII when he openly expressed doubts as to the veritable presence there of the relics of St Mary Magdalene.

The glory of the sizeable remains of the basilica of Vézelay lies in the narthex and in the sculptured capitals in this vast vestibule. No one is quite certain what the function of a narthex (in architectural terms, a vestibule stretching across the western ends of early Christian churches) was. It may have been for catechumen[1] or for 'penitents' not yet 'reconciled with God through the church' or it could have been a waiting place for women. The fourth suggestion is that it was a shelter for pilgrims who, after a long journey, felt themselves too dirty and spiritually unready to enter the church proper.

From Vézelay the pilgrims went on through Perigueux until they met the main Paris–Tours stream south of Bordeaux.

Le Puy, the third of Picaud's starting points, now a town of thirty thousand inhabitants, is practically on the river Loire; it has been called the most picturesque place in France, a geological freak, and the best place in Europe in which to study the evolution of religion. The claim to picturesqueness is dubious, but the curious topographical features of the landscape and the bizarre but beautiful cathedral, the enormous bronze statue of the Virgin and Child built on a pinnacle, and the old Byzantine chapel built on yet another pinnacle, make the other two claims valid.

The cathedral, built over a miraculous healing 'fever stone', a little like Santiago, has been described by a great French writer, Émile Mâle, as 'one of the most beautiful Christian monuments in the world; more than all others it sets the imagination at work by its mystery, its strange half-Arab design, its confusing reminder of the orient, its lovely cloister and its black and white arches, which remind one of the great mosque at Córdoba'.

The cathedral is built on a pinnacle of rock within the present town and Émile Mâle also makes a reference to the most astonishing aspect of the building; an immensely long and imposing flight of steps leading to the main façade. It is called the Rue des Tables because of the women sitting outside their houses tatting and has been painted by every artist visiting Le Puy for the last hundred years. The street starts as a very steep cobbled road until it changes into a stairway of 132 steps, which takes you to the summit.

From here departed one of the most famous, the earliest re-

[1] Candidates being instructed in the Christian religion and awaiting baptism.

corded, also the largest and most publicised pilgrimages to St James. It was conducted by Bishop Godescalk in 951 and what a crowd there must have been! They met at the bottom of the Rue des Tables, ready to ascend the flight of steps on their knees and throw themselves upon the Fever Stone. As they would be away for over a year they were accompanied by daughters, wives and sweethearts, and we have some idea of the size of the crowd when we recall that there is extant an old guide book (not Picaud's) in which pilgrims were exhorted not to pick up anything they might drop for fear of being trampled underfoot.

Le Puy, which in the Auvergne dialect means the peak, was formerly the Roman town of Ancium and it has been suggested that Anis, then Ancium, derives from the name of the Egyptian goddess Isis whose cult was introduced into the Roman Empire and became popular mainly on account of the splendour of its ceremonies.

The town's gastronomic speciality is a green and highly potent liqueur (which the French call a *digestif*) called *verveine* (there is even an hotel of that name) and we call Verbena. The pilgrims[1] would not have sampled this since its distillation was not begun for another hundred years. Nor would they have seen one of the most massive religious monuments of the whole world. Officially it is Notre Dame de France, which the locals call 'The Virgin of Le Puy'. It stands on yet another crag called the Rocher de Corneille, behind the cathedral, and is made entirely of bronze and is over fifty feet high.[2] It has an extraordinary story, since much of the metal comes from Russian guns.

The French Commander-in-Chief, General Pelissier, had several times stayed at Le Puy and knew of the unusual Rocher de Corneille. He wrote to Bishop Morhon suggesting that he (the Bishop) ask Napoleon III for the cannon that *would be captured at Sebastopol*. His Majesty replied 'yes' if indeed they were. They were captured, on 8 September 1855, and so the statue got from the 125 bronze and 200 cast iron cannon, 150 tons of metal.

The statue was erected to perpetuate the memory of the proclamation of the dogma of the Immaculate Conception and was blessed on 1 September 1860 before a crowd of 120,000 persons.

[1] When I refer generally to the pilgrims, walkers, Jacquaries, etc., I always mean those of the eleventh to fourteenth centuries.

[2] The Virgin holds the infant Jesus in her hand and, to get some idea of the size of the statue, be it noted that the head of the child alone is taller than a man.

How footsore the Jacquaires must have been when they finally left Le Puy, for they certainly would not have failed to visit that which I have saved to the last to describe, 'for all the other sights of the town become mediocre compared with the astounding St Michel-d'Aiguilhe or "of the needle",' sayes Émile Mâle.

The rock on which the miniscule chapel is built is such a dramatic little freak of nature as perhaps to be unique in Europe. For though it is over 289 feet high it is only 500 feet in circumference at the base and completely isolated from the flat surrounding land; a natural obelisk, a perfectly round tapering cone which geologists think could be the chimney of an extinct crater filled with volcanic rock and isolated by millions of years of erosion.

You need sturdy legs to make the ascent, but this is child's play compared with the climb the pilgrims did long ago, for there are still traces of the original steps which are almost perpendicular. No wonder Bishop Truannus, who had the notion to build the chapel in 962, said 'In other times even the most agile men could hardly climb up', and so one assumes that before he started building there was an even steeper stairway.

The chapel itself crowns the rock so perfectly that the ensemble has been rated by many to be the eighth wonder of the world, while others have said that the building seems to have been placed there not by man but by time itself.

Two hundred years after Truannus started the chapel, further extensions were made and it is noteworthy that even in those remote times they took care to enshrine and build around the tenth-century work; and on the minute space available they managed by some miracle of ingenuity to add a five-tier belfry – similar to the one at the cathedral.

After Le Puy the pilgrims went on through the Armagnac country and the land of *foie gras* (the forcible stuffing of geese had not then been 'invented'), through Eauze (present headquarters of Courses des Vaches Landaises), and on to Roncevalles in the Pyrenees.

Returning now to route number one, from Paris they started from the very centre of the city at a church consecrated to the Sons of Zebedee of which only the Tour St Jacques remains today. On the day of departure the pilgrims attended a service at which their staffs were blessed and they were accompanied at the service by the 'Friends of Mister Saint James'.

After leaving the capital by the Notre-Dame bridge and the rue St Jacques (still extant), they passed a huge hospital built for pilgrims coming from Flanders. Then there were two routes to choose from: via Chartres, to admire the stained glass with scenes from the Song of Roland; or, more popular, via Orleans, where in the cathedral they were able to use the miraculous chalice of St Evert, or they could visit the churches of Saints Agnan and Samson. On then through Blois and Amboise to Tours, where they went to a remarkable eleventh- and twelfth-century cathedral which, along with St Martial de Limoges, Conques and St Sernin at Toulouse, served in part to inspire Compostela. Picaud mentions this architectural cousinship (*ad similtudiem ecclesie Beati Jacobi*), but alas nothing remains of the enormous and remarkable edifice except two great towers. This church was dedicated to the great St Martin, who cut his coat in half (it was forbidden for a Roman soldier to return with less than half his belongings). It is interesting that our own words 'cape' and 'chapel' are derived from the *cappella* or cloak of this St Martin; for the name *cappella* was applied to the sanctuary where it was kept under the care of its *cappellani* or chaplains.

But the pilgrims also went to the present cathedral of St Gatien, who was especially venerated then because it was he who brought Christianity to the region in the third century. They then went on through Chatellerault, where they prayed at St James' church before a statue of the saint dressed as a pilgrim, and got to Poitiers. There they met their English fellow travellers who had come from Mont St Michel.

The fourth and southernmost starting point was Arles, to which a later chapter is devoted.

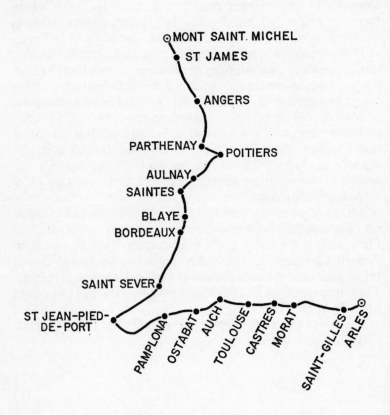

MONT SAINT. MICHEL
ST JAMES
ANGERS
PARTHENAY
POITIERS
AULNAY
SAINTES
BLAYE
BORDEAUX
SAINT SEVER
ST JEAN-PIED-DE-PORT
PAMPLONA
OSTABAT
AUCH
TOULOUSE
CASTRES
MORAT
SAINT-GILLES
ARLES

Chapter 5

MONT ST MICHEL TO ST SEVER

Said Sir Walter Raleigh:

> 'Give me my scallop shell of quiet,
> My staff of faith to walk upon,
> My scrip of joy, immortal diet
> My bottle of salvation
> My gown of glory, hopes true gage,
> And thus I'll make my pilgrimage.'

I too, carried a few bottles – empty screw-top mineral bottles, invaluable if you buy a full bottle of wine and can only drink two-thirds; the balance keeps indefinitely if well screwed down in these little containers.

Weymouth and Bristol were about the most popular English ports to sail from, and Fécamp, Caen and Mont St Michel the three most used ports in France. I put up at the spacious motel outside Mont St Michel and was soon on my way to dine at the famed Mère Poulard restaurant on the Mount, where the omelettes are cooked over such a scorching hot oak fire that four-foot handles to the pans are needed.

On foot – sometimes the crowds are so great that one has to walk a mile from one's car – to the Mount I got into conversation with a party who told me they had come from Paris, not to visit the Abbey, but to watch the high tide come in at exactly six o'clock. 'It comes up at the speed of a horse at the gallop and goes out again as quickly.'

As a place of pilgrimage Mont St Michel is older than Santiago, having been built and dedicated at the very beginning of the eighth century on the command of Archangel Michael. The Pope sent relics to Bishop Aubert and immediately royal pilgrims started to arrive from Paris, King Childebert III of France being the first.

He and others following him, just before they got to the flat sands, passed through the tiny village of St James and there followed a rise in the ground from which an astonishing *vue panoramique* is afforded. It was here that the early French pilgrims had their first view of the spire of the Mount's abbey church. It is therefore called Mont Joie de Mont St Michel.

The village of St James was founded by William the Conqueror in 1067 as a peace offering to the English for his having won the battle of Hastings, hence the anglicisation of St Jacques. But why did William choose that particular saint's name? Could it have been that pilgrims were already disembarking at St Michael's Mount – it is depicted already on the Bayeux tapestry – in great numbers?

Maitre Houssard, Mayor of St James – the Americans built their impressive military cemetery close by on account of the curious English name – is sure that there is no connection with Santiago and bases his assertion on a book very rare and very long, written entirely around the history of the village. There was and still is an abbey there, but this was primarily for pilgrims from Paris to St Michel.

Maybe. But the local curate, M. Gallois, showed me the relatively modern (1850) church, built on to the old tower of the Abbey and he thinks it was connected with the Santiago pilgrims. At all events, in the church is a large statute of St James which shows him bareheaded but with a great pilgrim's hat and scallop shell held across his stomach.

On we[1] went, then, through Rennes and Angers, whence a detour was made to Parthenay le Vieux for the good reason that this is the town that Aimery Picaud is supposed to have come from; here too is the twelfth-century Tour St Jacques at the entrance over the river to the old town, with its Rue St Jacques and its little old wooden houses.

At this point a book comes into my pilgrim's tale. In 1947 I launched a light claret – called appropriately Aquitaine. Seeing a book with this name in a junk shop I bought it for half a crown as

[1] Myself and the pilgrims of the Middle Ages.

a lucky omen, but because the back was torn it would not fit my shelves, it was put aside until, by an extraordinary coincidence, I unearthed it as I was setting out on my journey. When I opened *Aquitaine, Traveller's Tales*[1] I found a wonderful drawing of St Porchaire at Poitiers, which is specially mentioned by Picaud because, in the road that leads up to it, he recalls the miracle of the pilgrim who asked for a crust of bread from a woman who was doing her baking; her bread was turned to stone on her refusal.

There are some splendid etchings of the marvellous church of Notre-Dame-la-Grande with the market stalls surrounding it, and it was my plan to take lunch at a café with the same viewpoint as the artist of 1897 and note the differences. I was just too late to do this; I therefore detoured just outside Poitiers to a charming little village through whose centre a wide stream meandered on both sides of which were green public gardens and well-planned, unobtrusive parking places shaded by willows and pollarded poplars. In the middle of this square was the usual statue of a French soldier with a list of the fallen of three wars 1871, 1914 and 1945, and I saw that the town was called Vouille-la-Bataille. During a pleasant sunlit lunch at the Cheval Blanc I wondered which of the three wars 'la Bataille' referred to, and this in turn made me think that at none of the periods mentioned had any battle been fought so far from the Franco-Prussian border. As I paid my bill I asked madame which battle it was and to my astonishment she replied that it was 'a battle between Clovis, King of the Franks, and Alaric of the Visigoths'.

I found details of this battle in the *Traveller's Tales* book. The year was 507; the battle was short and sharp and it was all over by noon. Alaric was killed by Clovis in a single-handed encounter. This battle changed the course of Spanish history, for had the Visigoths won, surely they would have stayed on in this lush part of central France and not returned to Spain, and a warrior saint would not have been needed for the reconquest. Anyway it is certain that Vouille is so close to Poitiers that many a pilgrim would have detoured to see the battlefield.

Poitiers was a most important stopping place for the pilgrims, but exceptionally so for the English, for it was here for the first time that they met fellow penitents from Paris and Tours. A very few would have read Picaud's guide, but many may have memorised

[1] By Wickham Flower, FSA; illustrations by Joseph Pennell. Chapman & Hall, 1897.

what was to be seen and so they would have headed immediately
for the romanesque church of Notre-Dame-la-Grande, so called
because there was also a smaller Notre-Dame in the town.

The first is of the eleventh century, built by Gui Geoffroi, Duke
of Aquitaine, and by his son the ninth Duke, William the famous
crusader, troubadour and poet, after the great fire which devastated
the city in 1085; and though the date of the older church (there
are foundations of at least two other buildings beneath it) is open
to some question there is an ancient tradition – and there are good
grounds to believe it is true – that the present building replaces and
partly incorporates an earlier Christian church built in the middle
of the fourth century by Bishop Aliphius in the time of Emperor
Constantine.

Wickham Flower spent five summer weeks in Poitiers and every
day, 'with the assistance of a powerful glass examined minutely
some portion of the building; the whole of the west front is from
the ground to the top literally apparelled in pictures in stone'.

Most of these pictures are by Byzantine workmen and it is believed that they were originally decorated in colour and in gold.
Here are Adam and Eve in the garden of Eden, Nebuchodonozor,
as the French in the twelfth century called him, Joseph in magnificently embroidered dress, Mercy shown as a male figure, Truth as
a young girl, and a charming picture of the Nativity. But the most
interesting thing of all is that in the picture of the Anunciation
the Virgin is shown wearing *pointed shoes*, to which is attached
a most curious story, as a contemporary historian, Ordericus Vitalis,
a saxon monk, related in his history of England and Normandy,
written early in the twelfth century.

Fulk le Rechin – the quarreller – a Count of Anjou (great grand-
father of Henry II of England), in 1089 married the lovely Gertrude,
a daughter of Simon de Montfort, who later eloped with Philip,
King of France, and married him. Fulk had deformed feet and
in order to conceal his deformity, this may have caused him to have
shoes of great length made with very pointed toes. This soon became fashionable in the western world; Ordericus says that 'rich
and poor were greatly taken with [the fashion] so that now the
people insert their toes in things like serpents'. And this fashion
– of *souliers a la pointaine* – lasted for about three hundred years.

Poitiers was full of delights for the medieval pilgrims, and it still
is. There is a very good hotel, the France, in the main square, where
I stayed in comfort and ate in luxury before starting to look round.

The cathedral of St Pierre has strong connections with Britain, for in 1162, after the destruction of the older church by fire, the present cathedral had its first stone laid by King Henry II of England and Queen Eleanor, then Duke and Duchess of Aquitaine. The building was not completed and consecrated until October 1379.

St Hilary is jointly patron saint of the city of Poitiers, with Ste Radegonde, Queen of France in the sixth century. It was she who built her own beautiful church (ready for her own burial) just outside the city walls, since by Roman law burial within the city was not allowed.

St Hilary, too, has his own church, which was sadly spoiled in the seventeenth century but which previously knew days of great glory. It was dedicated on 1 November 1049 at a ceremony at which thirteen archbishops and bishops assisted; part of the funds for the building was given by Queen Emma of England.

Splendidly ramparted, yet modern within its walls and made gay by the pretty girl students who invaded the shops of this university town, Poitiers is indeed a place to return to.

Aulnay de Saintonge comes next, with its exuberant little twelfth-century church of St Peter. The setting is unusually pleasing, for it is set back in a well-kept graveyard, which makes it stand out magnificently. St Jean Angely comes next and later pilgrims would have walked under the fifteenth-century tower in the Rue de la Grosse Horloge, which the tourist brochure in English calls 'Big Clock Street'; but this is not as bad as the Mont St Michel brochure with a picture of the high tide coming in, described as the 'arrival of deep sea'.

Medolianum Santonum or Saintes comes next and I put up, with a pleasant welcome from Monsieur Typhonet, at the Hotel Central, Place de la Gare, a leafy cool, clear square at the far end of the town. I have in mind one day to write a guide to French railway station squares, because no amount of map study can tell whether they are alive and have atmosphere, with good restaurants around them, like Strasbourg, Colmar and Orange, or whether they are out at the dreary end of nowhere, like Beaune, Bordeaux and Dijon. The only general rule is that in German-influenced Alsace and Lorraine the gay life is centred more upon the railway station squares than elsewhere in France.

Saintes is a very easy town to understand; every ship, bank, café, or what you will, indeed the entire life of the place revolves around one very long road which runs dead straight, right through the town from one end to the other.

For students of Roman Gaul the town is of great importance, for in the first place there are the considerable remains of a splendid amphitheatre in a most beautiful setting and capable of taking 20,000 spectators; its dimensions are correspondingly impressive, being 414 by 334 feet. It was built towards the middle of the first century, has been badly defaced in the course of subsequent centuries, but is now used for summer pageants which are a great attraction. Then there is the magnificent Roman arch which, however, does not stand now where it was originally built early in the first century, as part of the ancient Roman bridge which linked the two parts of the town. It is now splendidly sited on the Place Bassompierre, but you can still see the dedications to Tiberius, Germanicus and Drusus on top.

This is a double arch, both being of the same size, big enough for chariots to pass through. Both this type and the single triumphal arch are fairly common, but what is rare and I think the one at Medinaceli is unique in Spain, is the triple arch, with a central arch for chariots and a smaller arch on either side for foot soldiers.

Saintes also has one of the best displayed archaeological museums of Roman Gaul in southern France; everything, the death masks, inscriptions, altars and sarcophagi, friezes and columns, all come from excavations of the city of Mediolanum Santonum done during the course of a century and a half.

But the most emotional place for the pilgrims was the beautiful double church, right on the highway to Santiago, of Saint Eutrope who suffered martyrdom in the third century. Aimery Picaud has a very detailed account of his life, occupying almost a whole chapter. He was born the son of the Emir of Babylon called Xerces and his Queen Guiua, 'who engendered him of their own flesh'.

When young he was brilliant but he wanted to see the world and especially to attend the court of Herod. Here he happened to see Christ work a miracle and he immediately wrote back to his father: 'I have today seen a man who is called Christ and there is no one in the world like him.' This was the turning point, and after many journeyings he accompanied (possibly) St Denis to France to share his apostolic labours. At Saintes the people expelled him and he went to live in a cell on a neighbouring rock, but he did make a few conversions, one of whom was the Roman governor's daughter Eustella. When her father discovered that she was a

Christian he told the butchers of Saintes to kill Eutrope; Eustella, finding him dead with his skull split by an axe, buried his remains in his cell.

The present spire, built in the fifteenth century, is nearly two hundred feet high, but of the church that was consecrated in 1096 (and at that time there was an immense nave which served both the upper and lower churches, which stretched right out into the present square) the most important thing left is the crypt; it is enormous, one of the largest I have seen.

Blaye, which comes next, was also an important staging post for the pilgrim. I stopped there for lunch in late September. It is a curious town: in the first place it has so many parts that one cannot believe that there are only 4,500 Blayans, as the inhabitants are called; also it stands on the estuary of the Gironde, which is so wide here that land on the other side cannot be seen, and as there is a long wide promenade one fancies oneself beside the sea. There was a row of cafés facing the water, all quite empty, and I chose one which was enormous, where a man and wife were just about to sit down to an elaborate and almost sumptuous lunch. No, they said, they did not sell any food of any sort and yes, of course, I could bring in my picnic lunch and could they please supply knives, forks, plates and condiments. To save them from getting up again I ordered a Ricard, a large glass of muscadet and a large red wine. This was not an act of thoughtfulness only, for if a small glass of wine costs say Frs 1.80, a large glass is invariably three times the liquid content for only twice the price! This was the time of year when the tomatoes ripen to the size of grapefruit and with one of these, *pâte du campagne* and bread, and a mound of butter, I am content. After lunch, partly out of curiosity and partly out of politeness, I said:

'I suppose you are madly busy in the summer.'

'No,' replied the couple affably.

'But you must be busy at some time of the year, or perhaps a lot of local fishermen come in,' I persisted.

'No,' they said, 'It is like this all the year round.'

It was on the precipitous jutting rock that the Roman legion first built a town here and called it Blavia; the medieval city was razed to the ground in the seventeenth century to make way for a citadel, finished in 1689 by that indefatigable military constructor, Vauban. It is a weird, haunting, almost self-contained village nearly half a mile in length, and a few families still live in houses built into the fortifications. Adjoining are two remaining towers of the medieval castle where Jaufre Rudel, the twelfth-century troubadour, was born. He it was who, though never setting eyes on her, fell in love with his 'princess from afar', Melissande of Tripoli. Eventually he set sail to visit her, only to fall ill on the ship and expire on arriving in the arms of his beloved!

> 'Loved one from a distant land,
> For you my heart does ache.'

But the importance of Blaye to our pilgrims was that Picaud strongly recommended a visit to the basilica and abbey of St Romain founded there in the sixth century. Now St Romain, a disciple of St Martin of Tours, was the patron saint of travellers, and Gregory of Tours tells us that he saves from drowning all those who invoke his name during a storm at sea. But in the abbey-church (the abbey was destroyed by the English in 1441 and the church by Louis XIV in 1676) was a great personality: blessed Roland, martyr and issue of a noble family, and Count in the camp of King Charlemagne. He was the hero of Roncevaux, who conquered kings and then, worn out by hunger, cold and excessive heat, flagellated unceasingly, pierced by arrows and lances, died of thirst – so they say in the valley of Roncevaux.

Roland's tomb was visited by thousands and thousands over the centuries and Francois I, passing through Blaye in 1526, caused it to be opened so that he could gaze on the bones of the warrior. It also had a great place in the poetry of the early Middle Ages.

There was no very definitive route from Blaye to Bordeaux and indeed many took boats to Bordeaux, as shown by a French song here translated, printed in the nineteenth century entitled: *The Great canticle of True Pilgrims to Great Saint James in Spain Sung to a Known Air:*

> 'When we left France, greatly desiring,
> We left our fathers and mothers unhappily,
> And we left behind all pleasures
> To make this holy voyage.

> 'When we got to the port of Blaye
> Near Bordeaux we entered a boat
> To go over the water a good seven leagues
> By sea. Mariners go quickly
> For fear of storms.'

Alternatively, they could have taken a ferry across from Blaye to the left bank of the Gironde and walked down through mile upon mile of vines, through what is now the Médoc, by far the greatest red wine-growing district in the world.

Or they could have trudged straight on, not taking to the water but simply hugging the river's right bank. I took this curving road instead of the big highway because it was marked as a beautiful wine road for tourists and was surprised at the profusion of flowers in front of the little houses and by the general beauty of the drive. Surprised because I spent two years in Bordeaux as a youth, when I won the Worshipful Company of Vintners' Travel-and-Work-in-the-Cellars Wine Scholarship, and Bordeaux was the first and most important starting point. I got around a bit and remembered that the countryside was deadly dull, especially in the Médoc, which is nothing but a green sea of vineyards. When they are really well kept and seen from certain angles, they can look remarkably like a huge military cemetery.

There was wine in plenty, too, for the pilgrims eight hundred years ago, testified by a later verse in the poem I have already quoted above:

'When we got to town called Bordeaux
The Confrérie invited us to drink the new wine,
The new wine and white bread in abundance.
This was for the unhappy pilgrims who
Had to traverse the Landes.'

This reference to the Confrérie or Brotherhood I find most interesting; some thirty years ago the Bordeaux growers, as a public relations operation formed the Commanderie de Bontemps and designed for themselves a most dignified, flowing, claret-coloured robe and a round hat of which the centre colours are egg-yolk yellow surrounded by white. You will not find *bontemps* in your French dictionary, for it is a rare word for a little wooden bowl in which the whites of eggs were whipped up and then put into hogsheads of clarets to fine them. All good wines in my time (1928–30) were thus treated (isinglass was used only for cheaper wines), so much so that in the port wine lodges of Vila Nova de Gaia (twin town of Oporto) in Portugal so many egg whites were used that the pastrycooks of the region created special little cakes with the left-over yolks.

I was made a commander in 1971 – it is not all that much of an honour, mainly a question of paying for a very expensive banquet – at a fabulous evening at Château Pontet Canet in the summer of 1971. The evening divides itself into three parts: speeches in praise of those to be made Commanders of the Bontemps; then what the French call *manifestations*, which can best be described as musical high jinks; and then the banquet, scheduled to take place at around midnight and always two hours late.

For the long congratulatory speeches a huge overground cellar had been whitewashed and hundreds of very small hard wooden folding chairs had been hired on which bottoms had to be content for several hours. There were some thirty of us to be 'done', which involved ascending the rostrum from one side of the hall, while one's sponsor ascended from the other and made a speech – frequently long – praising one's services to wine and especially claret. Most of my fellows were proprietors of supremely luxurious restaurants all over Europe, with cellars of claret which nearly took one's breath away, or gastronomic journalists of repute, and though I had certainly written more in hard-cover books than all the journalists put together, I was no more or less distinguished than the rest. But my sponsor was by far the most distinguished person there that evening, Professor Georges Portmann, world-famous surgeon and *sénateur* of the Gironde.

For the pilgrims Bordeaux was important not only because Aimery Picard told them they must visit the basilica of St Seurin, but especially because of the relic which was to be seen and venerated there.

St Severnus, or St Seurin,[1] was Bishop of Bordeaux around 420 and had apparently been Bishop of Trier (Treves) before going to France. An abbey was erected in his name and was at first administered by the Benedictines; the western door and the crypt, which are still standing, are of the twelfth century. The Roman–Gaul crypt is interesting as it contains the seventeenth-century tomb of St Fort. Though he is an imaginary Bishop of Bordeaux, historians suggest that he may have evolved from St Seurin, but anyhow from 15 May till 19 May each year mothers can be seen placing their babies on the tomb so that they should become *forts*, strong.

But Picaud did not send his pilgrims to this; he wanted them to see a horn made of ivory, the olifant which poor Roland blew at Roncevalles. Picaud makes quite a point of this, for, after telling us

[1] Not to be confused with the far more famous St Sernin of Toulouse.

of the powers of his mighty sword, he continues: 'It is recorded also that in sounding his horn the power of his wind broke it in the middle.' This ivory horn, thus split, is to be seen at Bordeaux at the Basilica of St Seurin.

My friend Dorothy Sayers, in her splendidly readable translation of *The Story of Roland*,[1] has written:

'They[2] storm Narboune[3] and leave it by the way,
And reach Bordeaux a city of great fame.
There, on the altar of Seu'rin the good saint,
Filled with gold mangons, the Olifant they lay,
(Pilgrims may see it when visiting the place)
And cross the Gironde, where much good shipping waits.
So the King brings his nephew back to Blaye,
With his companion, Count Oliver[4] the great,
And the Archbishop, that was so wise and brave.
All in white tombs these noble men are laid
They lie there still, good lords in Saint Romayne's
The French commend them to God, His Power and Name.'

After Bordeaux the pilgrims passed the wine-growing region of the Graves (gravel) and then the sweet white wine-making district of Sauternes. I wonder if grapes suitable for making these sickly, mawkish white wines were available in the tenth to fourteenth centuries.

Then they reached the very old priory of which the arched porch can still be seen right on the main road today. But you only see the top half of the door; the road, as at Bury St Edmunds, was once a good six feet lower than today. No one could be a more fanatic would-be preserver of ancient monuments than I, but here should be an exception; the remains have caused a deadly dangerous Z-bend to exist on the main road to Spain, with giant lorries charging along at break-neck speed in both directions. I pulled my car up well off the road, I thought, to photograph the portal but when I got back into it my companion was visibly shaken at the near-collisions which had occurred.

The pilgrims were now entering the Landes and Picaud tells us

[1] Penguin Classics, 1957.
[2] Charlemagne and his army.
[3] Far more important in the Middle Ages than now.
[4] There is a discrepancy here between Picaud's Guide and *The Song of Roland*; the former has him buried at Belin.

they took three days, 'for people already tired', to cross it. It was not exactly pleasurable. 'If you cross the Landes in summer,' says Aimery, 'do take care to protect your face from enormous flies which breed there and which are called wasps or hornets; and if you do not watch your feet you will find yourselves sinking rapidly up to your knees in marine sand, which is everywhere.'

Things have hardly changed; I remember well that in the 1930s French tourist brochures of the Landes showed women up on their tall stilts.

Motorists leaving Bordeaux for Bayonne, Biarritz and Spain will know how quickly, after first seeing the beauty of the handsome pines, the attraction soon wears off. The reason, I think, is that the road is too straight, too fast; it gets monotonous and so I do suggest that after Belin you do just what the pilgrims (at least some of them) did and strike off, still in the Landes, through a side road via Pissos [*sic*] and Mont de Marsan and rejoin the Bayonne highway at Dax – you will lose about forty minutes, but the scenery makes it worthwhile.

This is what I did and arrived at nightfall at the lovely little town of St Sever to find that my room reservation at the pleasant one-star Hotel de France et des Ambassadeurs was certainly in order, but, said patron Dupjouy, they were so pleased to meet me. Yes, the Rotary Club would love a talk from me on St James and all was fixed for next week.

Only then did the correspondence come back to me! Never write letters without keeping a carbon copy, and never write in a foreign language after you have had a bibulous lunch.

I would not spoil my book by doing the pilgrim's route backwards, so I had to set off long before dawn to do the (fourth) route from Arles to Saint Sever and then on to the Pyrenees.

Chapter 6

ARLES TO THE PYRENEES

To arrive at a lovely town, to call at the best hotel to hear that the price is far beyond your pocket, then to wander round in the rain and find all the other hotels *complet*, to go back to the expensive one and hear, having decided to pay up, that it is now full, such has twice been my experience at Arles. So it was pleasant to book in at the Hotel Jules Caesar in Arles, worth every penny of what I had to pay.

I am not the only person who thought that Arles (which the Roman Emperors called Gallula Roma Arelas) a beautiful city; what was good enough for me was good enough for Emperor Constantine; so much so that he hesitated for quite a time, when he wished to abandon Italian Rome and transfer the seat of the Empire, over the choice between Arles and Byzantium. Apart from being obsessed with the beauty of the town, Constantine loved it also because it had been one of the first places to embrace Christianity; *Arles le blanc* it had been called because she had been untainted by heresy.

The bedrooms of the Hotel Jules-Caesar have been reconstructed around a seventeenth-century *chapelle* and to look out upon the quiet and beautifully kept cloister is enchanting. The hotel restaurant is called 'Lou Marquis' and is one of the great eating spots of southern France. On the menu was Quenelles de Brochet á la Nantus – fresh pike meat pounded with breadcrumbs poached and covered with shrimp sauce – which is my favourite fish dish, but only when made in the restaurant's kitchens.

The town has one of the best preserved, most beautifully sited arenas in Europe, where present-day bull fights[1] attract huge

---

[1] They are illegal in France, so the fine is paid automatically.

crowds. These sports stadiums, as they were, existed centuries before the pilgrims passed along but we hear nothing of travellers visiting them, which at first thought seems odd. But not, surely, on reflection; they were in the main religious people and as such would hardly have been interested in the light-hearted spectacles which took place in the arena.

But they were sent by the Guide to worship at the shrine of St Throphime; 'the first Bishop sent to this town to preach the gospel of Christ. And without doubt, and this is definitely confirmed by Pope Zozimus, it was from this source that all France received the faith,' says Picaud.

Before entering the town, however, the pilgrims encountered what was perhaps the most poignant sight of their whole tour – Les Alyscamps. Call them the Elysian Fields, call them a necropolis, a Roman burial ground, a Christian cemetery, or just a vast collection of tombs; call them what you will, but even now, despite plundering and desecration, the place, which is on the very borders of the present city, with its black cypresses and double lines of poplars, is a haunting sight.

In ancient Roman days this cemetery was not yet called the Elysian Fields, for it was just an alley lined with rich Roman sarcophagi, a word from the Greek meaning 'consuming of human flesh' because certain calcareous stones from which they were hewn had the property of dissolving flesh in a fairly short time. It was called the necropolis of the west and dated from the establishment in 47 BC of the Julia Paterna colony. But the reason why it became the most important of burial grounds was just because it was on the main road from Rome to Spain, long before St James came upon the scene, but when Spain was an important part of the Roman Empire.

The area covered was vast, nearly a mile long but only half a mile broad. This was because expansion in one direction was restricted by the marshes (*marais*), over which went the Via Aureliana on a viaduct, and travellers were protected from the sun and wind by a long line of cypresses.

That was in Roman times, but in the early Middle Ages the Avenue des Alyscamps became so famous that many a pious Christian wished to be buried there. The place was really adopted by the Christians, for excavations in several other cemeteries around Arles show that in the latter pagans only were buried.

It is generally assumed that Alyscamps is the same as Champs

Elysees, Elysian Fields, but Professor Armand Dauphin, the accredited archaeologist of the region, has put forward an almost irrefutably sound case to show that this is incorrect. The letter A, he says, never changed in course of time to E; rather the other way around. Anyway, Elysian comes via Latin from the Greek *elysei* not *aelysei*. He then says that no necropolis in antiquity was thus called the Elysian Fields, since this mythological name was only for good persons, whereas in a cemetery all sorts are buried.

So, he asks, why not look for a geographical meaning? Alys- camps was Aliscans in the period when the *chansons de geste* were the vogue; thus we have simply the plain of the *alysse*, or alyssum (or popularly 'gold dust'), and in that period it grew there more profusely than now.

The reason that so many Christians wished to be buried here arose out of a legendary tradition that Charlemagne had fought a mighty battle on the plains around Arles and that the twelve heroes of Roncevaux (or Roncevalles) were buried in the cemetery. The massacre had been terrible; so great that it was impossible to distinguish the bodies of the Christians from those of the Saracens, but that by a miracle all the bodies of the former were taken to sarcophagi that lined the Avenue.

Some idea of the size of the place can be gathered from the fact that at the height of its popularity there were nineteen churches, chapels and basilicas within the precincts and that the monks of the monastery of St Victor had a full-time job burying bodies within the shade of the many trees. So keen were Christians to find their last home there that they left orders for their bodies to be strapped to coffins and floated down the Rhone to Arles with sufficient money aboard to see that if the raft got stuck in a back- water it was pushed back into mid-stream. And even Dante in his *Inferno* mentions 'this plain filled with tombs', which he saw.

Picaud confirms that the cemetery was a mile long and that the number of tombs there in marble was unequalled anywhere. 'They are all worked in different ways and carry ancient inscriptions in a language which is unintelligible. As far as the eye can see there are these lines of sarcophagi.'

So much for the story up to the fourteenth century. What of subsequent times? Alas, it is a tale of desecration which would be of exceptional interest if it were not so harrowing. Stone has to be quarried and what could be easier than to go down to the cemetery and help oneself to a few tombstones for building purposes? Then in the sixteenth century it was the vogue for French kings to present sarcophagi to visiting princes.

Today what one sees – and so well worth while – is not the original alley of Alyscamps, or Allée des Tombeau, nor is it even on the same spot, but a nineteenth-century reconstruction. It was done when the people of Arles wanted to save something from the destruction of the necropolis brought about by the construction of the PLM railway.

After Arles comes the decadent little town of St Giles, some twelve dull miles away, but the 'bible-in-stone' carvings of the triple front of the abbey-church are even more beautiful than those of the romanesque Arles church of St Trophime, which is saying a lot. This church of St Giles must have been enormous, as one can see by wandering round the ruins at the back. There is a pretty little triangular square at the front of the precinct and one of the gift shops had some comfortable tables and chairs out, and three students, seeing that all the other tables were full, invited me most deferentially to sit down.

'Is the coffee good?' I asked. And on their saying yes, and on the understanding that I be allowed to pay for my own, I sat down. On a hard-working trip like this the instant you accept a drink from another you are tied by the rules of courtesy to say a certain length of time and if you feel in your bones that you should be on your way and that the next stopping place will be more worth while, the enforced wait is agony.

I told them what I was about and they started to tell me about St Giles and they were far too nice for me to correct when they were wrong. Says Picaud:

'Oh! How wonderful it is to profit by visiting his tomb! And from the very day you have prayed with fervour you will be exorcised without any doubt. Why, I saw someone who had invoked the Saint escape from the house of a certain Peyrot, cordwainer of the town, and as soon as he left the building the whole place – which was in a shocking state – collapsed ...

'Then a man bitten by a serpent was cured; the daughter of Theocrites was cured after a long illness, and a bitch, formerly a savage animal, was tamed and served its master.'

Picaud then continued with a minute description of the altar and every carving in the church; it is more detailed than any he describes along the route, save Compostela, and then he reverts to his favourite warning: that other places and their monks might claim what is not in truth theirs.

'Such then is the tomb of the Blessed Gilles, confessor, in which his venerable body reposes with honour; and may the Hungarians blush with shame when they pretend that they have his body. And may the monks of Chamalières be confounded when they think they have his whole body. And likewise may the Normans of Cotentin be equally troubled with fear when they pride themselves on having his entire body. But as many will witness, none of his holy bones have been transported from here.

'There are only four holy bodies, it is said, that have never been taken from their sarcophagi, that is if one is to believe a number of witnesses: Saint James, Saint Martin of Tours, Saint Leonard of Limousin and Blessed Gilles.'

Some idea of the importance the cult of this saint (who died in 721) who at one time had a pilgrimage to his relics as important as the pilgrimage to Santiago may be gathered from the fact that in the early Middle Ages there were 30,000 inhabitants in the city as compared with only 5,000 now.

Actually St Gilles, who was born in Greece of royal stock and is always pictured with a gazelle pierced by an arrow which he nursed, is credited with as many miraculous cures as is Santiago Matamoros. They are the familiar ones, but the story of him and Charlemagne is rather touching. It was the King of Gascony and Toulouse who, out hunting, shot the gazelle, and the animal later led him to the saint, also pierced – by mistake – by an arrow. So impressed was the King with Gilles' piety that he commended him to build an abbey. Then the story came to the ear of Charlemagne, who later confessed to the saint all his sins save one, which was too heinous. For twenty days Gilles offered prayers that Charlemagne would confess this one too and at the last minute an angel brought a letter from God giving him permission to give the King complete absolution without the confession.

It was late vintage time when I was there and the route traversed mile upon mile of flat vineyards, some stripped to the last berry and others heavy with bunches so tightly packed that you could not drive a pin between one grape and another. They were all black and all within feet of the highway unfenced. Why some were harvested and others not I shall never know, but I was soon to know why none were pilfered when I reached out to snatch a bunch. The skin was thick and unmasticable, the huge pipes were rock hard and the juice was minimal.

After Montpelier came a division of the ways; some pilgrims went south through Béziers and Carcassonne, while others went on to Toulouse. I spent several nights in Toulouse at the Comtes de Toulouse hotel and then the Caravelle hotel, because to omit a visit to the most important basilica along the entire route, even including Spain, was impossible.

Like the whole of Toulouse, St Saturnin – shortened to St Sernin – is built of long, thin bricks the colour of onion skin. I suppose they are handsome; if I think that Coca Castle in Northern Spain is one of the loveliest of buildings, I ought to think the same about the older buildings of Toulouse. But I do not.

Unlike St Gilles, who died comfortably in his bed, St Sernin was a martyr and, as Picaud tells us, was 'attached to bulls furious and untamed and then precipitated from the citadel of the Capitol down a stone stairway a mile long. His head was broken and his brains came out and the whole of his body was done to pieces; he gave up his soul in a dignified way to Christ.'

There are many references to the likeness of the basilica of St Sernin to Compostela, but that surely is only so far as the interior is concerned. At Toulouse, and again one sees it at León, a new church design, based entirely on the need to accommodate the pilgrim crowds, was needed and carried out, which was so to arrange matters (by building double aisles on each side) that they could make a complete circular tour of the building without the flow being stopped – surely the first forerunner of a one-way traffic system.

The church and the high altar – the original one a superb table of marble now reinstated (it was lost for centuries) – were consecrated in 1096 by Pope Urban II in the presence of a host of nobles, as well as fifteen bishops from France and Spain; just one indication of how important it was to the Spanish Church.

The crypt is so rich in relics that it is supposed to have the largest collection in any church after St Peter's, Rome. There are caskets containing the relics of no less than six saints, a gift from Charlemagne on his return from his Spanish expeditions.

But when all is said and done the outside is a sad disappointment and to me a mystery. What had gone wrong? If one looks down on the church from the air, one certainly does get an idea of its present size and of the majesty of the vast octagonal six-storey bell tower. Also, I stumbled upon a painting in the Museum of Old Toulouse by A. Monserie entitled 'An assay at reconstructing the abbey'. I do not think the artist has exaggerated its past beauty and when the pilgrims saw it they must have gasped with wonderment; no wonder the town was so popular.

The mystery to me is the total lack of animation around the present; it is set in an oval space beyond some dull iron railings, between which and the church grow a few stunted trees; on the perimeter of the oval there is a single café, so aloof from the church's world that it does not deign even to sell postcards. Could it be that though we inveigh against souvenir shops, by their very tawdriness they enhance the beauty of the churches from which they get their living?

One road leading from the church square is called the Rue du Taur, with a charming old *église du Taur* – Taureau, in memory of poor Sernin and the wild bulls.

Nothing could be further from the drab muddle of the present St Sernin than the fortress-like starkness of the church of the Jacobins, which was built around 1230 by the Dominicans, following the Treaty of Paris, to see that the Toulousians followed the straight and narrow path of orthodoxy. Inside is one of the most remarkable sights in any church on the Way or elsewhere: twelve round stone columns have brickwork radiating away from each so that they look like palm trees and have therefore been called 'St James' Palms'.

But though the town was exceptionally 'full of delights' some pilgrims became ill on the way; if they had certain ailments which were then considered contagious they were forbidden to enter the walls of the town. Furthermore, many travelled part of the way by boat up the Gironde, which is exceptionally wide at this point. I was just leaving the town by a great bridge and thinking that I had done all my work when I came upon the hospital where they were cared for. I saw in the courtyard of an agglomeration of thin red brick buildings an enormous modern concrete replica of a cockle shell twelve feet square; then I saw the words 'Hospital Saint Jacques' on the wall. The place was thronged with doctors of both sexes in white coats; two officials at the entrance gates told me that I could under no circumstances take my car in, but that I could wander round if I wished. Parking was miles away and I was about to move on when a young man came up and asked what my problem was; by a stroke of luck he too was a student of the *chemin* and so I was allowed in and went round with him. It was a splendid modern hospital, but it was noteworthy that a large part of the building was constructed of the usual brick and clearly many hundreds of years old; not only were the pilgrims cared for here, but I was shown vaulted moorings constructed so that really sick pilgrims who had come to Toulouse by boat could be ferried from the river Gironde and taken straight to their sick beds.

The pilgrim crossed the Pyrenees by two passes about sixty miles apart, as the crow flies, but nearer 120 miles by car. The pass nearest the sea and much the most frequented, serving the Paris, English, Vézelay and Le Puy routes, was Roncevalles, at a height of 1,057 metres.

The more easterly pass was that of Somport Canfranc (1,632 m.), and travellers leaving Auch to get there would have gone through L'Isle de Noë (Noah's Island), Mirande, Maubourget, St James,[1] Pau (Eglise St Jacques), Oloron and then up the Gave[2] d'Apse to Urdos, and then over Somport and Canfranc. The first town in Spain was Jaca.[3]

Jaca was for the pilgrims the alpha of their trek which would end in the omega of Santiago, and so far as the cathedral went it did not disappoint. In 1063 this little Romanesque jewel, founded by Ramiro, first King of Aragon, was well advanced in its building and a few years later the sculpting in granite on the capitals of the front porch was finished. They have a surprising vigour: vegetation, serpents, the history of St Sixtus and, especially famous, the sacrifice of Abraham.

The town of 11,000 inhabitants has a good hotel, The Gran, in the half-way to luxury class, and it is a good jumping-off point for visiting more lovely monasteries near by than any other town of north-west Spain.

But if from Auch the pilgrims did not want the higher climb but did want to see Roncevalles more than Jaca, then they took my route due west and, passing through Vic-Fezenac – a charming little town with a pretty square under leafy trees – then Nogaro –

[1] North of Arles is a hamlet named St Martin-de-Londres. Why?

[2] A mountain torrent in the Pyrenees.

[3] But after leaving Arles and then St Gilles a number of pilgrims turned south for Somport, via Carcassonne, and St Gavdens. If they did this, then of course they missed Toulouse.

famed for its walnuts – and on to Aire-sur-Adour, where they met the main stream of pilgrims coming from Le Puy.

This little town, so quaintly situated on the river, tempts one to rest a while and I did. Rather proud of itself in its quiet way, Aire keeps itself clean, produces several little leaflets proclaiming its virtues and tourist attractions and has persuaded its shopkeepers and café owners to be polite and patient with those like myself who have a foreign accent. It always seems to be such a pity that it is the next restaurant owner who has to pay for the rapacity of the one before and I behaved like a boor in asking the price of every single item in a nice little café-restaurant in the town on account of a nasty little swindle the day before. Incidentally, the modern traveller need not feel that out of good manners he need ask if he can bring into a café his bits and pieces of picnic lunch and eat them with a glass or so of wine and a coffee; it is so much the normal thing that usually the *garcon* thinks you are asking for something which he does not understand.

That day I amassed a splendid collection of farmhouse butter, *pâté de campagne*, crusty bread, tomatoes, endive (chicory) and the rest, but I suddenly had the urge for a hot meal. I went into a café, explained my problem and the woman said that up the road was a *Routiers* restaurant which specialised in just that sort of thing. The place was clean but scruffy. Yes, said Madame, she quite understood; some grilled veal, some cheap red wine and absolutely nothing more, but why not let her take my vegetables and make up a nice salad of them. That sounded like a splendid change, so I gave up all my food, including the butter and *pâté*, and the next thing I knew was that as well as the bread and wine an omelette was served to me. Then followed the meat, some chips, my vegetables and, when I said no to fruit and coffee, a huge bill was presented with no suggestion of my provisions being returned.

Pride made me protest and so I was brought another piece of paper with the words *'un repas'* and a reduction of about ten per cent. Mustering up my finest French, I explained my disgust but said I would not 'create' if I could have a properly detailed bill. This did produce a bill with the details set out and another tiny reduction and so I produced the cash and started to fold the bill up. This clearly agitated the lady.

'Look, let me have the bill and I'll knock off twelve francs,' she said.

But at the café in Aire they were so nice that I offered drinks all round and then, out of curiosity and mainly to give myself a chance to talk about my early Bordeaux days, ordered – not dreaming they would have it – a liqueur which was made in that town thirty years ago, called Cordial Médoc; they had it. It is far more subtle than the usual over-scented liqueurs and I can only describe it as distilled wine – which is, of course, brandy – with the essence of Bordeaux grapes then put back.

Along with Dax, Aire is the oldest (50 BC) town in that region, known as the Landes, and was called Atura by the Romans, being on the river Atur, now Adour. At the beginning of the fifteenth century the town became the capital of a Visigoth kingdom, which is how a glorious little romanesque church came into being. Many students of Christian history have wondered if a lady who became known as Ste Quitterie ever existed, but it is fairly certain that she did and the evidence is that Gregory of Tours, in planning to write the history of the saints of the Visigothic fifth century, gives a sort of synopsis of chapters: 105 St Tetricus, Bishop; 106 St Orens, Bishop of Auch; 107 Ste Quitterie, Virgin; 108 St Paulin, Bishop. It was the usual story; she was the daughter of a king and she was converted to Christianity without her father's knowledge and against his wishes, as the king wished her to marry a Visigothic prince, whereas she had vowed her virginity to God. Her cult started in 589 when a Council of Toledo, presided over by St Leander, solemnly affirmed their conversion to the orthodox faith. The relics of Ste Quitterie were in a little church and cenobium[1] in a tiny hamlet of Mas which, adjoining the town of Aire-sur-Adour, is today called Mas d'Aire. Here in 1092 was built the great abbey of Ste Quitterie and it soon became an important station along the pilgrim's way to Santiago. Now the English appear upon the scene.

In 1288 the abbatial was ravaged by a terrible fire, and as at this time the region was under English domination it was from the English treasury that a new church was built – Gothic this time instead of Romanesque and higher than the previous church – and it was consecreted in 1309. Even before this, in 1242, the Queen of England, then in Bordeaux, had asked that she should be brought from Mas d'Aire the relics of the saint which were then venerated in the cathedral. The present church has a lovely sculpted portal and a huge impressive crypt. The place is, however, rather tucked away; it should not be missed.

[1] Middle Ages ecclesiastical word for a convent.

St James on his feast day at Santo Domingo de la Calzada

9 St James with the hens at Santo Domingo

Aire's other connection with England is that on 14 March 1814 a deadly battle took place between Wellington (12,000 English and Portuguese troops) and Soult (10,000 French) and the place became known as 'The Passage of the English'.

Aire also claims to be the home of *foie gras* and a number of other gastronomic delicacies, in particular chicken with *chanterelles*, a pale yellow edible fungus which abounds there.

A nice room was again waiting for me at the Dupouy Hotel, and after a pleasant dinner and some good local wine I gave a little talk – my first in French and also my first on the *Camino Frances*. That was to the Anglo-Spanish Society some ten years ago after 'The Road' had been my hobby for a couple of years.

Set in a lovely undulating plain with forests which make it a perfect centre for the more serious tourist, St Sever is an unusually attractive town with the considerable remains of an abbatial so large that I nearly made a mistake in thinking that the enormous church in the centre of the town was all there was to see. But the chance purchase of a postcard sent me back inside the church, where on a wall was a coloured pictorial map, eight feet square, showing the abbey, its outbuildings and the grounds as they were at the end of the sixteenth century; and so the convent des Jacobins, which I now walked along to see, must have been part of the whole complex.

The exterior is in sad need of repair and a few thousand pounds spent now on some minimal cement patching could arrest total decay for another century. Inside is a huge courtyard under a corrugated perspex roof. 'We use the courtyard in winter for the monthly fair, where we sell the uncooked goose livers; then in summer we remove the roof and the courtyard is used as a car park for tourists,' said a man who was getting a wedding banquet ready in a hall to one side. The refectory or dining-room which the pilgrims would have used is a magnificent sight, with some splendid rafters; it is now used for the monthly winter sale of goose livers, this time the cooked ones.

Hagetmau comes next, with the curious, very old and small crypt of St Gines in the grounds of a private house; then Orthez; then St Palais, very much a tourist centre, where down a lane and in the grounds of a tiny farm is the Stele Discodiale[1] of Gibraltar, erected at the meeting-point of the Jacobites from Paris, Vézelay and Le Puy.

[1] An upright slab in the form of a discus.

For three of the four great routes had virtually fused at St Palais. I do not know on what grounds the erectors of the stele chose that spot. It certainly is panoramically open, but the hamlet that all the records state was the meeting place was at Ostabat, a little farther south. Of all the dirty, forlorn, dilapidated villages I have had to visit for the sake of this book, this was the worst. Perhaps some hamlets which have been literally abandoned save for a couple of families, between León and the Cebrero mountains, are more tragic, but Ostabat is in a rich part of France; it has not a single bar, though you can get a beer standing up (be satisfied with a mug) in a smelly grocer's shop.

And so we reach St John-Pied-de-Port, an enchanting and clean historical little town where I put up at one of the most friendly and best-run hotels in France. Monsieur Chiriquin has been the owner of the Central Hotel now for thirty years, and because he keeps the place spotless, serves good food and employs efficient and polite staff, he has my warm blessing.

This is another townlet that the energetic Vauban was asked to fortify, though there are so many that one can only assume that he merely rubber-stamped most of the work. At any rate there are fifteenth-century (pre-Vauban) ramparts; the main street is called the Road of Spain, and there is a Porte St Jacques from which pilgrims had a fine view over the plain of Cize. The town is on the River Nive and only 500 yards from the present bridge, along a quiet sandy footpath, shaded by tall poplars, is a very ancient pilgrim bridge in an idyllic setting.

Five miles farther south the modern traveller passes into Spain at the little frontier-hamlet of Arnéguy. You present your passport, the customs man waves you on. You hold out your green card as if to say, 'Please at least look at this'. The customs man waves you on. You point to it and raise your eyebrows.

'Look,' you say, 'it's correctly dated. The last time I passed through Calais the policeman noted that it was dated one day late and I had to pay nearly three pounds for a temporary certificate. I didn't half kick up a row with the insurance company. Fortunately the covering receipt showed it was their mistake.'

He waves you on, not wanting to know.

Before – that is twelve miles before – the pilgrims reached the Ibaneta pass, 3,000 feet up, they went through the pretty little village of Valcarlos – Charlemagne Valley. This is where we must deal with the question of Charlemagne, the Song of Roland,

Turpin's Chronicle, and Compostela: a remarkable story in which history comes first and the legend follows.

Because he wished to defend himself against the Abderraman dynasty of Córdoba, Ibna-el-Arabi, a Saracen knight of Zaragoza, sent a deputation to Emperor Charlemagne in 777, asking for military aid and promising in exchange to become a Christian with all his followers.

Charlemagne, who was already at war against the Saxons, accepted the invitation and, after placing garrisons to fortify his frontiers, marched into Spain with all his available forces. He divided his army into two parts, one of which crossed the Pyrenees to the east and conquered Gerona and the other under his own command crossed the Pyrenees nearer the sea and conquered Pamplona, razing it to the ground so that on his way to Zaragoza there would be no fortress at his rear. Both armies then laid siege to Zaragoza but without success. Trouble with the Saxons then forced the Emperor to abandon his Spanish expedition.

But as a reprisal for the destruction of Pamplona, the Navarrese lay in wait for the army in the defile of Roncevalles or Roncevaux (*ronces*, thorns; *vaux*, valley) and there on 15 August 778 the famous battle was fought. Charlemagne's troops were divided into two corps, the van being formed by some four thousand men under Charlemagne's command. Bringing up the rear was Roland with booty taken on the victorious way to Zaragoza and hundreds of slaves as hostages. The Navarrese allowed the vanguard to pass and then attacked Roland, who fell, together with the Peers of France, after an epic combat.

There seems little doubt that these are historical facts; they were recorded by Chronicler Eginhart in his *Vita Caroli* in 830 and an epitaph in Latin verse confirms the date. Then the tale of Roncevaux goes underground for a couple of centuries and we get the extraordinary occurrence of history turned into legend, and that is where our Santiago pilgrimage comes in; for with the Way actually passing the bloody battlefield, what should be more natural than that monks, minstrels and poets should tell, sing and write about the event, embroidering the story in the process?

From internal evidence of feudal customs, language, accoutrements and arms, and names of historical personages, and the probably authentic knowledge of the territories held by the Saracens, it was probably written in the twelfth century and not long after the First Crusade.

What interests scholars, however, is how the oral legend grew out of the historical fact, for the man who wrote it – possibly a Norman called Turold – must have had something to work on and that something was a tale told to the pilgrims in the heights of the Pyrenees. What is significant is that the Song of Roland, by far the earliest, the most readable, famous and greatest *chanson de geste* (song of deeds) of four thousand lines – short as epics go – is told as though the reader knew a great deal about the story before he settled down to read, or rather to listen.

After the godlike Charlemagne with his white flowing beard, doubly valiant and honourable Roland, wise Oliver, nasty Masilion, the Saracen king, and the traitorous villain Ganelon, the next most important person in the *Chanson de Roland* is Archbishop Turpin, who may well have had a real existence in an Archbishop Tilpinus of Rheims of the eighth century. His personal charm and extraordinary bravery have been highly dramatised, for in the second assault on the pagans he is given the honour of opening the battle, and he is the last left on the battlefield of Roncevalles when all the rest are slain; yet he was by no means out of character, for the period of the fighting and crusading priest had not yet given way to that of the contemplative cloistered monk. But was Turpin ever at the battle at all? Did Roland ever see the great Archbishop lying with his bowels gushing from his side? Did Turpin say just before dying:

'Alack brave champions;
May your souls rest with the all glorious God
In paradise amid the rose blossoms?'

Modern scholars say not and that while the battle raged he was saying mass a few miles away.

This does not matter. What does matter is that this Turpin was the person whom the monks of Cluny wished people to think had written the fourth of the five books called the *Codex Calistinus* or *Book of Saint James*.

Now Charlemagne was such a great person that the Cluniac monks, as historians see it, wanted him to be involved in Compostela because until that time there existed two parallel traditions concerning Charlemagne and his Twelve Peers, one burying them along the Paris–Bordeaux route and the other along the Arles–Toulouse route.

The thing to do, and it was a superb piece of public relations work, was to write a 'history' which would fit both traditions. Weary and old, Charlemagne wished to rest, but one night he saw a starry road which crossed Spain to Galicia where the body of St James lay at that time unrecognised. Many times he saw this but did not understand its portent until the Apostle appeared to him and commanded him to recapture the road that led to his tomb, so that all people could go in pilgrimage till the end of time. In exchange God was to offer the Emperor a crown in heaven.

So the story has it that Charlemagne undertook three expeditions to Spain: the first via Pamplona, which he captured, pushing on afterwards to Compostela and farther to El Padron, where the boat from the Holy Land arrived that carried the body of the Apostle. Then Charlemagne rode into the sea and thrust in his lance as a sign of his dominion even to the ends of the earth. His next sortie to Spain was to chastise the Saracen knight Agolant; after defeating him on the banks of the River Cea, Charlemagne built an abbey where Sahagún now stands. On his third visit he assembled a great army in the Landes of Bordeaux and, crossing the Somport Pass, conquered all Spain and captured Saragossa, but he was then attacked in the mountains and his thousand knights were slain. At last the Emperor died and all the deeds of his life were placed in the balance on the Day of Judgement. It was touch and go, but a headless Galician threw in the stones of all the churches Charlemagne had built; Charlemagne rose to Paradise.

The person who unravelled the profound significance of this propaganda operation by the monks of Cluny was the great French writer about the pilgrims' road, Joseph Bédier.

The scheme – and I translate – was to group around southern France every hero in all the *chansons de geste* and to set them marching with the same crusading spirit to the tomb of the Apostle and then to bring them back via Roncevalles, so that on this last stage back from Spain St James could give them a feeling that they had shared in the joy of martyrdom. It was a wonderful idea, this twilight of heroes reborn to eternal light. It was a wonderful idea to distribute their remains along the routes to Compostela so that they of the militant church could thus be guardians, models and patrons of these triumphant pilgrims.

Valcarlos was then an evocative name, for it was there that Charlemagne encamped whilst his rear guard was being massacred. Then came the peak of Ibanesa in the Pyrenees which, says

Picaud, 'is so high it appears to touch the sky; those who make the ascent believe they can touch the heavens'. Here the pilgrims rested at the monastery of San Salvador, where on foggy days a bell was constantly rung to guide them to their temporary lodgings, and afterwards on a gentle slope to Roncevaux.

Though the scenery has not changed since 776 a great number of buildings have gone up for the comfort and care of the pilgrims. I am in a dilemma here; if I were certain that no one would ever go to Roncevaux I could describe it in the fashion of travel brochures. But the sad fact is that the place is dismal. What I cannot forgive are the coloured brochures showing the complex of buildings and what appears to be superbly slated roofs; it is a terrible shock to discover that the roofs are of grey corrugated iron, slightly rusted. However, there is the chapel of Sancti Spiritus, the oldest building in Roncevaux, situated above a cave which used to serve as an ossuary for the remains of the pilgrims who died in the hospital.

The chapel of Santiago, next door, is in better condition. It used to be the first link in Spain of a whole chain of churches dedicated to Saint James. On the bell gable they placed the old bell from Ibaneta which had saved so many lives by its clangour when straying pilgrims were beset by bandits or wild beasts.

The most important building is the *Colegiata* or Collegiate Church, built and richly endowed by Sancho 'the Strong' between 1194 and 1215. The former chapter hall, which is now a royal vault, dates from the fourteenth century and contains the remains of Sancho, who was in fact a giant, and the carved figure lying prone above his tomb is seven feet four inches long. But the most interesting things to be seen are the links of chain captured from the Saracens which the King brought back after the battle of Navas de Tolosa, down in the province of Jaen.

Two miles farther into Spain is the very well kept little village of Burguete, with several good pensions; then follows the most lovely countryside, with Espinal, Erro, Zubiri, Urdaniz, Larrasoana and, almost in the suburbs of Pamplona, Huarte, where a marble gothic statue of the Virgin Mary was venerated.

Chapter 7

THE PILGRIMS' ROAD AND THE RECONQUEST

We left St James just half-way through the ninth century with the Reccareds and Roderics of the Visigothic era of Spanish history and we now move on for five hundred years or so to the Ramiros, Sanchos, Ferdinands and Alfonsos of the Asturias, León, Navarre, Aragón and Castile.

The confusion is daunting; this is because, when one kingdom merged into another, King I of a given name of the former became for instance King III of the same name of the latter, but often it was the other way round.

The oldest kingdom was that of Asturias and León, starting with the semi-legendary Pelayo, 718; then, with seven short-reigned kings between, we reach Alfonso II ('the Chaste'), who was on his throne when St James' body was found. Then come Ramiro I, 842; Ordoño I, 850; Alfonso III, 866; Garcia, 910; Ordoño II, 914; Fruela II, 923; Alfonso IV, 925; Ramiro II, 930; and Ordoño III, 950.

About half a century before this Navarre had had its first King Garcia I, 885, followed by Sancho I, 905; Garcia II (called 'the Trembling' or alternatively 'the Timid'), 924; and Sancho II ('the Greater'), 970. We may here note in passing that Garcia's timidity at least kept him on his throne for a great number of years for those days.

Castile, during this incredibly confused period of Spanish history, was a dependency of León and the Asturias and later had its first king in Fernan Gonzalez, 932; then came Garcia Fernandez, 970; Sancho Garcez, 955; Garcia Sanchez, 1021; and then Sancho 'the Greater', 1027; but this Sancho is the same king as Sancho II of Alvarre above.

Now we come to Aragón. This was partly held by the Moors, but the western section was possessed by the Christians, being a dependency of Navarre. The first King of Aragón was Ramiro I, a son of Sancho the Greater.

Now let us return to the Asturias (on the Bay of Biscay, with Covadonga and Oviedo as main cities) and León. In 955, taking over from his brother Ordoño III, Sancho I (the first Sancho of this kingdom) came to the throne and was named 'the Fat'. He was indeed so obese that he offended Christian opinion of the time and was forced to retire into exile by a usurper. Sancho then did something extraordinary; he wrote to Abderrahmán III, the Calif of Códoba, asking if he could consult some of the famous hakims[1] of the Moorish capital about his obesity. The Calif answered favourably; Sancho was superbly slimmed down by the use of herbs and then made himself so popular that Abderrahmán gave him an army of Moors to reconquer his kingdom.

When we come to the Alfonsos the confusion is far worse, and we must simply say that within a period of under a century there were kings with this name on the thrones of León, Castile, Navarre and Aragón. It was these kings who, with Ferdinand III, did most for the Pilgrims' Road. Most of them had descriptive names. Of León, Alfonso I was 'the Catholic', II 'the Chaste', III 'the Great', IV 'the Monk', V 'the Noble', VI 'the Fearless', VII 'the Emperor', VIIII 'the Good', IX 'the Holy', X 'the Learned' and XI 'the Just'.[2]

One of the most important of these was Alfonso VI (the Fearless). He had six wives and the second was a woman who had grown up under the influence of the monastery of Cluny. She was Constance, daughter of the Duke of Burgundy, and it was she who restrained his nationalistic impulses and turned him towards the idea of a church with greater control from Rome. In this he had the strong support of the Pope, who was determined to employ Cluniac monks to rid the Spanish church of its Visigothic traditions. With this plan in mind St Adelemas – called Lesmes in Spain – was sent to Spain from La Chaise-Dieu (Haute Loire) in France, where he had been abbot. He arrived on an ass and

[1] Moslem physicians.
[2] Then a break for five hundred years to XII 'the Peacemaker'.

immediately started to work miracles in front of Alfonso, who was so impressed that he gave him a monastery to help the pilgrims at Burgos.

The King had an ulterior motive for fostering the pilgrimage of St James, for he was eager to attract foreign merchants and workers to Spain and for this reason encouraged them to settle down in the 'Frankish Quarter' of towns on the route, like Belorado, Burgos and especially Sahagún. And it was during his reign that remarkable character El Cid appears on the scene: 'The history of the eleventh century in Spain is full of examples of the employment of *chevaliers d'industrie*; but none of these has ever obtained such celebrity as the Cid the national hero of Spain.' So says Stanley Lane-Poole in his book, *The Moors of Spain*.

The Cid's (Arabic Sidi, lord) proper name was Rodrigo Diaz of Bivar from a town of that name near Burgos, but he was called by the other, more popular Arabic name by his Moorish followers. He was also called El Campeador, which in Spanish means something rather more special than champion. A *campeador* was a man who had fought and beaten the selected single fighting man of the opposite side in the presence of the two armies. Rodrigo had earned this name not fighting a Moor but a Christian, having as a youth killed a Navarrese champion in a war between Castile and Navarre.

Although he used him for military skirmishes, Alfonso VI never liked the Cid because of an incident connected with his gaining the crown. Alfonso's brother Sancho was murdered by one Bellido Adolphus, such a traitor that he has had his name linked with the other infamous Spanish traitor, Count Julian, and even with Judas. The death of Sancho left the Castilians no choice but to make Alfonso, ex-King of León, their own king. This they were unwilling to do, since they feared that Alfonso would make Castile subject to León. It was indeed touch and go and some of the nobles suggested a compromise, that as a condition of being nominated king, Alfonso should swear that he personally had not had any part in his brother Sancho's death. But which of the nobles was to put the proposition? The only person who so dared was El Campeador and before twelve select nobles the King did duly swear; and the true historical event has been recorded in one of the best ballads ever.[1]

[1] James Young Gibson, 1826–86.

> 'Alfonso and ye Leonese
> I charge ye here to swear
> That in Don Sancho's death ye had
> By word or deed no share.'

The Cid then rubs things in and says that if he does not tell the truth he will be slain not by nobles of Castilian blood but, to his eternal shame, by Asturian peasants, a fierce and cruel race.

> 'Three times the Cid has given the oath,
> Three times the King hath sworn,
> With every oath his anger burned
> And then he cries with scorn,
> "Thou swearest me where doubt is none,
> Rodrigo to thy sorrow,
> The hand that takes this oath today
> Thou hast to kiss tomorrow. . . ." '

The Cid's answer sums up his character; he was first and foremost a mercenary who would burn and slay his opponents whenever it suited him, but his morals were above reproach:

> ' "Agreed Señor!" replied the Cid,
> If thou wilt give me pay
> As other kings in other lands
> Do give their knights this day;
> Whose vassal I consent to be
> Must pay me like the rest,
> If you agree to do so now
> I yield to this request!"
> The king grew pale to hear these words
> And turned him from the Cid,
> And from that hour for many a day
> His wrath could not be hid.'

But the King needed his vassal and this is where his connection with the Pilgrims' Road comes in.

Alfonso VI wanted to strengthen the pilgrimage by any means he could; he also wanted to strengthen the bond between Castile and León, so he took a number of Castilian nobles together with the Cid on a goodwill mission to Oviedo. This was in 1075.

Ever since the days of Alfonso III 'the Great', the cathedral of San Salvador (the Saviour) in this town had been a place of pilgrimage second only to Santiago and indeed there grew up the saying:

> '*Quien va a Santiago*
> *Y no a Salvador*
> *Sirve al Criado*
> *Y deja al Señor*'
>
> (He who goes to Santiago
> And not to the Saviour
> Waits on the servant
> And rejects the master)

The cathedral at Oviedo is unique in Spain as being the only one which incorporates substantial pre-romanesque remains above ground. This is the Cámara Santa of the early ninth century and was built by Tioda, who had completed the adjoining basilica by 802. The Cámara Santa, now known as the chapel of Santa Leocadia – a noble maiden of Toledo, d. 304, who, imitating another saint, Eulalia of Mérida, begged God to let her die by torture for Christ – stands on a low subvault obviously so constructed in order to preserve the relics from damp. Placed in a holy ark constructed by disciples of the apostles, these relics were almost the most sacred of all, being those of the Passion of Christ, viz. fragments of the Cross, drops of the Redeemer's blood, the napkin that enveloped his head and crumbs of the Last Supper.[1]

These relics were so holy that no one had dared open the ark save some foolhardy clerics, who may not have fasted properly or correctly beforehand and who in 1030 did open the chest, from which there emanated so stupendous a light that some of those present were struck blind.

Alfonso VI, however, following the example of his father, Ferdinand I, made his followers and the clergy prepare themselves for the ceremony by fasting and penance and then, after divine service on the fourth day of Lent, 6 March 1075, in Oviedo and in the presence of Dona Urraca (his sister), the Bishops of Oviedo, Oca,[2] Astorga and Palencia and the Cid, the ark was opened. Neither this entourage nor the King were blinded this time, but the latter saw to it that reports of this impressive find – they

---

[1] They had been brought to Oviedo by Visigothic nobles when they fled to Asturias and Cantabria after the Moorish invasion in 711.

[2] An important man in that period.

included relics of the Virgin Mary[1] – were circulated all over Christendom to add to the prestige of Oviedo and the shrine of St James as well.

All the time the Christians in the north were engaged in this feverish round of publicity, anti-bandit precautions, forest clearing and hospital building, the Moors in the south were quietly beautifying Córdoba but noisily quarrelling among themselves. It is not our duty, however, to trace the history of the Moors in Spain until nearly three hundred years after their arrival, when the mighty Almanzor arrives upon the scene.

Starting life as an insignificant student at the University of Córdoba, where his father was known as a lawyer of a good but not influential family, Almanzor al Allah (meaning 'victorious by the grace of God' – an epithet which shows that he intended to go on a crusade) was so certain that he would come to power that, confidently predicting that he would one day become Master of Andalucia, he even asked his schoolfellows which posts they would like when that moment arrived. His career is an interesting example of what latent courage and selfishness could do in a Moslem state where the road was open to fame for a genius who did not necessarily have access to the corridors (at first, at least) of power.

Starting as a mere court letter-writer to the great chamberlain – equivalent to our prime minister – he used his charm and winning ways to gain the favour of the ladies of the royal harem and especially Aurora, who on the death of Calif Hakim found herself placed in a position of great importance.

But while Almanzor's meteoric rise to power was taking place, the fame of the pilgrimage away up in Galicia was beginning to cause such a stir that it was feared that the shrine would make a greater appeal to the pilgrims of the world than the Mosque at Córdoba. Every year, therefore, Almanzor proclaimed a Holy War against the enemies of Islam, hoping thus to strike terror into the souls of the Mozarabic Christians who might possibly be wavering in their loyalty.

The greatest foray of all was to be to the shrine of St James and the expedition was meticulously planned. A fleet was sent to cooperate on the river Douro and Almanzor, advancing from the south, scored an initial triumph at Zamora, where news of his mighty army had so frightened a number of Spanish counts or petty chieftains that with the true selfishness of this period in

[1] They were recorded in a manuscript at Valenciennes in the eleventh century.

Spain they sided with the invaders to secure their own safety and to share in the spoil.

Almanzor entered Santiago on Wednesday, 10 August 997, and like Napoleon at Moscow, found the city deserted, the inhabitants having fled from the merciless infidel whose method of warfare was extermination. He sacked the town and so completely demolished the church that, according to a Moorish chronicler, on the morrow no one would have supposed that it had ever existed. But surprisingly he neither destroyed the tomb of the Apostle nor carried the ashes back to Córdoba, because according to Christian chroniclers the saint 'had the power of surrounding himself with an obfuscation of his own making', as Richard Ford puts it. It is further added for good measure that Almanzor did find one person in the deserted city, a monk still praying before the holy shrine.

'What doest thou here?' the Moor asked.

'I am at my prayers,' replied the monk.

Thereupon his life was spared and a guard was placed around the tomb to protect it and the monk from the licentious soldiery.

Though Almanzor did not take St James' ashes back to Córdoba, he did carry back a vast amount of booty and something else which may well have been a psychological mistake, for it served to keep the Christian crusading spirit alive. He transported, with the help of the strongest Christian captives, the bells of the Cathedral of Santiago back to Córdoba to be hung up, reversed as lamps, in the great Mesquita. And there they stayed, but only for 329 years, when they went back to Santiago!

Alfonso VII the Emperor was crowned King of León and Castile in 1126, and having been brought up in Galicia – indeed he called himself king of that country before he assumed the title of Emperor – took a great interest in Santiago. He it was who persuaded the Pope to elevate the cathedral to the status of a bishopric, a consequence of which was the setting up of further French settlements along the road. But he also set up a rival shrine at that town where it is said that the map of Spain folds exactly in half. Although I do not like it overmuch, for it is too tourist ridden, Toledo certainly has more Moorish-Christian history within its walls than any other town in Spain. Anyway, Alfonso VII, after capturing Córdoba in 1144, decided that Islamic culture had so much to offer to Europe that it could not and should not be lost. Thus it was that he employed a number of Jewish scholars who were masters of Arabic, Hebrew and Greek thought and gave them help from his own churchmen to translate a great number of works from these languages into Latin and Castilian. Toledo became a goal for students from France, Germany and England and a new pilgrim route was opened to that town as a rival to Santiago. Toledo is and has been for about fourteen centuries the home of the Primate of Spain, but in the twelfth century efforts were made to transfer it to Santiago but without success.[1]

Alfonso VIII became king as a minor in 1158 and ascended the throne at the age of fourteen in 1170. In that same year he married Eleanor, daughter of Henry II of England. He was nicknamed 'the Good' or 'the Noble' and remained on the throne for nearly half a century. He did every bit as much as any of the other Alfonsos to continue the popularity of the Way. He persuaded merchants from England and Gascony to work in Burgos and in the opposite direction organised safe passage for others to take Castilian wines, wool and hides to Cantabrian ports for shipment north; but these commercial ventures were done not so much to help the Castilian merchants but to see that the Way became safer and easier to traverse; and, generally, according to the chronicles, Alfonso X 'the Wise' was the greatest monastery giver of them all and was 'crowned by God'.

Though not connected directly with the Way, Alfonso VIII's main claim to fame is that he won one of those decisive battles that change history. This took place on 16 July 1212 at a place in the present province of Jaén called, as was the battle, Las Navas de Tolosa,[2] and the Moors were so decisively beaten that their kingdom never again presented a threat to crusading Christian Spain.

Five years after this there came to the Spanish throne a king whose single-minded crusading spirit won him a posthumous reward in canonisation as a saint. In Rome they seem to be weirdly inconsistent in the number of years they take to make a saint. With St Teresa of Lisieux, whose life and work I find dull and uninspiring, they dispensed with the fifty-years-before-you-can-be-considered rule and she was canonised twenty-three years later. Both St Ferdinand and St Joan of Arc have their saint's day on 13

---

[1] The pressure to make the change must have been very great; for writing in the fifteenth century William Wey erroneously says that of the archbishoprics in Spain the Primate was at Santiago, the next at Seville (at that time Spain's largest city) and the third at Toledo.

[2] Nava is an old word signifying a small plain among the mountains. It is contained in the name of Navarre. Las Navas de Tolosa is not to be confused with the Tolosa in Guipúzcoa.

May, but they had to wait 419 and 489 years respectively for canonisation. Ferdinand (the real founder of the University of Salamanca) was by all accounts a remarkably fine man; for twenty-seven years he waged tireless and totally successful wars against the Moors, not to gain territory but 'to rescue Christian people from the domination of the infidels', as Butler tells us in his *Lives of the Saints*.

Butler further tells us that 'It was at the battle of Xeres,[1] when only ten Spanish lives were lost, that Saint James was said to have been leading the host on a white horse', and this must have been just before 1236, the year of St Ferdinand's most famous re-conquest of all. Says H. E. Watts: '. . . a still more valuable prize was made by the Christians, the fame of which resounded through Europe. The great city of Córdoba which had been the pride and glory of Mahommedanism – the seat of the highest civilisation to which Islam had ever attained – the centre of light and learning, the second Mecca to the faithful – fell easily into the hands of Fernando.'

He then reconsecrated the great Mosque or Mesquita as a cathedral but sent the bells back on the backs of Moorish captives to Compostela.

[1] Now Jerez de la Frontera.

⊙ SANTO DOMINGO

● NAJERA

● NAVARRETE
● VILLA ROYA
● LOGROÑO

● TORRES
● LOS ARCOS

● IRACHE
● ESTELLA

● LORCA
● PUENTE LA REINA

⊙ PAMPLONA

10a Sculpting of the miracle hens at Santo Domingo

The hen-coop in the cathedral at Santo Domingo

11a Thirteenth-century hermitage of St James at Valdefuentes

11b The favourite church of Alfonso the Wise at Villarcazar de Sirga

Chapter 8

PAMPLONA TO ESTELLA

It is only a morning's drive from the French frontier to Pamplona, or as the French insist on calling it, Pamplune, the ancient capital of the kingdom of Navarre.

The façade of the cathedral[1] is so ugly that surprisingly few people visit the Gothic cloisters which are of consummate beauty. In one corner is a fountain very rarely seen in such a position, especially built by the monks for the pilgrims on their journey. Leading off the cloisters and thus making the whole Gothic ensemble the most important of its kind outside France is an even rarer ancient building, a kitchen with five huge chimneys to take away the smoke; the only similar one is at Fontrevault on the Loire.

The oldest church in the town is the oldest Gothic church in Navarre – for we are now in this province[2] – built by King Sancho el Mayor when he introduced the Cluny reform into Spain. The tower is famous and outside in the porch is a very fine statue of St James, dressed unusually in a raincoat, perhaps an indication of the weather in this part of Spain. This church of St Cernin has the closest of connections with the huge St Sernin at Toulouse.

The importance of the town in the early days of Compostela can be judged by the size of the former Hostal de San Miguel, now the Museum of Navarre, worth mentioning because of the beautiful way the exhibits have been laid out and because it contains the best collection of Gothic murals in Spain.

[1] The name for a cathedral in Northern Spain is *Seo*, which is confusing.
[2] Only three provinces in Spain are not named after their capital city. Navarre, *cap*. Pamplona; Viscaya, *cap*. Bilbao; and Alava, *cap*. Vitoria.

But Pamplona today has 150,000 inhabitants, though the city which came into being, flourished and stayed prosperous as a convenient junction on the pilgrims' way, has another saint who to the inhabitants is much more important. Martyred in 287, St Fermin was born in the town and his saint's day is (most conveniently for the tourist industry) on 7 July, when one of the most dangerous bull-fighting spectacles in all Spain – the Running of the Bulls – takes place. Thousands of words have been written to describe this event, but reduced to simple terms, the bulls which have been brought in from country farms to be fought and dispatched are, instead of being lodged in a corral or pen adjacent to the bull ring, kept in an enclosure outside the city. From there to the ring all the streets are barricaded off save the one along which they are intended to charge in their fury.

The *encierro* (driving bulls into the penfold) is marked by the roar of rockets, which is only matched by the roar of the crowds, and it is no wonder that 'even trained runners who give themselves a generous handicap find themselves pressed by the racing bulls, and as the animals approach the ring the crowds of more timid runners conglomerate and there is pandemonium'. Thus Walter Starkie in his *The Road to Santiago* described what he saw, and he continues: 'For the bulls, maddened by the shouting people, stampede and charge over those who have fallen in the melée, and gore those who block their way. They race on like an avalanche over the writhing mass of human beings.'

The great Manolete was fighting the bulls during this particular *corrida* and Starkie remembers seeing him each evening in a small but smart restaurant and describes him as 'one of the most retiring and unaffected young men I have ever met; his physique was delicate though wiry, his expression serious and full of melancholy'. Not a word of this description is exaggerated; Manolete, who played the bulls more gracefully than any other toreador and was gored to death at Lérida, will be affectionately remembered when all the other fighters have been forgotten.

I have eaten often in the restaurant in the Paseo Sarasate (named after the famous violinist and composer born in the town in 1884) which was started by seven pretty young sisters around 1937. The food and service is good, the restaurant prospered and so it got into the guide books all over the world by its very charming name, 'Las Siete Pocholas' (the Seven Pretty Ones). These young women not only had excellent taste – and still have – but they had that sort of ambition which led them to buy up an adjacent building and expand. They decided its new name must be a dignified one, so they wished to call their place the Hostal del Rey Noble; a noble name indeed, but they misjudged the incredible popularity of the old one. Still, they persevered and won, or nearly won, for the official name of the most luxurious and best restaurant in Pamplona is now 'Hostal del Rey Noble, "Las Pocholas".' The word 'seven' is now missing; the restaurant is still there.

There are two hotels in this university town which I like: the Perla in the busy Plaza Castillo (get a back room), and in the spacious Taconera gardens the more expensive, modern, luxury hotel, The Three Kings.

The pilgrims leaving Pamplona had a pleasant though tough walk in front of them, for they had to ascend and afterwards descend the Sierra de Perdón. They then certainly made a detour to visit a Templar church, the chapel at Eunate, which is a bizarre construction. It has worried architects for a hundred years, for it is octagonal and is not unlike the Holy Sepulchre in Jerusalem. But around the church is a puzzling cloister, also octagonal, with thirty-three arches suspended upon twin columns; the most recent explanation is that it was a funeral chapel.

It was at Puente la Reina[1] that the two pilgrims' roads, the Aragon Way passing through the town of Jaca and the Navarre Way passing through Roncevalles and Pamplona, met. This town, now of some 2,000 inhabitants, sprang into importance because in the eleventh century Queen Dona Mayor,[2] wife of Sancho the Great, caused the bridge which was named for her to be built over the river Arga, solely for the use of the pilgrims.

It is not unreasonable to feel a little emotional about this town because the main street runs dead straight from the Hospital of the Crucifix (its 'Y' shaped cross, with the arms upstretched, is famous throughout Spain) to the beautiful bridge which has been in constant use for eight hundred years; so has the street.

The road from Puenta la Reina to Estella is of great interest because you can find detours from the present road where the old road is clearly definable. Such a place is Cirauqui, which in 1965 had a population of only a thousand inhabitants. Then came the village of Bargota, of which nothing now remains, but it was important because it belonged to the Knights Templars. Here the

---

[1] In the eleventh century it was called Ponte de Arga or Ponte Regina.
[2] Or it may have been Dona Estefania, wife of Garcia of Najera.

pilgrims crossed a little rivulet by a tiny but very old bridge which is still standing. Here is still to be seen an ogival Gothic church with a splendid façade of curiously oriental style.

The road then goes on to the Lorca, of 267 inhabitants in 1965, where there the single main street is the very one the pilgrims would have taken. On the left is a small church, somewhat restored, with a single nave and an interesting Romanesque apse. In front of the church a hospital once stood, given in 1204 by Gutierrez Gascon, son of Gascon de Murel. Actually he gave it to Our Lady of Roncevalles and in the same century the two establishments were run as one.

There are four kilometres between Lorca and Villatuerta, but since the old road runs more or less parallel to the present one few if any physical signs of it can be seen. Outside the village, which now has only 730 inhabitants, are the ruins of what was the monastery of San Miguel, where the pilgrims were well refreshed; then, five kilometres farther on, comes Estella.

The month of July 1959 was a scorcher. Paris ran out of ice cream; London ran out of beer; old people died of the heat and newspapers in their ignorance predicted that it would be a fabulous year for wine, not realising that if there is too much sun the vines get roasted and the wine is rather harsh. Still, they said so much about it that they temporarily pushed up the forward buying of clarets and cynical wine merchants called it *'l'année de la presse'*.

During the worst week of this scorcher one of my innumerable wine-discovering holidays drew to its close. This time it had been to the Rioja district of which Haro, a pleasant town and proud of its storks, which nest annually on the top of the town hall, is the centre. We were exceptionally late for lunch, as we had been tasting much wine at the *bodegas*. It was market day, too, and I feared that all the restaurants might have sold out, so that when after circling the square twice I found a parking place and my son, George, suggested we put the car in the shade, I roughly replied 'for heavens sake let's get some grub in our bellies and to hell with the heat'. After all these years I offer my apologies, for when we went back to the little Ford and I opened the door, the heat was so terrific that we had to fan the inside with our hats. But that did not do much good and as we bowled along past the bright red soil of the Rioja vineyards my thirst was so great that I declared we must stop at the very next place we came to, which was Estella.

This town of 8,000 inhabitants has been called the 'Toledo of the north' on account of the great number of beautiful churches and other buildings. In 1956 the *barrio* (or precinct) of San Pedro de la Rúa, which included that part by the river along which the pilgrims used to walk, was declared a National Monument. Although *Estella la Bella*, as it was called from the fifteenth century, was a most important halt for the pilgrims, I think that most Spaniards think of the town in connection with the two Carlist wars of the 1830s and 1870s.

Its greatest moment in the nineteenth century was June 1874, when the Republicans under General Concha marched on Estella with the intention of capturing 'the holy city of Carlism'. It was an impossible task, for the town lies in a hollow of the mountains and the Carlists had taken up strong defensive positions to guard the approaches. Furthermore, when it was known that the Republicans were on the way all the women, children and non-combatants left the town and went up into the mountains, taking not only food but every scrap of property they could remove. All of which proved unnecessary; the Republicans were decisively routed and the fugitives returned to the town, which indulged in scenes of rejoicing more jubilant than those seen in London at the relief of Mafeking. Three days later, Don Carlos (Carlos VII) and his wife Margarita set out from Tolosa to honour the town's defenders. They were driven to a village near by and then, mounting the two pure white Andalusians which were waiting for them, the royal couple rode into Estella. There is a black and white sketch of the King returning from mass in that town which is quite moving.

There are at present two visible signs of those stirring events; there is the Casa de Carlos VII at 13 Plaza de los Fueras,[1] where the King stayed when Estella was the Carlist military headquarters from 1872 to 1876, and a far grimmer reminder, a stone recording the execution by firing squad, under the orders of Carlist General Maroto, of five generals of his own camp for alleged treachery. The stone is outside the modern Basilica of Our Lady of Puy, which houses a statue of the Virgin said to be of Visigothic origin.

I may be right in saying that Estella has more anicent buildings

---

[1] It is said that Carlism flourished so vigorously in the north-east because the Basques were very proud of the chartered right or Fueros which dated back to the Middle Ages and which the Madrid Government was trying to whittle away. This is grossly exaggerated.

and churches than any other town of its size in Spain. It is also claimed that it 'is a living museum, showing the transition from the purest Romanesque architecture to primitive Gothic'. There are four churches still entire, two very old churches of which vestiges can still be seen. Of these San Miguel, of the twelfth century, has a Romanesque doorway with a sculpted tympanum of incredible richness, and San Pedro de la Rua has a superb cloister. But in the little quarter which has been declared of historical interest is the only non-religious building in Spain that is fully worthy of the enthusiasm showered upon it. This is the Palace of the Kings of Navarre, built at the end of the twelfth century by Sancho the Wise. The Arab influence is very strong and there are some picturesque carvings on the front, including a duel to the death between Roland and the Saracen villain Farragut.

But Estella's greatest interest lies in the story of its foundation, since 1090 it was not on the pilgrims' road at all. For at Villa Tuerta the travellers went straight on to a place called Zarapuz where there was a small monastery-hospital. Then, mounting the slopes of the Montejurra hills, it went straight to the Santa Maria la Real monastery at Irache, still extant in its rather sombre entirety.

But in 1090 King Sancho Ramirez decided to build a village for Franks[1] at Lizarra, three kilometres to the north of Zarapuz. Sancho had quite definite plans as to how to set about raising the money for the construction of a new pilgrims' resting place, for he decreed that a tenth of the royal rents and of the rents of all churches in his kingdom should be devoted to the project. He outlined his schemes in a manuscript written in Latin:

'I wish that the monks of Saint Juan de la Pena should found a town of free peoples where the road to Santiago passes Zarapuz and I wish to deviate the road to Lizarra and to build there a castle and a population of *francos*. And as this spot is much more healthy than the other place, I say to the monks that they should build of their own enthusiastic free will, and that I will give them a tenth part of those things which for the love of God are given to me. The monks will from kindness accede to my supplication.'

.   .   .   .   .

[1] *Francos.* But the word had two meanings in ancient documents, and in the eleventh century it stood for free or privileged people and not for French origin, as it did later.

They repeated themselves in those days, but they also knew how to get the message over.

Saint Juan de La Pena was the most important monastery in that century and was called 'the cradle of Aragonism'. It is not strictly on the pilgrims' route and most writers on our subject are torn between a desire to include it because of its impressiveness, yet not wishing to 'cheat' by bringing in everything everywhere. But the Spanish tourist leaflet on the Pilgrims Way does list the monastery, which it describes as being in 'picturesque surroundings!' An understatement, since Saint Juan de la Pena (it is twenty-eight kilometres from Jaca), the ninth-century pantheon of the first kings of Aragon, with its underground Mozarabic church, is set in an awe-inspiring site of extreme mountain desolation. One has a frightening sensation of being about to be crushed by the overhanging mountains. It is hard to imagine that so many buildings can have been built in this starkly restricted ravine, but there were far more in the past than today, there being undivided cells for all of the monks, two houses for the abbot, a library, a hospital, guest houses and a garden with a fountain which still exists. This place was to the east what Covadonga was to the west, a sanctuary from whence Alfonso I, the Battler, went out to win Spain back from the Moors.

After leaving Estella, which now has a small but comfortable hotel – the Tatan – by the river and the Capa restaurant next to Don Carlos' former residence, the pilgrims' route passed on along a road that is today exactly as it was, beyond the sanctuary of Our Lady of Rocamador[1] to the mighty monastery of Irache, built as a hospital in the twelfth century by King Garcia of Najera. The church is a resplendent building with strong Cluny influences and there is a seventeenth-century cloister with some fine sculptures on the columns.

Irache is very much alive today. Indeed, there is what the Americans call a winery attached to the establishment which is commercially successful.

In the second Carlist war this monastery was remembered by most Spaniards as the hospital used by the Carlist forces after the famous battle of Montejurra, when the Republicans tried to re-capture Estella some months before the events I have already described. Both sides claimed victory in this battle, but the Carlists

[1] A dramatically situated town in southern France beneath enormous mountains.

certainly saved Estella. Don Carlos shocked his generals by insisting on going into the front line, where a grenade exploded at his horse's feet.

Villamayor de Monjardin is a big name for a hamlet with only 122 inhabitants, according to an official survey. But it was quite important in the early Middle Ages, since it has a nice little Romanesque church with a doorway containing a number of well-composed sculptures on the capitals. One of these is of the well-known battle of knights. Inside the church the thing to admire is the magnificent silver twelfth-century processional cross. This came originally from the huge fortress-castle of San Esteban de Deyo, which dominates the region and which contains the sepulchre of King Sancho Garces I, who in a number of bloody battles with the Moors recaptured the castle and liberated the valley of the Ebro. Nothing remains of this important fortress save a strip of wall, but there is a modern hermitage which houses the sepulchre King.

The next place along the road is Los Arcos. This townlet of 2,000 inhabitants had a bad reputation in the early Middle Ages; for although Aimery Picaud in his great guide says of Estella that 'the bread is good, the wine excellent, the meat and fish abundant, and it abounds in all delights', he utters a dire warning about Los Arcos: 'The town is watered by a river whose water brings death to horses and men who drink it.'

He is terribly inconsistent, however, for although the rivers at Puente la Reina and Los Arcos are deadly, while the river at Estella, which lies between them, is healthy, Picaud tells us that all the rivers until one gets to Logroño have fish in them which are death to all who eat them.

'Whether it be the fish which is vulgarly called the barbel or that which the Poitvins call the Alose (shad) and the Italians the *clipia* or eel or tench, in no part of Spain nor in Galicia should you eat them, for without any doubt you will die soon afterwards or fall ill. If by some chance you eat them and you are not ill that is because you have more health in you than others. All the fish and meat of beef and pork in Spain and Galicia makes foreigners ill.'

Los Arcos is a strange and beautiful but sad little place. The parish church is charming, but of many styles and periods; it has a plateresque[1] doorway, a late fifteenth-century Gothic cloister and a superb painted retable of the fifteenth century. The beauty of the town lies in the tawny-coloured sandstone of which it is all built and the fact that it is almost entirely enclosed by a single wall.

As for the sadness, this derives from the fact that the inhabitants are slowly leaving the place. In 1965 the population was 2,040 souls; in 1969 it was 1,900 and in 1972 it was down to 1,700. That number is not so very small for a tiny village, but the area inside the Los Arcos walls is quite large and it is this that gives the place its melancholy aspect.

[1] Named for the silversmiths of the sixteenth century, in architecture it stands for an almost grotesquely ornamental design.

Chapter 9

LONGROÑO

For the pilgrims at this point there would certainly have been great excitement; they were shortly to leave one country, Navarre, and enter a new one, Spayne.

And the modern pilgrim must here make a five-minute detour by car to visit the hamlet of El Busto, where there is a relatively modern church with an incredibly ornamented plateresque retable which, with its gleaming gilt and scores of images, is stupendous.

The church was murky when I entered, but I knew that here was something exceptional; so I quickly went out into the sunlight and accosted a passing woman to ask her where I could find a priest and explained why.

For answer the woman fumbled in her purse and then said, 'follow me'. We went back into the dark church and the woman dropped a coin into a metal box and immediately the floodlights blazed on the retable.

I was quite moved by this utterly unmotivated kindness and, the beauty of the golden screen.

'Oh! thank you, thank you!' I said. 'Can I pay you back?'

'It is nothing,' said the woman.

The lights soon went out and I put in another coin and we dallied. The woman had a large wicker basket on her arm and she told me she was taking clean linen back to the shop.

'What shop?' I asked.

'My husband has a barber's saloon in the main street and I'm off to tidy it up.'

I felt the back of my head; too long, as usual.

'I need a cut,' I said and walked with her.

After Los Arcos comes Sansol and then, only a couple of kilometres fartther on, the hamlet of Torres del Rio. Here, dominating the place, is a very ancient church of the Holy Sepulchre, denoting its connection with the military order of the Holy Sepulchre of Jerusalem. It is built on an octagonal plan which makes one think immediately of the curious Eunate. It has a Byzantine arched roof and, outside, a round tower from which the hamlet obviously got its name.

Leaving Torres I had to slow down behind a huge lorry and some youths, wearing rather bogus pilgrim garb, thumb-signed for a lift and, when I indicated no, hurled abuse and made obscene signs. But the route always had its playboys, its pinchbeck pilgrims, mingling with the real pilgrims. Indeed, as late as the end of the seventeenth century, the Sun King, Louis XIV, was forced to make a second regulation to prevent people going on gadabout trips outside the country:

'Louis, by the grace of God, King of France and Navarre, Salutations.[1]

'The abuses which have crept into our Kingdom under the pretence of holy devotion and pilgrimage have reached such an excess that many of our subjects have left their parents without permission, have left their wives and children without sustenance, have stolen from their masters and have abandoned their apprenticeships to pass their life in one continuous debauch.

'Furthermore, some have even taken up their abode in a foreign country where they have married, although they have legitimate wives in France.

'We have thought to put a stop to these disorders by our Declaration of August AD 1671, in which all those who wished to go on a pilgrimage to St James in Galicia, Our Lady of Loreto[2] or other holy places outside our kingdom should present themselves to the bishop of their diocese, who would examine them as to their motives for wishing to make the pilgrimage and this attestation shall be in writing. Furthermore, they must get from the Lieutenant-General of the place where they abide a certificate containing their age, status, vocation and if they are married or not, which certificates

---

[1] As there is not a single full stop in the whole of this proclamation, I have added a few.

[2] Just south of Ancona, Italy, famed for its sanctuary of the Holy House of Nazareth, transported there by miracle.

shall not be given to minors, young married men (*enfants*) or apprentices who have not received the consent of their parents and masters.

'And if a pilgrim cannot present such a certificate to the magistrates or police of places through which they shall pass they will be arrested and punished; the first time by the carcan,[1] the second time by whipping as a corrective punishment (*par manière de castigation*), and the third time condemned to the galleys as a vagabond.

'Now we have been informed that certain sons of families, in a spirit of libertinage, go on the pilgrimage and try to avoid towns where they know that their certificates will be asked for, while others travel with false attestations, confident that the signatures of the bishop or judge will not be recognised in far-off places where they stop for the night. And most of them flatter themselves that if they should be arrested somewhere without a certificate they will only have the first punishment meted out to them as the judge will be unable to prove that this was not their first offence.

'Under these circumstances we now ordain that any pilgrim travelling without our royal permit signed by a secretary of state and the bishop will in the case of men be condemned to the galleys for all time and in the case of women any punishment that our judges consider appropriate.'

Louis' regulation had nothing original about it; in fact it was a shortened version of a very similar one promulgated by King Philip II of Spain in June 1590, which went into far greater detail.

The preamble states that by the Grace of God Philip is King of Castille, León, Aragón, Jerusalem(!), all islands of the ocean and both the Indies, Archduke of Austria, Duke of Burgundy and six other places, and a lot more. He then addresses himself to his son and every conceivable person of rank and every possible official, including rectors of universities, and informs them:

'that it has been brought to our notice that a great number of people of the realm are causing a lot of harm by not working and by marching about thieving, robbing and committing other offences and that to commit these crimes with greater freedom of movement they deceitfully pretend that they are going on an excursion[2] to

[1] An iron collar used for punishment.
[2] The Spanish has *romeira* and not *peregrinacion*, which former word means a ramble, a day's outing, a roaming. Connected today with a gipsy trek to a shrine.

some house of devotion and they put on the habits of pilgrims wearing slavins[1] and other woollen clothing of diverse colours and large hats with all the insignia. Thus attired, they trick the justices into making them believe that they are genuine *romeiros* and *peregrinos*.'

Philip's edict goes on to say that as from that moment it is forbidden to anyone to wear pilgrim habit unless on a pilgrimage and unless they have the necessary certificate which – more restrictive than the French edict – had to state the towns to be visited en route. And even when the licence had been obtained a pilgrim was not permitted to wander – to seek alms – more than four leagues (twelve miles) on either side of his prescribed road.

Having dealt with Spain itself the proclamation next turns its attention at great length to foreign pilgrims. Foreign pilgrims might certainly dress in excursion clothing without any let or hindrance whatever and during the time allotted to them, provided they have a certificate duly signed. The foreign justices were given precise instructions regarding the visa.

The visa was intended to prohibit the pilgrim from wandering more than four leagues from the sea port or frontier town – or from straying more than four leagues from the prescribed route. The day and date of entry was to be noted. A description of the clothing worn by the pilgrim was to be written out so that he could be recognised. Finally the visa had to state how far each pilgrim could go each day.

No exact punishment was stated but a vagabond was to be punished according to the laws of the kingdom and was to be 'castigated with great rigor'.

The edict was signed by Philip II at San Lorenzo (the Escorial) on 13 June 1590.

The distance of four leagues on either side of the pilgrims' official road is interesting. Four leagues are twelve miles and a swathe of twenty-four miles across Spain seems a huge area if one is trying to prevent robbers from pillaging the countryside. The year 1590 was quite late in the history of the pilgrimage and it was certainly after all the sanctuaries, hospitals, monasteries and abbey churches had been built. And although by this date the route would have been fairly well defined, it was still far from being a metalled road and only a walking or bridle track; as such there would have been scores of points on the route where the pilgrim had a choice

[1] A pilgrim's mantle.

of two different ways or even more. So, had buildings been erected for the pilgrims' use near one or the other choices it would have been harsh to have put them out of business by preventing visits.

Allowing my fancy again to roam, I am certain that the police of the Middle Ages would have scrutinised visas with extra care at Viana, for instance, because this was the last town in Navarre for pilgrims passing into Castile – more important, the first town out of Castile for returning pilgrims. These would, of course, have been the wise guys; they had completed the outward journey and were now on the way back, and it may be safely reckoned that if there were any drinks on offer it was not they who would have to pay.

'What about Logroño?' the pilgrim on his way out would ask timidly.

'Not bad. The river Ebro runs through it and the river water is pretty decent. Good fishing too.[1] But it is not all like that, for when you get into Galicia there is very little wine and only bread made from rye. Still, the cider is good and so are the milk and honey.[1] Thanks, make it a double.'

The 'very noble and very loyal city' of Viana (the population has dropped from 3,000 to 2,000 inhabitants in ten years) is now a tragically decaying town, but with innumerable historic buildings still standing, reminders of a turbulent and mightily impressive past. It is situated on a little hill just before Logroño and was founded by Sancho the Strong to defend Navarre from attacks from Castile, and right through the Middle Ages it was the most important place in the region from the point of view of defence. Its importance to pilgrims is attested by the fact that at the entrance to the town there were two fountains and once inside there were four hospitals (one was certainly in existence in 1270) and that as late as 1784, at the Hospital Mayor of Señora de Garcia, the first to be founded, they always kept six free beds for poor pilgrims.

Even now the town is full of historical monuments and the parish church, built between the fourteenth and sixteenth centuries, is so enormous – and incidentally very beautiful – as to be of veritable cathedral dimensions. Here is buried Cesare Borgia whose father was Pope Alexander VI. Cesare was killed here in 1507 while in the service of the King of Navarre. Opposite the church is one of those lovely old town halls which always remind me of the Con-

[1] Aimery Picaud's Guide.

quistadors' period, perhaps because so many buildings in Chilean and Peruvian towns are in the same style.

A few miles farther on we leave Navarre and come to the first town of Castile, Logroño. Purchas, the English pilgrim who went to Compostela in 1425, says:

> 'There to Gruon in Spayne
> That is the last towne of certain
> Of the Realme of Naveron.'

Being the centre, with Haro, of the Rioja wine trade, I have had to stay many times in this provincial capital and in my opinion, together with Valencia, Orense and Cartagena, it is one of the dreariest towns in Spain. There are two hotels in this city of 60,000 inhabitants, the Rioja-Carlton which is brash, and the Gran, concerning which I must digress. The main square is a huge rectangle in the centre of which is a gigantic statue of Espartero, a great general of the first Carlist war, a garden and an enormous bandstand; if the whole place could be tidied up it would look magnificent. At one end, on the other side of the road, are some fine, tall, iron railings in the centre of which is a pair of handsome wrought-iron gates. Behind this is a large gravel courtyard and beyond this, up a flight of gracefuly curving, palatially wide steps, are the spacious doors of the Gran Hotel. The interior is even more spacious; the foyer is of ample proportions and the dining room even more so, while above and at the back, along seemingly endless corridors, are no less than seventy-six bedrooms.

My guess is that it would have been built about half a century ago and that when it opened its doors it would have been an establishment of considerable luxury. Now, though it does have central heating, it has a rather low rating in most tourist books, but the bedrooms are correspondingly cheap. I like it, and not for its cheapness; it is not for me to explain here why others might not.

There is no mention of Logroño in the early days of the pilgrimage, since at that time, when Ordoño II of León linked forces with Sancho Garces of Navarre, the capital of the kingdom was Najera; Logroño only became important when Alfonso VI incorporated Rioja into Castile. It became more important still when St Dominic of the Causeway built a superb twelve-arched bridge, with three defensive towers, over the Ebro, which was later rebuilt by his disciple San Juan de Ortega (St John of the Nettles), which survived until the nineteenth century.

The unanimity with which modern guide books state outright that there is nothing to see in Logroño is remarkable. There are at least four churches: Santa Maria del Palacio; the curious Santa Maria la Redonda, 'which in addition to its fine late fifteenth-century Gothic has a kind of oval hall at one end like a salon in a ducal palace which gives a note of incongruity to the whole building';[1] St Bartholomew, with a fine façade crowded with carvings of his life; and Santiago el Real. This last has, set in a covered arch but very high up, what I think must be the largest carved stone statue of St James on his charger in all Spain. But it is difficult to photograph; the nearer you get to it the more acute is the angle and the less gets into the picture, while if you walk down a very narrow street immediately opposite the statue a lot of little shop signs get in the way.

Wise travellers will here detour to visit the stark castle at Clavijo, a place of immense strategic importance in the wars of the Reconquest. The castle is built on a great crag and when you climb or motor up to inspect this mighty ruin you will easily see how it dominates the valley leading from León to Castile.

Though not quite so 'verifiable' as the battle of Simancas (see page 113), it was here a century earlier that St James appeared on a charger – alone this time – to help the Christians, and it is from this date that he really became Spain's warrior patron saint. And it was at this date, too, that the Bishop of Compostela started to receive a tithe produce rent from the first fruits of the year's harvest and vintage, which caused such bitterness in later centuries.

Leaving Logroño, the pilgrims passed through Villarroya which has now completely disappeared but is mentioned in the Pilgrims' Guide as Villa Rubea; they then went on to Navarrete, of great importance in the twelfth century. Here, to remind us of its existence, is a forlorn little porch or stone doorway, all out on its own in the fields, which was the hospital of the Order of St John.

Though we picture the pilgrims trudging peacefully along and perhaps a little bored, many a side show was provided from the sixteenth century onwards, as past events became history. This would particularly have been the case just before Najera, for just by the river Najerilla, on 3 April 1367, John Duke of Lancaster, pretender to the Castilian throne, and Edward Prince of Wales, more commonly known as the Black Prince, fighting with their

[1] Walter Starkie, *The Road to Santiago.*

armies alongside Pedro I, routed the opposing forces of usurper Henry II of Trastamara.

It was 'a mighty victory', as has been said of another battle, and early in the fifteenth century the holy wayfarers were parting with their sous to local guides who showed them *un grand champ moult long et ample ou le prince de Gales gueagne la bataille et esconffit le roy Enric*.[1]

Najera is a dismal little town now, but it has a splendid mausoleum, the burial place of several kings of the region and especially Don Garcia, 1035–54.

I have stressed that the pilgrims would often leave the route to visit any shrine, sanctuary or monastery that took their fancy, but nearly all of them left the road between Najera and Santo Domingo and walked some twelve miles to visit the monastery of San Millan de la Cogolla,[2] who was known as the 'twin moor-slayer'.

We must not let our enthusiasm for St James and the fact that he was patron saint of Spain blind us to the fact that many other saints also had fervent votaries, and Abbot St Emilian Cucullatus (574), to give San Millan of the Cowl his correct name, was one of them. He was not a very forceful character; a shepherd in his youth, at twenty he heard a call from God, became a hermit and then, on the insistence of the Bishop of Tazazona, took holy orders, but was quickly 'reduced to the ranks' for giving too much to charity. He spent the rest of his days in contemplation at the spot where he was later buried.

His connection with St James and his great moment came around the very end of the tenth century at that vital battle of Simancas, when Asturian King Ramiro II refused to hand over sixty virgins to the Emir of Córdoba, the annual tribute payable for not being molested by the Arabs. Ramiro dug his toes in, because there had been an eclipse and it was thought that this was God's way of showing his displeasure at their pusillanimity in giving those lovely girls away. Emir Abdul-Rahaman II was so furious that he gathered an enormous army together and the opposing forces met at Simancas – it now houses the historical archives of Spain – outside Valladolid. This battle was 'verifiable history' (Sir Thomas Kendrick's excellent phrase), though the ratio of one thousand Moors to one Christian is suspect. No matter; Ramiro encouraged

[1] A large field, very long and wide, where the Prince of Wales won the battle and harried King Henry.

[2] In modern Spanish it is *cogulla*, a cowl or a monk's habit.

his troops by saying that they must put their faith in St James, at which point Count Fernan Gonzales of Castile and King Garcia Sanchez of Navarre, who were fighting the battle along with the Asturian king, said that another holy saint in Spain, the sixth-century San Millan, would give succour. Then came the drama. The Christians went forth to the battlefield and knelt down to pray. The Moors thought they were surrendering but were quickly disillusioned, for Santiago and San Millan appeared, on white horses and clad in silver armour, brandishing their swords, accompanied by a host of angels, and brought the Christians a great victory. From then on a tithe payable to the San Millan monastery became payable.

The siting of this majestic monasterial pile is one of rare beauty. It stands in a valley below the monastery of Suso, an even older monastery where the saint was first buried. This is a hilly spot honeycombed with caves in which hermits like San Millan are reputed to have lived.

The road to Yuso will not have changed much in the past centuries and is winding and forlorn. But I was in a happy mood as I motored along, and when I was stopped by a man with his plough and two mules straddled across the road, I halted willingly to make conversation and accepted a swig of red wine from his *porrón* and not a drop went down my shirt. I then repaid the gesture by donating a nearly full bottle of wine and asked him what time he got to work.

'Eleven o'clock,' he replied.

'That's a bit late,' I said.

He retorted that, apart from the fact that it took him a full hour to get to his fields from his home, the ground was anyway too frozen to plough before that hour.

Like so many pilgrims who are on record as visiting the place for the same purpose as myself, I was there to gaze at one of the most impressive church treasures in Spain. The best description of it is to give a translation from the little booklet which is sold at the monastery: 'In the middle of the ninth century there was constructed in this monastery a small chest of wood lined on the inside with a Persian fabric and covered on the outside with a gold veneer and sown all over with precious stones.'

From an artistic point of view the most interesting feature of this relic-chest of San Millan is the twenty-five carved ivory panels depicting incidents in the life of the saint.

The door of the monastery (it has been called the Escorial of north-eastern Spain) was opened to me by a priest to whom I took at once. He told me he was sixty-eight and had been born in the village. Until he was twenty-six he had been learning to become a priest. Then he had gone as a missionary to China for twenty years, from whence he had returned to Yuso and for the last twenty-two years had, with five other priests, been running the monastery. He took in very good part my request that my visit might be very quick, but when I said that I did not think I would bother to inspect whatever treasure was locked away, he insisted with such vehemence that I agreed to wait while he fetched one of the most enormous keys I have ever seen.

We soon found ourselves in a large, bare, clean and impressive salon, in the very centre of which was the relic chest, all by itself. As I stood admiring the chest and thanking heaven I had not hurried after all, the priest made one of the most endearing remarks I had heard for a long time:

'You see, I had to force myself to persuade you to look at these ivories, because if you had got back to London and then you had heard how famous they were, you would never have forgiven me and I would never have forgiven myself.'

The story of the life of the saint, given on the ivories, has been told by poet Gonzano de Berceo (1180–1246), named after a village very close to the monastery, where he served for many years. His reputation as a poet is low, but he is remembered as the first writer in the Castilian language whose works have come down to us.

According to the ivories, San Millan certainly had a very full life and Gonzano makes the most of it. In the twenty-two panels he is seen having his bed set afire by demons, who are so piqued when the saint awakes in time that they laid about each other with burning brands; how he casts out devils; how he robs two horse thieves from afar so that they had to restore his pack animal before he would give them back their eyes; and so forth.

Back on the road again, the pilgrims trudged on to the next town, where they heard of a very endearing personality. One Spanish writer has given him the charming title 'the celestial roadmaker'. He was rejected by the Benedictine Order as too illiterate, yet he is the only person in the entire history of the pilgrimage to have been remembered sufficiently for a stopping place – and a very important one – to have been named after him. Born near Belorado,

Santo Domingo de la Calzada (St Dominic of the Causeway), after he had been spurned by the monks, settled down as a hermit at a spot where the forests were thickest, and the highwaymen and wild beasts most active, and started to clear the wood from the little cell and chapel he had built for himself. Increasingly the wayfarers stopped there for the night, so Dominic built them a hospital and tended them personally; so the town took the name of the saint who founded it.

The present town of some 5,000 inhabitants is a great favourite of mine because in the actual hostel built by St Dominic and so exquisitely converted is one of my favourite *paradors* or state-run hotels. Though the entrance hall inside the enormous converted castle at Olite may be loftier and larger, though the foyer at another fortress conversion at Fuenterrabia may be more striking, the huge room at Santo Domingo combines such dignity and charm with imposing dimensions that it must win the palm.

The bedroom they gave me overlooked the minute old square and I could easily have flipped a sugar lump into the doorway of the cathedral where they have kept a live white cock and hens in a coop for over 400 years.

My double room – the singles in the *paradors* are almost non-existent – was luxurious. I entered the door of my bedroom from the landing and was confronted by a little corridor with a number of coat hooks on the left, and on the right two huge sliding ward-robe cupboards with twelve coat hangers and a range of drawers in each. On the right was a bathroom with five separate light switches, with a large, deep, sunk bath and shower. Another door led into the wc. In the bedroom itself were two large double beds. each with side tables and huge reading lamps with individual switches. There was a writing table and small chair with a standard lamp; an arm chair and another table. The furnishing was of excellent taste and quality, there were French windows leading on to a small balcony, and the central heating was efficient. All this, with a porter day and night to take up your bags, a restaurant generously staffed and with linen for the table, a coffee bar and a drink bar always open, carries a rating by the Spanish Guide Michelin as fourth out of six . . . a 'good average hotel'.

The Spanish Ministry of Tourism have officially classed all hotels in the country with from one to five stars and they put the great majority of their own as only three stars. This I can understand for political reasons, but what in heaven's name does the

'Guide Mich.' mean by down-grading these splendid hotels? By French hotel standards they would be two grades higher.

The remarkable Romanesque–Gothic cathedral which I looked out upon each morning was consecrated, but only as a church to begin with, in 1106 and became a cathedral in 1232. Inside is a huge mausoleum and underground crypt with relics of the saint and a plaque stating that in 1939 he was made patron saint 'of the Ministry of Public Works'.

Behind the mausoleum, about eight feet up and with the appearance of being let into the wall, is a huge, gilded, painted, sculpted, flamboyant chicken coop in which are a live cock and hen – when the cock crows tourists nearly jump out of their skins! – surely the most unusual sight in a church in all the western world. It commemorates by far the most popular miracle legend of St James, of how the judge was about to have his Sunday lunch of two roast fowls, when he was told that the boy falsely accused of thieving was still alive on the gibbet. He said 'I'd as soon believe that yarn as I would that these two chickens could get up and fly away'. And they did!

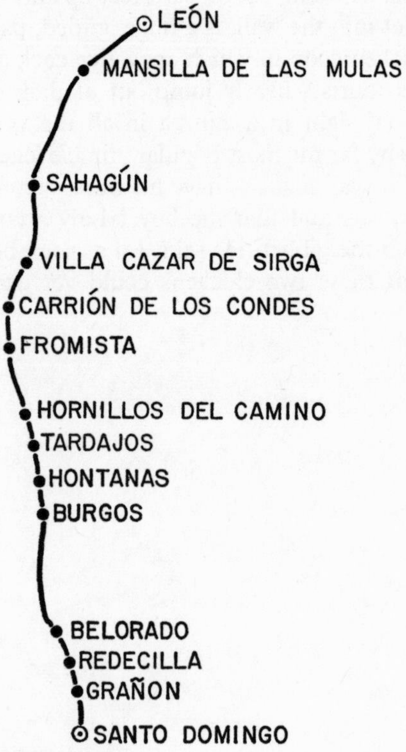

⊙ LEÓN

● MANSILLA DE LAS MULAS

● SAHAGÚN

● VILLA CAZAR DE SIRGA

● CARRIÓN DE LOS CONDES

● FROMISTA

● HORNILLOS DEL CAMINO

● TARDAJOS

● HONTANAS

● BURGOS

● BELORADO

● REDECILLA

● GRAÑON

⊙ SANTO DOMINGO

Chapter 10

BURGOS. SAHAGUŃ

Something was always happening; at Grañon, on the way out from Santo Domingo, the Jacquaires were shown the 'Cross of the Heroic Ones', in memory of a combat between the townspeople of Grañon for the possession of some coveted fields. Not everyone did battle but only one man on each side, and because Martin Garcia won for Grañon a mass was said for him every Sunday until 1967.

Redecilla del Camino is next, followed by Belorado, the largest place (3,000 inhabitants) before reaching Burgos, with a classical porticoed square (try the restaurant Alaska there), a magnificent parish church and a good sculptured St James as a Moor Slayer.

Then come, a little to the right of the present road, three tiny hamlets of Tosantos, Villambista and Espinosa del Camino with nothing to remind us that they were on the old road. After this a road from the north joins the main pilgrim's road and there is also an important detour to be made to the monastery of St John of the Nettles. Here, too, are the hills of Oca which once traversed bring us to the city of the Cid, the largest on the main road from the French frontier to Madrid, the capital of Spain for a time during the Civil War, and the fifth stop in Aimery Picaud's pilgrims' guide, which houses a cathedral whose lace-like spires caused Philip II of Spain to exclaim 'It is the work of Angels'; Burgos.

Philip must surely have been referring only to the outside, for the inside is a dark and dreary affair. At close range it is impossible to see the building as a whole because the immediately surrounding area is so tightly packed with buildings, but if you motor a mile or so out of the town, south towards Madrid, and have the courage to turn right across the dual carriageway, you will come to a cart track which ascends steeply to a field from whence you see Burgos cathedral dwarfing all the other buildings of the city. The sight is unforgettably beautiful. There are three groups of pinnacles, pale ochre spires which force their way up into the sky, giving the town a look of chivalry and romance.

Though there was an earlier church on the same spot no vestiges of it survive, and what we see is a Gothic church begun in 1221 (the first mass was celebrated in 1230) and only finished, so far as the structural essentials are concerned, in 1568. St James is very well represented in every nook, aisle and corner of the cathedral, which, being 379 feet long, is one of the largest in Spain, though 'examined in detail Burgos cathedral is less satisfying than it seems from a distance', says John Harvey in his *Cathedrals of Spain*, which agrees with what I said above.

Though I do not like Burgos very much as a town, my enthusiasm for it as a Jacobean centre is unbounded. I have said that Puente la Reina was the place where all the pilgrims' roads met, but at Burgos another strand came in, bringing those pilgrims who did not want to go over the Pyrenees but who took the coast road from Bayonne, San Sebastian, Vitoria and Burgos.[1]

This city of 120,000 inhabitants (the population has increased by 30,000 in ten years) has two parallel histories which are not greatly connected with each other. This is quite different from a town like Estalla which became famous during entirely different centuries.

Burgos began to be re-populated in 884 by Conde Diego Porcillos under the order of Alfonso III the Great, King of Leó; shortly after this it became the capital of Castile. Then in the eleventh century Ferdinand the Great added the Kingdom of Galicia and León. In that century, moreover, some say 1026 and others 1043, was born Rodrigo Diaz de Bivar,[2] known as El Cid, who became the prototype of a Spanish gentleman; Burgos has claimed him for her own. In the fifteenth century Burgos declined considerably, when the Spanish kings moved the capital (Madrid did not become the capital until as late as 1606) from there to Valladolid.

In 1812 Wellington laid siege to the town, but the French

---

[1] But why was this apparently relatively easy way so much less popular? In the ten years that I have been studying the subject no one I have asked has come up with an answer. One can only assume that it was mainly that so many pilgrims wanted to pass through Roncevalles.

[2] A village near Burgos.

resisted so obstinately that it was not until a year later that Joseph Bonaparte began to evacuate the town and the English troops moved in.

The parallel history was the one based on its great importance on the Pilgrims' Road. All that is known about the pilgrims' movements in the town is considerable and well documented. They entered the town by a street called the Galzadas (highway) and, passing to the left of the convent and hospital of St John and to the left of the church of St Lesmes, and then crossing a stream by a tiny bridge, reached the cathedral. And in the eleventh century we know that they left the town by the arch of St Martin and passed thence to the *barrio* (town quarter) of St Peter of the Fountain and eventually to Villalonquejar and Tardajos.

As for the hospitals in the town, there are reported to have been no less than thirty-two at the beginning of the sixteenth century. This figure comes from a German guide-writer and pilgrim as important and even more quoted than Aimery Picaud and Purchas: Herman Kunig de Vach, a monk coming probably from near Strasbourg.

The first edition, entitled *Die Wallfahrt und Strasse zu Sant Jacob* ('The Pilgrimage and Road to St James') was published by Mathias Hupfuff in Strasbourg in 1495 and it is thought that it was printed quite soon after it was written. Four other editions were printed between 1495 and 1521, when Jobst Gutknecht ran off his press at Nürnburg – a good index of how much in vogue such guide-books were.

Outside Burgos there were, and still are, two monasteries which well deserve special mention, after I have said some words on these institutions in general. When Henry VII ordered his suppression of the monasteries in England he obliterated an order of things that had been then in existence for over a thousand years. The names of religious houses which are known to have existed before the Norman Conquest ran into thousands. They had been pillaged times out of number, they had been burnt by marauders, and yet they revived again and again.

To begin with, to give these places of worship the name 'monastery' is a mistake, for the word derives from the Greek and means the dwelling place of a person living on his own in seclusion. Be that as it may, the religious houses that were called monasteries were almost the converse, since they were places of abode for men and women who were supposed to partake of common meals, to sleep together in one common dormitory, to attend certain servises together in their common church, and to pursue certain employment in the sight of each other in the common cloister. And, when the time came, to be buried together in the common graveyard.

I am not greatly exaggerating when I state that at first a monastery was not intended as a benevolent institution; it was a way of escaping from the spiritual pollution of the wicked world. In passing their lives in the worship of God the inmates were making themselves more fit for a world to come.

The design of the complex of buildings that eventually became a monastery in the tenth to thirteenth centuries, of which I am talking, followed a remarkably uniform pattern. The church was the heart of the place; it was not that the church was built for the monastery, but it was the monastery that existed for the church. This was almost invariably built in the form of a cross lying east-to-west; the long limb of the cross we called the nave, the cross limbs being called transepts and the head of the cross the choir.

As a general rule this choir was occupied exclusively by the monks or nuns at the monastery, and casual servants, work people and visitors were not admitted to this area, since they were only there on sufferance. The church was built for the use of the monks; it was their private place of worship. Almost as essential and invariable was the cloister or great quadrangle, enclosed on all sides and always placed to the south of the church to gain as much of the sun's rays as possible. Round the quadrangle ran a covered arcade whose roof was supported on the inner side by stone columns. The part not roofed in was called a garth, often planted with grass and sometimes having a fountain. Living thus at least until the thirteenth century, mainly in the open air, the monks had their school, and generally pursued their daily life together.

The next most important room was the refectory, where the monks all took their meals together; then came the dormitory or common sleeping place for the fraternity, which was invariably constructed over a wide range of vaulted chambers and so approached by a flight of steps. The beds of the monks were arranged at regular intervals along the walls of the dormitories and, though in some monasteries a wainscoting partition protected the sleepers from each other, thus making a little cubicle with a door. A monk's cell was virtually unknown, at any rate in England.

Apart from domestic offices the other room common to all

monasteries was not the library – they had hardly any books then – but the scriptorium or writing room. By far the greater part of the work done in the scriptorium – on vellum and parchment, which were exceedingly expensive – consisted of inscribing day-to-day documents concerning the meticulous divisions of lands farmed out to the peasants; also producing school books and replacements of church service books. The similarity between the beautiful façade of the Miraflores *cartuja* at Burgos and the one at Jerez de la Frontera, both about three miles out of their respective cities, lost me a tidy bet. I had unearthed a Spanish pack of playing cards with photos of fifty-two of Spain's greatest monuments on them and was boasting of the number I knew. But I lost all I had won on doubling up on the ten of hearts, the Jerez Carthusia monastery and not the one at Burgos. My friend, Rose Macaulay, in her greatest book, *Fabled Shore*, was touched by the beauty of the Jerez monastery, the façade of which is so similar to the one visited by the pilgrims outside Burgos. The magnificent fifteenth-century Jerez *cartuja* was secularised in 1836 and for long was used as a stud.

'The rich façade and portal of the convent sculptured in tawny stone is very good, with eight great doric fluted pillars, balustrades and statues in niches topped by Saint Bruno and above him God the Father. The weeds and shrubs are all uncut, the whole place mouldering gently into decay, hot and silent, haunting, dreaming and desolate.'[1]

Just outside Burgos is a famous hospital and a more famous monastery placed so close together that many a guide book confuses them. First there is the Hospital del Rey, which was the most important of them all, though not the oldest. It was founded by Alphonso VIII at the end of the twelfth century and run by the friars of the Calatrava order. So large, so wealthy, and so well run was it that it was able to accept pilgrims by night as well as by day and Kunig de Vach adds to this snippet of information a note that when he visited the place at the end of the fifteenth century there was a pillar erected to mark the spot where a prior was killed by arrows after he had poisoned a hundred pilgrims. But though the monks were generous and allowed poor pilgrims a daily ration of twenty ounces of bread and twelve ounces of meat with bone, or ten it off the bone, and sixteen ounces of red wine along with some

[1] Thus Rose Macaulay, writing in 1948. The place has since been restored.

chick peas, bacon and potatoes, only two days' stay was permitted and pilgrims had to show their certificates on their way out and the Compostelan certificate proving they had made the journey.

The monastery of Las Huelgas was of the greatest importance in the past (and still is, but for another reason) and has had a remarkable and curious history. In the first place Huelga means 'leisure' or better 'relaxation from work', which gives a clue to its origins, for it started as a pleasure-castle and then became a Cistercian monastery.

It was Alfonso VIII, who married the pomp-loving Eleanor of Aquitaine, daughter of Henry II Plantagenet, who ordered the change from extreme piety; he made it clear that he wanted the establishment to be gay, splendid and powerful rather than too religiously austere. He succeeded; the place became the residence and also the burial place for generations of kings, queens and infantas of Castile, and the founder Eleanor, mentioned above, was the first to be buried there. In 1187 Alfonso gave it to the Bernadine nuns, and the first abbess, Dona Maria Sol, became so powerful and famous that it was once said that if the Pope ever wanted to take a wife he could not do better than the Abbess of Las Huelgas. He would also have had a bevy of daughters too, for the official number of inmates was fixed at one hundred, and they were of such noble birth that they had to be addressed as *Senora Dona* instead of the ordinary *Sor* (sister). Another of its claims to fame is that the Black Prince stayed there before the famous battle of Najera.

Museums are not for me and so I rarely recommend them, but the costume museum at Las Huelgas is a very different story, and the circumstances of its foundation are exciting and dramtic. The destruction wrought by Napoleon's troops during what we call the Peninsular War was terrible, and the pillaging of the treasures of the monastery was an abomination. But they missed a few things, and when a Spanish government commission in 1942 opened the sixteen royal tombs to the left of the nave of the great church, they discovered a windfall, for one of the few not profaned by Bonaparte's troops was that of Infante Don Fernando la Cerda, son of Alfonso the Wise. Inside the tomb was a pinewood coffin spread with two splendid pieces of Persian brocade and on these lay several golden medallions and a silver cross. The coffin was lined with Arabian silk and the mummified body of the prince was clothed in a light green tunic, over which was draped a rich cloak decorated with symbolic lions and castles. His face had been covered with a piece of green brocade, but on his head was a cap embroidered with the arms of Castile and León in gold, mother of pearl and coral. His right hand held a huge broadsword and on the third finger of his right hand was an elegant ring set with precious stones. Over his tunic lay the baldric[1] of his sword, ornamented from one end to the other with shields and the heraldic leopards of the arms of England.

Also displayed are other objects found in the tomb of which a number of astonishingly well-preserved (they are exactly 700 years old) garments of the kind so often seen on statues, made of finely woven linen or wool lined with fur. When the tourist brochures say that the costume museum is the finest in the world they probably exaggerate, but when they say that 'in a peculiar way the onlooker gains the impression of being actually face to face with medieval people' they are not all that wide of the mark.

From Burgos to León the Way is dreary, flat and monotonous, but it has more pilgrimage associations than any other stretch. I should like to expand on this point; Puente la Reina, Estella and Viana are pretty little towns in their own right; surrounded by attractive undulating countryside, but they are in a busy and fairly touristic part of Spain. All the hamlets and towns we now come to before reaching lovely León are decrepit and ugly, but all the churches and monasteries were built for the pilgrimage; indeed, the places came into existence solely because of St James.

Furthermore, there were no strands coming in from north or south, and there was only one short alternative route. Finally, from Burgos to Sahagún there were no monasteries, shrines or churches to visit on either side of the route.

After Burgos there was a bifurcation which is very well documented. It is quite a short one; the pilgrims went either northwards to Las Quintanillas, Villanueva de Argano, Citores del Paramo, Olmillos de Sasamon and Castellanos de Castro, to Hontanos. The other one went from Arrance de Tardajoh then via Hornaza and Hornillos del Camino and joined the other strand at Hontanas.

After Tardajos there is now no road whatever until the next stopping place, Hornillos del Camino. To get here you turn left off what is now marked by the tourist signs as the Pilgrims' Road,

[1] A richly ornamented girdle worn over the chest and under the arm to support the sword.

one of the very few places where they have been dishonest. Just before the village of Villanueva de Argano you go down a very minor road through Isar. Here you take another minor road, no more than a mud track, and you will find yourself in Hornillos. It has no shops, sheep wander in and around the lanes with the inhabitants and words can hardly depict the appalling conditions of the track in the village. My car's undercarriage kept hitting the baked mud ruts as I tried to steer between them. But I managed eventually to get through to the far side of the village and there meet a shepherd with a flock of sheep.

'Yes,' said the old man, pointing to a tree-lined track, 'that is the true old pilgrims' way. If you like, I will walk it with you to-morrow.' I declined the offer, got out of the car and started to trudge. After a few yards I came across a curious sort of fountain with a plentiful jet of pure water; it was marked by a huge stone perched on the top of three upright ones.

Hornillos del Camino was in 1156 given by Alfonso VII to the monastery of St Denis in Paris. A Benedictine monastery, dependent on Our Lady of Rocamador in France, was founded here and governed by a French prior with twelve monks. Then Alfonso VIII gave to this monastery everything in the town of Hornillos that had previously belonged to the St Denis monastery. There was also an inn and an infirmary for the very gravely ill.

The road from Hornillos to Hontanas is totally flat, arid and scorched by the sun, and it was here that pilgrim Laffi saw a cloud of locusts 'so great as to obscure the sun'. Hontanas (present population 192) he thought nothing more than a village which was lowly to a degree, and he goes on to state that the only people there were shepherds and that the huts were surrounded by a great palisade as a defence against wolves. He continues: 'In this disgraceful place we ate a little bread and oil, which was given to us by a German selling statues.' In conclusion he advises pilgrims to get up early but not actually to set forth until after the shepherds leave with their dogs.

Domenico Laffi was a clergyman from Bologna who made three separate journeys along the road in 1666, 1670 and 1673. Shrewdly observant, he has plenty of curious things to recount, but he is of great interest to students of the road in the seventeenth century. He confirms how the institutions which had grown up in the twelfth century hey day were still there in the seventeenth and how, with only a few insignificant variations, the road followed the old track.

The next village is Castrojeriz, which Laffi calls Castel Soris, which is better than the French pilgrim of 1627, who called it Quatre Souris. Just before this one-time town (population now 1,480) stood the great convent of St Anthony. The order of Antonines was founded in Vienna in 1093 by one Gaston whose son was cured of St Anthony's Fire (erysipelas), also called 'the sacred fire'; it ravaged Europe terribly in the tenth century. The imposing ruins of the convent can still be seen, as well as those of the stark castle on top of the hill.

Fromista is the same size as Castrojeriz and as flat and as dere-lict, but it gets infinitely more visits since it has a church which the Tourismo have put on more leaflets than any other along the road. It is old, Byzantine, and away from all other buildings; one can look at it and photograph it with great ease. But just because it is in every single book of the 'Spain in Pictures' type, there is no reason to deny its being a real little gem. Greatly restored, it is all that is left of a Benedictine monastery founded by Dona Mayor, widow of Sancho the Great of Navarre; it is referred to in the Queen's testament of 1066, where she left vines, money, lands and a herd of cows to the monks for its upkeep. The inside of the church is rather dark but it is worth getting the key from the care-taker, since the carvings on the capitals are fascinating.

Let us, however, get away from churches for a while and talk of food. One almost national dish is called *revueltos con tomate* which is scrambled eggs with tomato. Utterly unlike the English-man's conception of this dish, which would have the eggs scrambled on their own with the braised or fried tomatoes apart, the Spanish way is to blend a puré of pounded fresh tomato into the egg and cook this all together and serve with snippets of fried bread. But there are two methods; the quicker is to cook the mixture with some fat in a saucepan, but the more tedious way is to do it very slowly in a double saucepan with less fat. This was what I had, followed by a piece of veal and a lettuce, black olive and asparagus salad at the Hosteria de los Palmos at Fromista – one of the nicest, coolest, best furnished restaurants in Castile.

My equanimity was somewhat ruffled, however, by an incident which caused me much annoyance at the time. Two pretty women left the Palmos as I entered and went towards an English number-plated car of the same make, date and colour as mine. I rated this a good excuse to make contact, but I did not, for I was thirsty and hungry and so went in and victualled up. The Plaza Mayor, where the restaurant stood, was so quiet – the population has dropped by 600 to 1,300 in nine years – that I had not locked the car; but when I went to put my brief case into the back I saw that all my suitcases were in totally different positions from the way they were when I had left it. Though they were much more sensibly stacked, now affording me a proper view of the road through the back, I was mystified and furious and immediately half-accused a youth who had offered to keep an eye on the car and whose offer I had refused.

'What's all this for?' I asked, angrily pointing to the bags.

'I don't know what you mean,' he replied.

It was fortunate I had not actually accused him, for it transpired that he had been the astonished spectator as the two girls got my bags out with a rapidity which word and gesticulation showed had astounded him; they had extracted my jack, replaced a punctured tyre on their car and put everything back. When I got to the driving seat I found a note: 'Sorry! But we thought we might have to wait until you had finished your meal.'

There was nothing I could do save drive off in high dudgeon.

Next come three hamlets, after which, surrounded by a few miserable cottages, is Villacazar de Sirga, officially shortened to Villasirga, where is the huge, imposing and beautiful church of Santa Maria la Blanca. The fame of this sanctuary to the Virgin has come down to us in one of the Cantigas (below) by Alfonso X the Wise.

There were some people who had not been cured in Santiago yet regained their health in this church in Villasirga, as for example the honourable and wealthy merchant from Germany who, as a result of a long and painful illness, had become a cripple and destitute.

> 'And at that time
> He saw a great pilgrimage
> Of folk from his country
> Going to Santiago.
> He begged them
> To let him go with them.
> Faced with this request
> They were much embarrassed.
> For on the one hand they could see
> How ill he was,
> And on the other hand

How poor he was.
But since they had
Such pity on him,
They agreed
To take him with them.'[1]

Alfonso, incidentally, was somewhat prejudiced against the shrine of St James, preferring that of Villasirga, which was the third church in Spain owned by the Knights Templar; it had originally a lofty fortified tower. I consider the setting of the place and the porch, with its double row of apostles, its chapel of St James and its great sepulchres, to be the best sight between Burgos and León.

Carrión de los Condes is a little medieval town which, if tidied up a bit, could be a joy. Apart from its strong Jacobean associations it was the home of the warlike Counts of Carrión. At the time of the Cid the young counts who had married the hero's daughters ill-treated them shamefully. Then, challenged as traitors before King Alfonso VI, they were defeated in the Vale of Carrión and their town was given to the crown.

Carrión is also where, according to legend, the incident of the bulls and virgins took place; here it was that a hundred maidens, on the orders of cowardly King Mauregato, were annually handed over to the Moors in the days before the battle of Clavijo. Then one year a herd of bulls violently attacked the Moors but left the girls alone. In the twelfth-century Romanesque church of Santa Maria del Camino is a delightful picture of this event.

[1] Alfonso wrote in Galician Portuguese poetic verse of this period, so popular with troubadors and their love lyrics:

> 'El en esto estando
> uiú que gran romaria
> de gente de sa terra
> a Santiago ya;
> et que con eles fosse
> mercé lles pidia
> et eles d'este rogo
> foron muit'enbargados;
> ca d'ua parte uiyan
> ssa grant enfermedade,
> et ar da outra parte
> a ssa gran probridade;
> pero porque auian
> d'ele gran piadade,
> en o leuaren sigo
> foron end'acordados.'

In the Plaza Mayor of the town, in line with a row of houses, is the remarkable façade of the Romanesque church of St James. Its sculpted freize is considered one of the finest in all Spain. The centrepiece is not the apostle but Christ in a *mandorla*,[1] draped in a heavy garment with turbulent folds.

But the most joyous building of the town (which earlier was called Santa Maria del Carrión – and Aimery Picaud says it was rich in bread, wine and flesh) is the monastery and hospital of San Zoilo, founded by Count Gomez Diaz and his wife Teresa in the eleventh century and first dedicated to St John the Baptist. The change came through that extraordinary urge the Christians of the Middle Ages had to possess relics of the great saints. St Zoil had died a martyr's death in Córdoba during the persecution of Diocletian. His remains were taken to the church of San Felix, where presumably they remained for several hundred years until young Fernando, son of Diaz, brought them to Carrión, having claimed them from the then Emir of Córdoba for valiant services rendered. But it is the sixteenth-century cloister built by Juan de Badagaz which is the jewel.

The road continues through desolate, flat, blistering deserted villages of brown mud hovels until we come to Sahagún.[2] We must now discuss the Cluniac influence on Spanish architecture and sculpture.

At the very beginning of the eleventh century Sancho the Great of Navarre, who was virtual king of all the coastal territories of Viscaya and the Atlantic, was persuaded by his friend and counsellor, Abbot Oliva of Ripoll, to introduce monks from Cluny into countries under his rule. These Benedictines from Cluny, mostly French, began to impose their own rules on the monastic communities, mainly it would appear to organise a direct catholic rule from Rome. That was the beginning of the enormous monastery-church-abbey of San Benito at Sahagún, called 'the Cluny of Spain'. By the middle of the eleventh century Sahagún was the greatest power in Spain; it was the centre of French influence, it ruled ninety monasteries and the Pope gave it all the privileges of Cluny. So far as the St James pilgrims were concerned it became especially important from the time of Alfonso VI, when he asked Abbot Hugo of Cluny to send monks to hasten the reform.

But the town of Sahagún itself must have been a most important

[1] Religious sculpture: an oval-shaped panel like an almond.
[2] The seventh stop of the Aimery Picaud Pilgrims' Guide.

commercial centre, entirely apart from anything else. There were no less than nine churches in the place and in 1255 Alfonso X granted it the right to hold an annual fourteen days' fair; the population was by now so large that special quarters were reserved for Jews and for Franks. There were a great number of Moors, too, who were highly regarded as craftsmen and lived in the Christian section.

Of the four remaining churches, San Lorenzo is so old that it has traces of Moorish influence in the horseshoe arches in the apse, and this church, along with San Tirso, are as much photographed by the Pilgrims' Route publicity section of the Tourismo as are Eunate and Puente la Reina. I must say that these two churches in this incredibly decrepit town do combine beauty and unusualness in a startling way, and I am sure that it is on account of them that Gertrude Bone chose Sahagún as one of the places to describe in her great book *Days in Old Spain*. After stating that these two churches possess the first Romanesque towers in Spain to be built of brick, she continues:

'In a brick country, where the houses are built of sun-dried clay, and in the high warm sun of Castile sink into the insignificance of earth mounds in the day time, the rosy baked brick of the fine towers of Sahagún glows and flames at evening like that of some early and noble cathedral. San Tirso, with its quadrangular tower and pillared windows above the beautiful romanesque apse; San Lorenzo, more unusual, more solitary, with its tiers of windows and bells, its three apses of brick and its sombre tower.'

San Tirso is kept locked and I had to go for the key to a priest's house a few doors away. He was about to change his occupation from wine-drinking to a siesta, so he gave the key to his house-keeper.

'And don't forget to get a tip for the alms box,' he added rapidly.

When I left I gave the girl a quite generous tip and she pointed to the box.

'No,' I said, 'for you personally and not for the alms box.'

It is surprising that both the Cluny monastery and this one at Sahagún, given their vast dimensions, should be in such ruins, but it is incorrect to state, as most guide books do of the latter, that nothing at all remains.

'Something of the ambition and area of the notable foundation can be gathered from the gateway and clock tower,' says Muirhead Bone, and photographs of this imposing pile show the great size; in fact the present main road runs under the gateway.

The pilgrims left by 'The Street of the Route' to the south of San Benito and once on the road again they were in for a truly thin time.

Chapter 11

LEÓN THE LOVELY

Many a pilgrim died along the Way but it is likely that there was a higher incidence of fatalities along this next stretch than any other. Laffi, for example, travelling with companions, a few miles short of Burgo Ranero, found a dead pilgrim by the wayside being devoured by wolves. They went on in order to find a priest to give him a decent burial, and then managed to obtain lodgings in the village 'which were so poverty stricken we had to sleep on the ground' he says.

Very few pilgrims thought of making a will before setting out and in the early years of the pilgrimage rules were promulgated to cope with this contingency. Around 1228 Alfonso II produced a statute stating that if a pilgrim died intestate, the innkeeper of the place where he was staying could keep the pilgrim's chief garment but no more. The travelling companions of the dead man were charged with seeing to the burial and funeral rites and they had to swear to the chaplain that they would see to it that the dead man's belongings were returned to his relations. If the pilgrim was without companions then the innkeeper and chaplain on the spot were charged with the burial and any expenses were paid from the deceased's belongings, the balance going one-third each to the innkeeper, the King and the church where he was buried.

Later there was a variation, and the bishop kept the deceased's belongings in safe-keeping for a year; then two-thirds of his worldly wealth went to the upkeep of the boundary fortifications between the Christians and the Moors.

The burial of a pilgrim was the occasion of great solemnity in the big towns as well as in small places, and in the latter it was the custom for people to come from other hamlets all around and follow in the procession, which was always headed by the parochial cross.

Should a pilgrim have no possessions whatever, the nearest local religious institution was obliged to be of assistance and in the accounts of San Pedro church at Triacastela, for example, there were the expenses of five *reals* for a pound of wax for pilgrims who died in the hospital, and four *reals* for two masses for another pilgrim defunct there. It was the two Alfonsos, IX and X, who were so keen on passing laws to protect the *romeros* and they certainly did their best to prevent the potentially thieving innkeepers from robbing their guests.

These hosts were not only expected to be honest, but were obliged to fit good quality locks on the doors of their inns, and they were instructed to ask pilgrims when they set off in the morning if they had lost anything in the night. If they had and the lock situation had been unsatisfactory, then the innkeeper must make good the loss. The church, of course, was entirely on the side of the pilgrim, for without him the ecclesiastics would receive no payment for masses, candles and such like.

After leaving Sahagún the pilgrims embarked on the most forlorn stretch of the whole way and the one with the least number of inns, monasteries, churches and shrines. One assumed, though, that they went along quite fast because the flatness here is even more noticeable than it was before.

At Calzada del Coto there was a curious bifurcation, for the two ways run almost parallel and very close together; the north road went through Calzadilla de los Hermanillas; at one time it was called the *Via Trajana*. The southern way went by Bercianos del Real Camino, el Burgo Ranero and Religias. The road became one again at Mansilla de las Mulas, a terribly poverty-stricken town but worth a brief stop on account of the remains of its gigantic castle walls, formerly one of the biggest fortifications of the Middle Ages. Here some ten miles off the Way is the Mozarabic church of San Miguel de Escalda (the escalade or scaling).

This word Mozarabic occurs so often in Spanish history that it is necessary to explain that when the Moors overran Spain they did not over-persecute the Christians (at least, until they became intolerable) who, on condition of accepting allegiance to the Moorish throne, were allowed to exercise their own religion. They thus became musta-arabs or would-be arabs, or mixta-arabs, mixed arabs, which finally was corrupted to Mozarabs.

Of the monastery of San Miguel it is the church which remains, and this has been declared an historical monument, a status it richly deserves. It is the most important Mozarabic religious building along the Way and was founded by those Mozarabs who had escaped from Andalucia in 910. Apart from this it is the extremely isolated setting in the deep wilds of the countryside as well as its architectural interest and beauty that earns its enthusiastic press. Yves Bottineau in *Les Chemins de Saint Jacques* speaks of the place with unusual warmth.

'At the end of an involved route we arrive at San Miguel. Hidden from view until the very last minute and utterly isolated from all other habitation in a countryside of idyllic beauty the remains of the tenth-century monastery await out sight.

'In the oppressive silence of nature, along with the song of insects and birds unseen, we pass under the lateral arch of the gallery and enter the church. Inside the music of arches and columns already seen outside is repeated. The style of architecture is a unique and splendid poem of marble and the place shows how beautifully Mozarabic art places at the service of the one true God memories evocative of Islam.'

And even the laconic Guide Michelin, after saying that in spite of its extreme isolation the place *'merite une visite'*, goes on to speak with some warmth of the columns of marbles surmounted by rich capitals on which are horseshoe arches.

Back on the road again we pass the half-ruins of the little medieval hospital and then over a bridge; from here it is but a short step to León. *Urbs regalis et curialis, cunctisque felicitabus plena,* the residence of the King and his court and full of delights, says Picaud.

León was built over the site of the camp of the Roman VII Legion and was then called Legio. Its Roman remains are impressive, for the streets of the old part of the town still preserve the outlines of the former camp, and considerable portions of the wall still stand at the north end of the town as well as some thirty towers out of an estimated total of about seventy-five. After the Romans left, the place seems to have been forgotten and fell into complete obscurity for several hundred years. This trend was sharply reversed after Alfonso III the Great abdicated and his son Ordoño II in 914 transferred his capital to León; and it remained the most important town in Christian north-west Spain until it was swallowed up by Castile.

Why León (population 100,000), capital of the province, is not more visited by tourists I do not know. True you cannot make the visit from Madrid and back in a day as you can Avila, Segovia and Toleda, and the surrounding countryside is suicidally depressing, but the shops there are above average and the choice of hotels is excellent. All this apart from ancient buildings. These are unforgettable. In fact, there are three superlative items: the church with the best stained glass and purest outside lines in Spain, the finest polychrome Romanesque wall-paintings in the world, and the best hotel in Europe.

There is a saying about León Cathedral that

> *'Toledo en riqueza,*
> *Compostela en fortaleza,*
> *Y Leon en suitileza.'*[1]

'The front is so perfect that it deserves to be contemplated for a long while,' says Jean Secret[2] of León cathedral. The lower part is in the classical style, with three arched portals; but higher up are two bell-towers separated from the centre piece, where there is a rose window, yet brought together again by flying buttresses which are on the outside walls of most churches, but here join the two towers to this central piece.

The three entrance portals of the west front all have names; on either side are St Francis and St John, while the centre portal carries the name of the church itself, Our Lady of the White. Around the doors, and beside them and over the tympanum, is an astonishing collection of carvings by an anonymous artist of around 1250, representing, amongst a bewildering number of other things, the Last Judgement. Here, as at Sangüesa, the angel is weighing souls, while on one side the elect proceed joyously to Paradise and on the other the damned are being initiated into the torments of hell by monsters who devour their lower parts, afterwards dipping their bodies into boiling cauldrons.

---

[1] Toledo is rich,
  Compostela has a fortress,
  And León has slenderness.
[2] *Saint Jacques et les Chemins de Compostelle.*

As I am not enthusiastic for the interiors of churches, and as I had not done my studies in advance, I nearly missed what is the most beautiful thing about this lovely cathedral. I was reading that evening in León, after a long look at the façade of the church and a quick glance into the interior, that the silleras or choir seats had some 'striking' (polite for naughty) carvings underneath, very like those at Auch Cathedral and at Plasencia. I thought I must take a look at these and the next day I returned to the church in brilliant sunshine after the black clouds of the previous day. On entering some churches on such brilliant days one encounters total darkness until the eyes adjust to the change. I even had a flashlight with me and went quickly to the centre choir. It was railed off to the public, but with one neat spring I was over. Feeling guilty but clever, I made my way to the stalls, and turned up the first one: a fox. Or it could have been a dog – my flashlight was nearly out. The next: a bear. Then, after a few more animals, came a stall where the carving had been hacked away. So the naughty ones had been obliterated! I went to get out and this time my agility failed. I got stuck astride a rail and, looking up, I saw staring at me, all in black of course, the most enormous priest I had ever seen, with eyebrows like Bernard Shaw and the thickest of black horn-rimmed spectacles.

Visualising that I would be taken to the dungeons for examination, I gabled a great deal of incoherent drivel, giving every reason for standing where I was save the true one.

'I expect you wanted to look under the seats,' the priest replied and turned away.

By now my eyes were accustomed to the darkness, but it was no longer dark! I thanked the Lord for that Spanish sunshine that the Arabs, in the construction of their buildings, did everything to exclude. I realised too that when the jingle said that León Cathedral had style it was probably to the inside that it referred. I looked up and around and marvelled at the immense expanse of glorious stained glass, turning the place into a delicate greenhouse to the glory of God. More to marvel at is how the thirteenth-century architect had managed to build a cathedral of such imposing proportions while keeping the wall space to a minimum. Adjoining the basilica – its primitive ruggedness is very reminiscent of Jaca cathedral – is one of the most hallowed spots in Spain and was a shrine of supreme importance to the pilgrims: the somewhat mysterious royal pantheon of the kings, built between 1054 and

1067 by Ferdinand I the Great. It is extremely small but what has given it such significance along the Way is that on the walls, and more so on the domed ceilings, are – painted between 1167 and 1175, or 1181 and 1188, according to different experts – the finest Romanesque painting in Europe, or even the world, according to a *Daily Telegraph* Supplement; but can anything outside Europe be Romanesque anyway?

To stand and look at anything nearly a thousand years old is to me inspiring, but modern colour photography has been brought to such excellence that, if you want to study the details of these superlative allegorical paintings without giving yourself a crick in the neck, you get a far better idea of what is being portrayed from colour postcards. The theme is pure allegory.

In the vaulted ceiling is a Christ in a *mandorla*, seated on a rainbow with a book, and in the four corners are the four Evangelists with human bodies but with the apocalyptic symbols of animals – four heads each holding a massive book of the bible.

In must be stressed that the artist had to work in a room only some forty feet square with a very low ceiling and a stone column in the centre; this is the only aspect which no camera can possibly portray and one scene seems to run into another.

The most striking composition of all is the one representing the Last Supper, a miracle of artistic adaptation given the space I have described. The painting of the huge Christ is dramatic and mystical and the apostles are grouped around him in a most original way. Here is the stylised cock, St Martial bringing wine and St Thaddeus bringing fish; while near by is a rustic scene of goats butting playfully, cows quietly grazing and shepherds listening to the angels' announcement. In the corners of the roof painting are the seven churches of Asia.

León, like Estella and Burgos, was the place where a tributary, bringing many of those who came into Spain from the north, met the main stream; moreover it was especially a place where pilgrims who had come by one road could return from León by another. This is one of the few places where we find any mention of pilgrims returning from their *romeiro*, for at the convent of the Augustins, where there is a lovely sculpture of a monk washing the feet of a pilgrim, who is in fact Christ, they seem only to have accepted pilgrims on their way home.

When I was staying at the Hostal de los Reyes Cátolicos at Santiago I got lost more than once (not surprising considering its size), and one day got to the head of a stairway where there were some sculpted heads of people associated with the building of the hotel, which impressed me so much that when several years later a rather odd correspondence was started in *The Times*, entitled 'Signed Architecture', I quickly contributed a letter wherein I said that if people were sufficiently proud of their designs to wish to be remembered for them they should have their effigies sculpted somewhere on the building as had been done at the hotel in Santiago. I concluded 'which is the second most luxurious hotel in Europe; the most luxurious is, of course, the Hotel San Marcos in León'.

An entire travel book has been devoted to describing San Marcos from its beginnings to the present day, and yet in it there is not one paragraph which gives any idea of the size of the present hotel. I spent a happy week there and had time to do a little pacing. Firstly, there are three hundred bedrooms, which means that there are three-quarters of a mile of wall-to-wall-carpeted corridors, every one of the walls of which, on both sides, are lined with exquisitely framed prints, individually lit. Along these corridors are chests, wardrobes, vases, water carriers, all perfect reproductions of Spanish furniture through the ages; a museum in itself.

Secondly, the little room on the first floor – used for breakfasts only – is twenty three yards by nine.

Thirdly, the main sitting-room or lounge has a polished marble floor on which are a multitude of beautifully coloured Persian rugs; the ceiling is one enormous painting, and on the walls are tapestries between which are statues and carvings. People sit on groups of low chairs upholstered in magnificently tooled leather. It is twenty-eight yards (84 feet) square.

Fourthly, there is the cloister or covered courtyard, which is unusual in being on two floors. From one side of the second storey of this upper cloister you can see something both beautiful and unique. For the San Marcos hotel is cheek by jowl with the sixteenth-century church and separated only by sheets of plate glass – each engraved with the Marcos emblem – which are fixed between the stone arches, and one can look down at any time of the day on the whole church scene below.

The restaurant is a long narrow room giving on to the summer terrace, ornamental garden and the river Bernesga beyond. By the size standards of the other public rooms in San Marcos it is quite small, it seats ninety, and is twenty-six yards long.

The front, which is unquestionably the finest Renaissance façade in Europe, is eighty-four yards long, or one hundred and twenty if you include the church, the whole of the front of which is studded, like the Casa des Conchas in Salamanca, with Jacobean scallop shells.

There is no end to the wonders of this hotel; the arcade of shops, the museum with Iberian, Roman, Visigothic and Romanesque carvings, bronzes, statues, axes and the eleventh-century ivory Christ of Carrizo, found in the monastery of that name. Enough? Not quite; the entrance hall and the immense stone staircases are indeed a sight to be remembered.

Actually the early pilgrims did not stay here, but at a little low building next door. For the hotel was only opened in time for Holy Year on 5 June 1965, but behind that simple statement lies much drama. In the first place a Royal Decree of 1836 suppressed all military orders. In practice this amounted to very little, for it was merely aimed at preventing abbots and priors from interfering in state affairs; but in the case of the convent of San Marcos it had the effect of turning the place almost into a heap of rubble. In 1875 a local mayor wanted it pulled down and on this being refused it became a veterinary school, and then a military garrison and stables.

In 1961, the Church, the municipality of León and the army, having at last agreed to relinquish their claims to the building – and they all having been indemnified – plans started for the erection of the hotel. First the National Institute of Industry was charged with saving the fabric of the convent from actually falling down and then in 1964 [sic] the actual work on the hotel started. How the stonemasons, plumbers, electricians, heating engineers, floor polishers, the installers of kitchen equipment, the restaurant and bedroom furnishers can have worked together on this prodigious task I cannot fathom; only architect Fernando Moreno Barbera could tell, but I have one memory which sticks in my mind.

There is a square in front of the hotel, probably a little larger than Trafalgar Square in London, and when I was staying at the most comfortable Conde de Luna hotel in León in March 1964 I went along to see how the building was progressing. The whole square was barricaded off and no trick of mine could get me past the guards. As I could not get my way I twitted them, saying that the hotel would never be open in time. They assured me that it would.

'Why are you so sure?' I asked.

'Because we have fifteen hundred men working day and night,' was the reply.

Crossing the lovely and very old Roman bridge, the pilgrims soon reached the church of Santa Maria del Camino. There is an ultra modern church there now, with startling lines, where piped religious music is played all day long. The scenery at this point is very flat and dull brown, and the road is as straight as a ramrod. I stopped for an early coffee at a restaurant outside the *urbanizacion Santiago* and started to write. During this time and while I was having lunch I looked out across the great plain to an old man in the distance who was being trailed round and round at a snail's pace on a board five feet wide hauled by a mule. He looked like a water skier in slow motion. Beside him was a girl playing with a child who had a lot of modern toys; they were clearly not poor. I found that he was winnowing out the chick peas (*garbanzos*) which figure in so many soups.

The pilgrims next came to San Miguel del Camino and then Villadangos, which has lost its hospital but still has an ancient rustic church whose walls are made of dried mud and where some sculptures depicting St James at Clavijo can just be seen.

Next came St Martin del Camino and then, famous for pilgrims of all times, the Puente de Orbigo, then used to cross the river, still passable today. It is as fine an example of medieval bridge-building as the Puente la Reina, and several of the broad pointed arches remain. There would be more of these arches if Sir John Moore's troops had not blown up the rest in their retreat to Coruña. On the west bank of the road the pilgrims actually took there used to stand the Hospital of Orbigo, built by the Knights of St John, and although nothing now remains it stood in the present Calle Vega near the church.

The reason for the fame of the bridge of Orbigo is that it witnessed one of those ludicrous jousts of the fifteenth century which so obsessed Don Quixote. The Leonese knight, Suero de Quiñones, had for so long been enamoured, nay imprisoned by love, of a lady that every Thursday he would wear an iron collar round his neck. He wished to rid himself of this penance and so thought of holding a joust for which he had to have permission of the King, John II, who was then at Medina del Campo. Happily for history this was granted, whereupon Suero caused his twenty-two conditions of participation to be read out at all the Courts in Christendom. This all took place in 1434.

If the whole affair had not been written up by a royal scrivener – we even know that his name was Pero Rodrigez de Lena – and if the manuscript, *The Book of the Famous Joust which the Honorable S. de Quiñones held at the Bridge of Orbigo,* was not still in the library of the Escorial, one could hardly believe that the whole thing was not a fantasy.

Quiñones was no fool, for in the year 1434 the day of St James (25 July) fell on a Sunday and it was a Holy Year; furthermore his ticket of leave ran from 10 July for thirty consecutive days, when the maximum number of pilgrims would be passing along the way.

I do not know whether a knight in armour, who was a true chevalier on a destrier (a large warrior horse) was obliged, if he was on the pilgrimage, to fight or whether he could go peacefully on his way, but he would have missed a good party if he had not tarried. For in a forest by the bridge Quiñones erected an emplacement comparable with what we now erect for the Olympic Games: a stadium 146 paces long was cleared, enclosed by a palissade the height of a horse. Around this were galleries; one for Suero and his companions, where they armed themselves, another for the same group merely to watch the jousts, and others for foreign knights, and more distinguished foreign knights, and two for judges, trumpeters and heralds, and most important of all, for scriveners who had the task of recording exactly what took place.

Suero de Quiñones saw to it that the whole enterprise was linked to the cult of St James; for at daybreak (four in the morning) on 11 July 1434 the first notes of the fanfare were sounded, the bells of the hospital at St John chimed, and the knights with their ladies emerged from their coloured tents to say Mass at the church of the Jacobean pilgrims.

As the days passed more knights arrived at the bridge and more banquets were given by jousters to their rivals, and many a dramatic incident was recorded. On 15 July a famous knight-adventurer, the Catalan Mosen per Davido, put on his double armour to tilt at Quiñones who, 'scorning danger and throwing all caution to the winds', assumed only light armour and over it a woman's white chemise which, as he manoeuvred his prancing horse, 'made him appear like a whirling fleck of foam', said the chroniclers.

Quiñones was unseated but eventually won and so returned the blood-stained chemise to his lady, who was now honour bound to wear it even in its bloody condition.

Finally the Leonese knight felt he had done enough. Entering the lists for the last time, he made a long speech, stating that he had remained on guard at the passage for thirty days, 'awaiting the arrival of knights who would deliver me from such a ransom'. This was a reference to the 300 lances broken off at the haft. Then amidst immense applause from the crowd Suero dismounted from his palfrey, whereupon a herald removed the iron fetter from his neck, placed it on a tray and carried it to the judges, amidst fanfares of trumpets and flaming torches.

The big show was over, but there is a pleasantly touching ending to the Leonese knight's bombastic display. In a cavalcade Suero and his knights rode back to León and, amid the applause of the crowd, rode up the Rua Nueva (it still exists), which the pilgrims also took, and retired to the palace of his father Diego Fernandez de Quiñones.

But now that he had had his joust and was released from his vow he went as an ordinary pilgrim to Compostela and when he reached the cathedral he deposited a bracelet at the feet of St James as a reminder of his fetter.

The much earlier pilgrims, of course, knew nothing of this exploit, but they certainly traversed the bridge which was built in the thirteenth century, and then went on to San Justo de la Vega, where there was once a pilgrims' hospital, and then, crossing the river Tuerto, they could see their next big stage point.

SANTIAGO

SAN MARCOS

LAVACOLLA

ARZUA

PALAS DEL REY

VILLAR DE DONAS

PORTOMARTIN

TRIACASTELA

TRABADELO

VILLAFRANCA DE BIERZO

PONFERRADA

MOLINASECA

RABANAL DEL CAMINO

FONCEBADON

ASTORGA

The church of St Martin at Fromista

12b Capital at the church of St Martin at Fromista

13   Arch of the former monastery at Sahagún

Chapter 12

ASTORGA TO TRIACASTELA

Pleasantly decaying, a charming little Spanish town, and seemingly quite uninterested in modernising its streets as do other towns in Spain, Astorga was Asturica Augusta in Roman times, an imperial colony and the centre of Roman Legions. Later it was partly destroyed by Almanzor and later still it was fought for by the Castilians and Leonese; no wonder that only vestiges are left of the huge castle walls.

No tributaries from other pilgrim routes met at Astorga, but it was the scene of 31 December 1808 of another and much less happy meeting of the ways, for it was from here that Sir John Moore's army started its retreat from La Coruña (Engl. Corunna), an operation which some thought a military disaster but which met eventually with Wellington's approval. I have only read Christopher Hibbert's account and thought he seemed a little biased in Moore's favour; for Moore's efforts struck me as being totally inept and Wellington perhaps not unkind for obvious reasons.

The scenes of debauchery in the town were awful; the Spanish soldiers had been without food for several days and the cold was so intense that many men had fired the remains of their ammunition just to keep their hands warm and then had thrown away their muskets. The British soldiery was worse; they not only stole everything they could from Spanish officers, but when these latter protested they insulted them. But they also became paralytically drunk, staving in rum casks and scooping up the liquid with their caps.

Though so little remains, the importance of the place to the pilgrims is testified by well-documented details of what was there to succour them. They entered by the St Andres gate, and they left by that of the Bishop. Within the walls were five hospitals and convents, Sts Stephen, Felix, Martin, Francis and (still extant) John, beside the cathedral, which has a mention in a document of 1187. It was here, according to a vague and almost certainly untrue legend, that St Francis of Assisi fell ill and became a patient.

Next door to the cathedral, which has an extraordinary sculpture of St James on the roof and a huge, striking altar-piece by Gaspar Becerra, who has been called the Michelangelo of Spain, there is the modern bishop's palace, the design of which has called forth much vituperation.

Antonio Gaudi, the eccentric Catalan architect from Barcelona, will either soon be forgotten and despised or else remembered as a genius. I think he will be remembered because the façade of his Sagrada Familia Cathedral in Barcelona – started before 1900 and still unfinished – is one of the most beautiful sights in Spain and I am fairly sure that others are beginning to feel the same, since it appears on more and more travel brochures. He also built a few houses in Barcelona, all on the twist, and the Bishop's Palace in Astorga, in which the bishop refused to live, and is now a badly planned and inefficiently run Pilgrims' Road Museum. The place is shut when it should be open and freezing cold in winter, and the caretaker, having taken your money, sometimes refuses to put the lights on. But I think the place outside is odd and striking but handsome, and inside it is beautiful.

But for the English pilgrim in Astorga the most exciting thing was a reminder of home, for here was a sanctuary – in the suburb of Rectiva just outside the city walls – of Thomas of Canterbury. The 'devotion' of this saint started quite soon after his martyrdom, and was brought to Astorga from England by D. Pedro Franco, who was a personal friend of Becket. Franco started a festival day in his memory and he also founded a hospital outside the town for which King Alfonso granted certain privileges.

From Astorga the pilgrims looked down upon the vast expanse of the Maragateria, the country of the Maragatos, a curious people about whom George Borrow wrote so brilliantly in *The Bible in Spain*. There used to be one theory that they were sprung from that semi-legendary King Mauregato of the Asturias, but later a much more serious suggestion was made that they had descended from Spanish Christians who had accepted the Arab faith and who had penetrated the region centuries before the Reconquest had begun.

Borrow was in Spain in 1840 and tells us that the name Maragatos signifies Moorish Goths and that there can be little doubt that they are a remnant of those Goths who sided with the Moors on their invasion of Spain and who adopted the religious customs and the dress of the Moors, which they still retain, except the religion. It is, however, evident that at no time has their blood mingled with that of the wild children of the desert, for not even in the hills of Norway would you find faces and figures more essentially Gothic than those of the Maragatos.

In Borrow's time these people, who left the cultivation of the land to their womenfolk, were the *arrieros* or carriers of commercial goods in Spain and thought it almost a disgrace to follow any other profession. They were costly to employ but fantastically honest, and 'no one accustomed to employ them would hesitate to confide to them the transport of a ton of treasure from the sea of Biscay to Madrid'.

But this is the very region where another of those race mysteries can have occurred. Here, give or take seventy miles, British soldiers of the retreating army were dying from drunkenness, frost, the bayonets of Napoleon's army. Hundreds of these soldiers had their wives with them and it is true that most of these women died of the same causes or were raped and then killed by the French. But some of them might have escaped, have been accepted into a convent or into a Spanish home until the troubles were over and then married Spaniards. The idea is worth a little research.

The present road after Astorga becomes deadly dull and all the foliage is covered with a fine grey-white dust; it is depressing, too, having to pass villages like Santa Catalina, El Ganso, Rabanal del Camino and Foncebadon, which meant so much to the pilgrims but which are now so decayed. But then one gets to Molinaseca, which is so charming, so intact, so medieval, that, as it is very like Santillana del Mar near Santander, it should be declared 'of national interest' and protected.

To get to Molinaseca (which means 'dry mill'), the most important stop between Astorga and Ponferrada, you must go to Ponferrada first and then motor back five or six miles, for this place is one of the very few along the whole road which is still a village of reasonable size with a fair road to it from one direction and no motorised progress beyond. It still has a superb little church, a pilgrim bridge, and a stone cross; there used to be a mill house, mentioned as far back as 1188 as belonging to the cathedral of Astorga.

Ugly to a degree, the miners' town of Ponferrada (population 50,000) was an important place on the Roman road from Astorga to Braga in Portugal. In the eleventh century Bishop Osmundo of Astorga placed an iron framework around the already existing Roman bridge and the place became known as Pons Ferrada – 'iron bridge'.

This is a town of contrasts for, in spite of the sordid concrete erections in the lower part, higher up there are vestiges of its ancient glory, especially the mammoth ruins of the castle and the remains of a drawbridge of those quarrelsome Knights Templar who remained in proud possession until the extinction of the order in 1310. After Ponferrada comes Carcabelos, noted for its wine, and then with a sudden complete change to the most beautiful mountainous scenery imaginable comes the lovely little town of Villafranca del Bierzo, at the foot of the Cantabrian mountain range.

On the edge of the town and commanding one of the most beautiful panoramic views in the country is one of the Government's best run and pleasantest hotels. It is an albergue as opposed to a parador, which means that it is 'not usually possible to stay more than forty-eight hours'. In 1961 there was a total of thirty-eight paradors and albergues, of which eleven were the latter; in 1968 there was a total of fifty-seven, of which fifteen were albergues; now there are seventy altogether, of which only thirteen are albergues. The first inn went up in 1928 in the Sierra de Gredos in Avila province so that tourists could admire the superb scenery there.

The exact siting of the albergues makes a fascinating piece of motoring history. No consideration of grandiose scenery came into deciding upon a location, which had to be a day's run in a car from the previous stop, allowing for estimated speed and the condition of the road. Most of the routes radiated out from Madrid and the day's run (around 1934) averaged out at some ninety miles – between two and three hours' motoring in the seventies. Most of the albergues, for the reasons stated above, are therefore located in dull, dreary, barren spots, but the site chosen at Villafranca del Bierzo, on the very edge of the town above the wooded valley, is one of consummate beauty.

The Bierzo district is like a deep irregular bowl and so shut away from its neighbouring regions by the Asturian mountains and the twin passes of Rabanal and Cebrero that it is no wonder that here Sir John Moore again toyed with the idea of making a stand; when that came to nought the hugest bonfire of stores was lit to prevent the French from getting at them. No wonder, too, that this deep valley was in the seventh century the most popular of places for hermits seeking to get away from it all.

Just before entering the town the pilgrims always went, especially those who did not feel too well, to say a prayer at the fifteenth-century church of Santiago, where they entered by the lovely sculpted door called the Puerta del Perdón – the door of pardon – for according to tradition a pilgrim who was taken ill and could get to the doorway got the same absolution as if he had been all the way to Compostela.

From this little gem of a church, which is in a field but can be seen from the road on entering the town, a road which passes the huge palace-castle of the Marquis of Villafranca, was a stretch called the Road of the Virgin. Picture an 's' with a line through the centre from north to south, a sort of dollar sign. The 's' and the straight line represent two extremely steep descents into the town, the straight line the one the pilgrims took and far too precipitous for cars. Another road, the 's' one, had to be made. The second intersection is most interesting; from the motor road on the right you look up at what is now a flight of stone steps, but on the left is an iron rail guarding a sheer drop of some fifteen feet where the old pilgrim road continues down to a narrow street called the Road of Waters, lined with ancient houses, which give the final touch of charm to this little Swiss-like miniature Eden.

From Villafranca the pilgrims followed the valley of the river Valcárcel and the present road vaguely follows it, criss-crossing it here and there. But how much longer, here or elsewhere, will one be able to point with any certainty to where the pilgrims' road exactly ran? Along this stretch one of the most impressive and truly needed road engineering works of the twentieth century is taking shape, a highway to bring impoverished Galicia nearer to Madrid. But when in a few years it has bulldozed its way across mountains, cleared forests and thrown giant bridges over ravines the present road will disappear and so will most of the now dying and decayed villages which get a scanty living from passing trucks.

I fear already that paths the pilgrims trod are now in danger of becoming unidentifiable. In the most important work on the subject of this century[1] the second volume devotes 500 highly detailed pages to the actual roads traversed by the pilgrims. On scores of pages there is a statement to the effect that at such and such a point the old road went either only, slightly, or a few miles to the left or to the right of the present main road. These observations are based on the road as it was forty years ago; but what about the huge cuttings that have taken place since then? What about by-passes several miles away?

The more frequent statement in this great book is that from A to B the present road *does* follow the old road. True, but around 1946.

In the Bierzo region we have first the road the pilgrims took, second the road which the authors of *Las Peregrinaciones* took, third the road widened and straightened which I have traversed and which in parts does not follow the last named road, and fourth the gigantic highway which I have already mentioned and which will last for another fifty to a hundred years. Now, while the second road mentioned above can be identified for certain, the path the pilgrims took can be known by reference to *Las Peregrinaciones*; but should stretches be bulldozed back to agriculture then any means of identifying it will be lost. Thought should be given to this problem before it is too late.

Trabadelo comes next, then Ruitlan and we cross the river Herrerias, where there used to be a hospital 'of the English' whose privileges were confirmed in 1178 by Pope Alexander III. And even today four or five houses grouped together are still called Hospital de los Ingles. I went on asking until I heard one man use those very words; it was exciting to realise that the name had lasted nearly a thousand years.

Just after Herrerias there was a fork on to Lugo by the Piedrafita Pass or, far more popular, up into the mountains to Cebrero at a height of thirteen hundred metres. The church and tiny houses around it were 'discovered' around 1962 and nattily done up – not really a complaint, for the winds up here are so fearsome that if they had not been restored they would all have been blown away. There is a modern and comfortable students' hostel there now – a bit stark for winter – built in 1966 inside the church walls. I suspect that the revival of enthusiasm for this stop has been generated by a charming author-priest, Elias Valina *alias* Elias

---

[1] *Las Peregrinaciones a Santiago de Compostela*; see bibliography.

Valina Sampedro (he used the longer name for a much more serious book), who has written the best popular pocket guide (*Caminos a Compostela*) imaginable for it is terse, erudite in the extreme, accurate and with first rate photographs, including one of Sr Valina in priest's robes outside his church in the snow – which was where I actually met him. It was February; I was worried by the snow on the pass as I left the main road, but the car just made it and there was this extraordinary, little flint church with a man standing in front of it. The snow around was thicker here and if I was to get to my next place time was of the essence, as my solicitors say, so I bought two copies of the book referred to and left. Months later I was back, there was not a cloud in the sky, the mauve wild crocuses were still making a show and I was shown round.

Cebrero is without doubt – and the fact that it is at an altitude of 1,300 metres may be relevant – the oldest stopping place with buildings still extant on the Pilgrims' Road, its foundation having been put at 836. In 1072 Alfonso VI gave the hospital and priory to the French monks of the Abbey of St Giraldo of Aurillac, in whose hands it stayed until in 1486, when it passed by the order of the Catholic Monarchs into the dependency of the Abbey of San Renito at Valladolid. These monks abandoned Cebrero when Mendizabal secularised the churches in 1853; it is now under the diocese of Lugo.

Very early in the thirteenth century a miracle occurred which may well have diverted pilgrims from the other easier route, and was sufficiently impressive for Pope Innocent in 1487 to grant a bull acknowledging the miracle as genuine. The story goes that one day at Cebrero there was a terrible snowstorm and the priest who was celebrating mass was surprised by the arrival of a peasant who had struggled all the way from the village of Barjamayon. The priest secretly despised anyone so mad as to venture out on such a night, when he saw the holy form turn into flesh and the wine into blood. And when the Catholic Monarchs went on their pilgrimage they gave the church a reliquary of silver in which to keep the remains of the miracle – could Wagner have got the germs of Parsival from this incident? Sampedro thinks so.

The precinct of Cebrero has been designated of historical interest not solely because of the pilgrims' church but because of features which date from long before they trod the road and which attract ethnologists from all over Europe. These are *Los Pallozas*, circular huts or hovels some ten feet wide and thatched not with straw but what seems to be gorse. The square stone blocks for the walls are of grey granite and are as solid as can be, but the thatching could not possibly last many years, even with normal winds, without frequent renewal. So some have been re-thatched beautifully, while others away from the part shown to the tourists have been allowed to disintegrate, and I saw chickens picking over the fallen roofs. This is one of those examples when a decision to repair or not must be very hard to make. There is no chimney and it is only from the single door that the smoke from the fire escapes slowly, turning the walls quite black. Their origin is very much earlier than Roman times and they are so unlike our idea of a human habitation that had they been allowed to fall to pieces no one would have known what had been their purpose.

From now on the pilgrims would not have complained too much at having to walk along the rims of the mountains, for the scenery must have enchanted them; moreover, it was often shady and they were generally going down hill to reach Triacastela, which some have called wretched, though I would say that it has a decaying charm and is not nearly as bad as the villages between Astorga and Villafranca. The place has a St James church which was almost entirely rebuilt in 1890, according to an inscription on the front, and very little remains of the original.

But it was the eleventh stop in Picaud's great medieval guide, as Sampedro calls this book, and it was mentioned as having a monastery in 922; but to the pilgrim it was a special place for a curious reason, for it was here that 'the pilgrims received a stone which they carried as far as Castañola (now Castañeda) to make lime for use in the construction of the Apostle's basilica', says Picaud. This was a wonderfully symbolic idea; every pilgrim had a hand in the construction of the House of God, but it was practical too and it has been pointed out that if in the twelfth century enough people carried a single stone to Castañeda (modern spelling) they were being of great practical help.

That this actually happened is fairly certain, for Lopez-Ferreiro's third book of his eleven-volume *History of the Church of Santiago* says that there were limestone quarries at Triacastela which were particularly lacking around Santiago. At Castañeda there were lime furnaces and from here the lime was carried in carts to Santiago.

At Triacastela the road split and some pilgrims went north

along what is now only a track and ascended to the hamlets of San Gil, Pintin and Calvor; others went south and got to the Benedictine monastery of Samos. It is on a curve in the river and tucked away in a deep valley; otherwise its immense size would strike the eye even more forcibly than it does now. There is nothing left of the original building, which was built some time between the sixth and seventh centuries, and it is known that from the eighth to tenth it was occupied by Jewish ecclesiastics from Andalucia. In 1951 a disastrous fire gutted the whole place, which has been entirely rebuilt, housing about twenty-eight Benedictine priests, some of whom I met when they were taking an afternoon constitutional.

From this point the road was all descent and the sixteenth-century Italian pilgrim Laffi says 'We came to a region which was beautiful and fertile; there was much fruit and a good number of houses, farms and gardens. One passes a river where are many mills and then soon afterwards one gets to Sarria.' And here the two strands met again and the present Calle Mayor (main street) of this flourishing town of five thousand people – glazed tiles and marble – is the very one the pilgrims walked down.

Barbadelo is the next place. It had a monastery which was sufficiently old to have been annexed to Samos in 874, and it still has a Romanesque St James church of great beauty, which has excited the interests of architects for many decades.

But at Barbadelo the pilgrims had to be wary; it was one of those stopping places selected by fraudulent Compostellan innkeepers, to which they sent their servants, who deceived the travellers with fraudulent recommendations of inns in the city.

Still walking gently downwards and still amidst beautiful scenery, the pilgrims next descended to a town on the river Miño which the march of civilisation has caused to be totally submerged.

Chapter 13

PORTOMARIN. THE ORDER OF SANTIAGO

At one stage a decision had to be taken; should a townlet be so preserved that future generations shall know the ways of their forbears, or shall people have the comforts that modern constructions can give them.

The river Miño is wide and to have built a bridge across it was no mean feat; when it was done people came to live by the Pons Minee, Portus Marini or Puente Miña. It is regarded as one of the most important Roman bridges in this part of Spain; a few arches survive and they have been photographed and discussed for the past fifty years. Another huge bridge now spans the Miño and from it you look down on a great expanse of water and you know to your sorrow that under it lies the old town Portomarin; it had to be submerged to accomplish the construction of a great reservoir, with a huge dam farther down the river. I have a book in which there are a number of photographs of the old town, taken around 1959, which shows that it was rather decrepit but quite charming, with a number of very old and somewhat dilapidated buildings.

Portomarin was an exceptionally important stop for pilgrims in the Middle Ages and its privileges were confirmed and reconfirmed on numerous occasions and especially by Alfonso IX of León and Henry II of Trastamara. Its fame was assured when the Commandery of St John of Malta built a hospital there, which even in 1939 had ceased to exist. There was, however, an arched entrance, but it was in such a dangerous state that it had to be pulled down in 1944.

The building of the new townlet of Portomarin, the transportation of the two old churches and one fine town hall stone by stone to the new site and their reconstruction has been an architectural triumph. To add to the tourist's comfort an albergue has been built, where I stayed to study the story of the removal. The tiny church of San Pedro is just on the outskirts of the village on the way to the albergue, but that of San Nicholas is in the most dominating position in the Plaza Mayor, opposite the *ayuntiamento* or town hall. It deserves this position, for this little Romanesque gem of a fortress-church struck me as being different from all other such places in that, having no tower, spire, gable or anything above the roof, and from the front appearing just like a cube, it looks more like a castle than a church, whereas all the other fortified churches in Spain look like churches first of all and like castles secondly. It has a wonderfully sculpted porch and a gorgeous rose window above.

Overlooking the church and Plaza Mayor, which is smaller than a tennis court, is a bar-restaurant (which has bedrooms), and as I sat munching I noticed that every single one of the square stones of San Nicholas church had been numbered, the ones at the top being numbered 2,000-plus. The numbers will now have been there for around a decade; will time efface them? I hope not; it will be a testimony to the trouble taken and a proof, too, that the stone did come from below the grey waters.

The main road ascends steeply into the main square and is lined on either side by an arcaded side walk where the main shops and bars are. As Sampedro would say 'to be visited'. Portomarin's hobbies and industries are fishing, brandy and ceramics.

A wild desolate moorland follows and the true pilgrims' road is to the left of the present highway; it was here I decided to devote two entire days to locating the exact path the pilgrims trod. When I was writing *Wines and Castles of Spain*, I first read H. V. Morton's *A Stranger in Spain*, in which he describes the ancient Moorish walled town of Niebla in the deep south with considerable enthusiasm and then advises his readers not to spoil the memory of such a lovely sight by entering the decrepit, squalid city within. Two days later I admired the fabulous walls, disregarded his advice and spoiled my memories. I suggest following his advice. Who has done so? And who will do so if I say that to try and locate the place along the pilgrims' road which has so fallen from grace is simply a sad disappointment?

First, I motored along the main road several times and noted that there were about half a dozen cart tracks over the scrub land to where I thought the village of Gonzar stood; then I asked several shepherds which of these tracks was the most likely to get me there. The first did not know what I was talking about, and the second sent me along the wrong track. When I found the right one I motored perhaps a hundred yards along it, had to give up, lock the car and walk about two miles to a settlement of six or seven hovels. To approach them you must go down a track about eight feet wide, lined on each side by five-foot dry stone walls; the track itself is six inches deep in black mud, on which a carpet of dried gorse had been thrown so that carts and tractors might pass. Some twenty yards farther on comes an opening about fifteen feet square, where stands a minute church in great disrepair; then comes another stone wall and then fields. From the church four or five other tracks lead, mostly between stone walls, on to the moor, then they disappear.

So many questions must be asked. How old are those walls? Fifty years? One hundred? Could they be made from the stones of houses which had been used for buildings of any sort, say around 1275, seven centuries ago?

The present chapel-church is anything from two to four hundred years old; it is not seven hundred years old. Is the present one exactly where the pilgrims trod, or is it twenty or two hundred yards away from the route? Are some of its stones from the old church, redressed by masons? If the present church is where the old one was, then one of the tracks may well be the actual pilgrims' road. Is there any way of telling, short of a huge architectural dig?

Incidentally, since so many pilgrims trod the road, as we know they did, and if as many robbers attacked them as is known, would not many pilgrims have resisted and would there not have been a scuffle? And if the robber was repulsed, surely in the bustle many a pilgrim would have lost his badge, a button, a knife. Must there not be thousands of relics along the genuine stretches of the road only a few feet down?

After Gonzar comes Ligonde and then Lestedo, which was important since it was here that a tributary coming from the south (the first we hear of from this direction), from Pueblo de Sanabria, met the main stream. Then comes Villar de Donas.

Lying about a mile and a half to the north of the present road the convent of San Salvador de Villar de Donas was a commandery or convent of the Order of St James. This is the point at which we may discuss those military orders which evolved in the eleventh and early twelfth centuries from the concept of monasterial institutions with an emphasis on penitention and the desire of the Christian warrior to protect the frontiers of his faith from the Mussulmans. The two ideas seem incompatible at first, but this was a period when men wanted to get nearer to Christ and if that meant death on the battlefield, so much the better; but if they could not die fighting for Him then the other way to achieve this 'togetherness' was by prayer, hair shirts, scourges and fasting, and, if that was not enough, to go unwashed for years and be so unpleasant to the Arabs (who were quite happy to leave the Christians in peace) that Arabs had to punish the obstreperous Christians by death, thus making them martyrs.

It was in the time when the Roman Emperors were embracing Christianity that this ideal of warring against the infidels started, and with this came the especial veneration of the three dragon-slaying or Saracen-slaying saints, Martin, Michael and George.

There are two conflicting theories as to the exact way that these Spanish orders came into being, the more likely though less exciting one being that they were copies of slightly older but similar orders in Central Europe; but it has been suggested that they derived from the Mussulman, who had formed similar societies to keep pagans away from their frontiers in the East. The Mussulman did not look upon the Christians as they did the polytheists or idol worshippers, who were given the famous choice of 'Islam or the sword'. Jews, Christians and other 'people of the book' – that is to say, monotheists with written scriptures – were usually allowed to become 'protected groups', merely paying a tax and ruling themselves.

But the background to the order at Santiago, of San Julian of Calatrava, stemmed from the fact that the clergy, in spite of their passionate desire to spread Christianity, were not permitted by the rules of their order to shed blood in battle. On the other hand there was nothing to prevent a Spanish warrior from taking vows to lead a holy life and to form with others a religious brotherhood. Such organisations came into existence in several Spanish towns, as for example in Tarragona in 1129. Slowly these military brotherhoods became involved in social problems, as in Toledo, where they undertook the building of bridges and the maintenance of the defences of the city.

This is the way in which the Order of St James took shape, when in 1170 Ferdinand II of León reconquered Cáceres and, as a measure aimed to defend the newly won territory and to organise future reconquests, founded a brotherhood called 'Los Freiles[1] de Cáceres', to which he gave the town in custody.

By early in 1171 the brotherhood was already called 'The Order of St James', which name it probably took because Don Pedro, Archbishop of Santiago, granted them a standard of St James as well as protection and certain rents which accrued to the cathedral in return for the priests promising to become knights and vassals of Santiago and especially to defend and protect the village of Albuquerque.

By the end of the twelfth century the order had its 'Rules of St James', which stated that the foundation was formed of a group of Spanish nobility who, taken by the grace of the Holy Spirit, would abandon all vices and would take the cross and sign of St James to defend the Church and conquer the Moors. They further agreed never again to wage war against Christians, to abandon the vanities of this world, to live according to the scriptures and to fight for God against the Infidel. These rules were approved by the Archbishops of Toledo, Santiago and Braga (now in Portugal) and the Bishops of León, Astorga and Zamora; and after much discussion, on 5 July 1175 Pope Alexander III confirmed the rules and placed the order under the protection of St Peter.

The badge or emblem which they displayed is of great beauty, strongly linked with the pilgrimage and of great importance in Spanish heraldry through the centuries to the present day: a little blood-red sword (nicknamed *el legato*, the lizard) in the form of a cross charged with a scallop shell.

For 317 years, from the date of their official recognition by Rome until 1493, the order grew in favour, wealth and power, so that at its height it possessed more than 600 convents, hospitals, castles, villages and other properties.

When the need to reconquer became less demanding the order undertook other forms of social aid. By far the most interesting was acting as official intermediary between the Spanish monarchs and the Muslims of Spain and North Africa in connection with the rescue and ransom of captives. They were thus the true forerunners of the present Red Cross.

The most important and largest property of the order, which was also their headquarters, was the castle of Ucles near Tarancor

[1] A priestly knight.

in the present province of Cuenca, and it was there that it met its end.

The fact is that in spite of the good they did, in spite of the fact that they were still what they had vowed – lions on the field of battle and lambs in the convent – they had become a state within a state and Ferdinand and Isabella felt that the order was a menace to the future unity of Spain. With a percipience which typified her astuteness Isabella, on the death of the master of the order, the Count of Parades, paid a visit to Ucles and instructed the order to appeal to the Pope to grant her husband Ferdinand the mastership, with the result that in 1493 all the order's vast properties went to the crown.

Villar de Donas or San Salvador de Villar de Donas had much in common with San Marcos at León and was at first a monastery of patrimony belonging to several Galician nobles. At the end of the twelfth century it was given to the order by the dean of Lugo Juan Arias, who set out rules of conduct. It was to be run on the lines of the Order of St James and the clergy who lived there were to observe its regulations. Like those of St James they had to wear black capes in winter, and to wear their outside tunics throughout the year. They had to live in poverty and chastity, and were to be obedient to the prior who was nominated by Ucles.

In one respect the order differed from the others in that the priests were permitted to marry, though conjugal chastity was to be strictly observed. Utmost obedience was expected and so was poverty, to which end, on becoming a member of the order, all worldly wealth was forfeited whether one lived inside the convent or outside with one's family. Priests were allowed to marry after they had joined and if they were widowers could re-marry, but only with permission of their master. Those priests who lived with their families were expected to live inside during Lent and on other Holy Days; on the other hand, when the men went to war the women were allowed to re-marry with permission of the master.

At meal times in the refectory the priests ate in silence while some edifying book was read to them. Meat-eating was permitted on certain days and in 1247 Pope Innocent IV directed them to consume flesh when they were on summer campaigns, and they were forbidden to flagellate their bodies for the good reason that this would impede the one thing that mattered, namely the Holy War against the Infidels.

Their most important garment was the cape, which had to be worn everywhere, but which must not cost more than eight mare-vidis and had to last for two years. They were allowed to wear the cross-sword of St James on these capes from the inception of the order, but later, in 1259, another emblem was permitted, but on conditions: the *venera* or scallop shell, the symbol of Compostela pilgrims. Only *sacerdotes* (chevalier-priests) and monks of sufficiently high rank could do this.

Not all members of the order were able to live such spartan lives and so many deserted that it became necessary to bring in rules to prevent defection. Thus in 1251 it was promulgated that no priest could make any journey without permission of his commander and furthermore he had to promise to return within a certain time limit, nor were they allowed to leave their destination without the permission of that commander. If any members of the order in a fit of anger said that he intended to resign he was imprisoned and punished.

Reverting to the permission to marry, this of course meant children and the attendant problems. Sons and daughters were educated by the convent until they were fifteen years old, when they could enter the order if they wished, but if they chose to go out into the world they could do so and take any inheritance they had coming to them, and it was expressly forbidden for any father-priest to disinherit any of his children if they did not enter the order.[1]

Having said so much about Villar de Donas, the statement that it is just off the main road is not enough. The 'road', which is rather a smooth sandy lane, runs through desolate and high heathland, and about a mile and a half along this it reaches a clearing, on the right of which is a real gem of a Romanesque church with something I have never seen in any other European church, namely a minute stone cloister attached to the *front* of the main door. Of the convent nothing remains, but less than fifteen yards away is a farm house and a lot of outbuildings all of the same stone as the church.

Now from the time of the building of the pyramids – unless you like to go back to Stonehenge – one of the most time-consuming occupations of our ancestors has been the quarrying of stone

---

[1] But I cannot understand how, if on entering the Order of St James you gave all your worldly goods to it, there could be anything left later to will to your children.

4 León Cathedral

15 On the collegiate church of St Isidor and now shown on the back of a 1000-peseta note

for buildings in which to house themselves or their gods. And when a site had been selected as the best for security or for commerce, it may well have lacked the right type of stone or there was not enough of it to quarry locally. An example of this is one of Roman Spain's least-known monuments: an obelisk called El Medol, several miles to the north of Tarragona, which lies – or rather stands – plumb in the centre of a huge sandstone quarry, a reminder of the vast amount of stone needed to build Roman Tarraconensis.

I suggest that until such time as it became cheaper to transport breeze blocks or sand and cement to a site, as recently as only fifty years ago, the use of existing stones was a dozen times cheaper than the labour involved in quarrying new stone. Thus scores of convents and castles which have disappeared in Spain and elsewhere in Europe have not done so through wanton destruction but because the stones have been used in creating other structures near by.

After Villar de Donas the pilgrim made a gentle descent to Palas de Rey, then to Carballac. Not far from Carballac are the ruined remains of the castle of Los Ulloas, which belonged to the counts of Monterey.

The pilgrims then left the province of Lugo and entered that of La Coruña and got to a village now called Libuerio. Libuerio is an interesting and unusual example of a place that not only has retained the same name for nearly a thousand years, but is still famed for something that earned its name in the first place. Picaud speaks of Campus Leporarius and the French diarist travellers of the sixteenth century called it Champlevrier and both mean 'the place of hares'; it is still famous in Spain today for the abundance of this animal. When the name of the place went from Latin to Castillian it became Leporario and when in 1185 the place was given by Ferdinand II to the monastery of Sobrado 'the *burgo* (village) of Leporario' was mentioned.

As a modern pilgrim I got to Mellid (pronounced Mell-ith, as if lisped) on a last Sunday in the month, when in the winter a cattle fair is held to which cows, pigs and chickens are brought for sale from outlying villages. The scene that presented itself was the most rural, the most Spanish, the most animated that I ever remember witnessing in that country, primitive but not impoverished.

It was just three o'clock and every bar, bar-restaurant, meson[1] and café was packed with people eating, drinking, smoking and talking with exceptional gesticulatory animation. They were mainly men, for outside were the women, walking their cows up and down, looking for buyers. People had come in on mules, bicycles, motorcycles, buses and charabancs, but the most memorable transporter of all was a smallish charabanc which had been converted in such a way that the front half took humans and the back half took cattle.

Mellid was an important stopping place in the Middle Ages; at the entrance to the town the Romanesque church of San Pedro once stood, and on the way out there was and still is the glorious little Romanesque church of Santa Maria. Mellid was not only important to pilgrims on the outward journey; it was a special night stop on the return journey for those who wanted to turn north and visit Oviedo. Apart from its two churches there was the monastery of the Holy Spirit, with hospital attached, founded in 1375 by the notary Fernan Lopez. It had twelve couches 'furnished and with all the linen needed to receive and shelter the poor and impoverished pilgrims who needed help'.

Soon after Mellid the pilgrims arrived at the hamlet of Castañeda, formerly called Castaniola and it was here that they deposited the limestone which, referred to earlier, they had picked up at Triacastela.

Leaving the present main road after Castañeda the pilgrims took a short cut and descended the Rivadiso ravine where a hospital in the care of Compostelan silversmiths, called the Confraternity of San Eloy, once stood. From here they got to Arzua, the largest village of this last section of the Road, where there was a church dedicted to the Apostle, which is now the parish church. And here they met their fellow travellers coming from the coast road.

[1] Whatever the dictionary says regarding the translation of this word, I have found that in the smaller towns of Spain those restaurants which are called 'El Meson' are always very old-fashioned, spotlessly clean, but usually empty both at lunch time and dinner time, save on the occasional market day for the mid-day meal.

Chapter 14

THE SPANISH COAST ROAD

If the pilgrims did not wish to climb the Pyrenees they took the sea road and entered Spain at Irun. I like this gay frontier town and always stay at the Hotel Alcázar and eat in the Jantokia restaurant on the same premises. Richard Ford did not like the place:

'Irun, Irunia signifies in Basque the good Town, and thus, opening Spain with a misnomer, gives a hint to strangers not always to translate Spanish words or titles in a too literal meaning; here at least the reverse is nearer the mark, for to speak in truth, and not in irony, this is but a bad and good-for-nothing place, peopled with 4,000 paupers, who live on the crumbs of those who come and those who depart; placed however at the entrance of Spain, and on the high road to Madrid, it is at heart a good coast town, and means of escape are plentiful.'

For a modern author of almost any book or article about Spain, not to mention Ford, would mean that he had a greater confidence in himself than I have. Ford's hand-book to Spain of three quarters of a million highly readable, but abusive and self-opinionated words is remarkable.

Richard Ford was born in Chelsea in 1796, the eldest son of Sir Richard Ford, a Member of Parliament best known as the Bow Street Magistrate who created London's first police force. He went to Winchester, then Oxford, and married the illegitimate daughter of the fifth Earl of Essex. It was her delicate health which took them to Spain, where Ford and his family spent three whole

years, in the winter in Seville, in the summer at the Alhambra at Granada, while he travelled on horseback throughout the length and breadth of Spain.

On his return to England, he set himself up as an expert on Spain, and when John Murray sought his advice on a Spanish companion volume to that publishers' tremendously successful handbook to France, Richard Ford suggested himself for the task, though he was a fairly rich man. He spent four years on the job, but for John Murray there was a shock in store, for when completed it was far too long, discursive and above all violently phrased.

It did not, however, go on sale, for even Ford became nervous about the extreme offensiveness of certain passages; publication was abruptly cancelled, so that today there are less than twenty copies in existence of a work which is almost as rare as Lewis Carroll's cancelled first edition of *Alice in Wonderland*.

By May 1845, completely revised, the work, however, was finally issued and became a resounding success, mainly I think because it was only thirty years previously that the Peninsula War had been fought over part of the terrain covered by Ford and those grim battles were still within living memory.

But what is one to make of an author who talked of his 'well beloved Spain' and then could write of the Escorial that 'The edifice has nothing in form or colour which is either royal, religious or ancient. The clean granite blue slates and leaden roofs look new, as if built yesterday. It has the air of an overblown barrack or manufactory.'

Indeed, the Escorial is rather sombre but it is also majestic. When Ford saw it he was looking at a building which had been standing for three hundred years; surely any building which is as old as that deserves less harsh judgement. That may be a matter of taste, of course, but what are we to make of Ford on Córdoba? 'Córdoba is soon seen. This Athens of the Moor is now a poor Boeotian place . . . a day will amply suffice for everything. The cathedral or the mosque, la Mesquita, as it is called (*mesgad* from *masegad* to worship prostrate) stands isolated. The exterior is castellated and forbidding.'

Nor is he ever very accurate. St Dominic of the Causeway was born, according to Butler in his *Lives of the Saints*, at Viloria near Belorado in Northern Spain, but on a vague story never authenticated Ford has him come from Italy, 'sent to Spain in 1050 by Pope Damaso II as an exorciser at the request of the peasants who were being eaten up by locusts'. One cannot help feeling that Ford chose this version for its sense of drama than for its truth.

After Irun came San Sebastian, which Fords calls the 'Brighton of Madrid'. Well, yes; only one does not see Brighton, even if Prinny did go there very often, as the summer residence of the British Government and the Diplomatic Corps, as Baedaker's Guide tells us was the case with San Sebastian. Being so near to the French border I find it is hardly Spanish at all, but my daughter, who did a summer *au pair* job there, thought the yellow-sanded bay of La Concha (and it is indeed shell-shaped) a marvellous place for bathing.

The pilgrims next trudged on over Monte Igueldo to the tiny little hamlet of Orio. Here the Catholic Monarchs (Ferdinand and Isabella) in 1484 granted the townspeople permission to keep two boats in the river to take passengers and merchants from one bank to the other. The tariff was one maravedi per person, two for a beast without any baggage and three if the horse or mule was loaded; but it was established that poor people and pilgrims should pay nothing.

After Orio comes Zarauz, where I spent a short holiday in 1935 and of which I subsequently wrote in my book *Table for Two* (1942):

'Thank the stars for Zarauz! It is the nearest to a perfect place that I have ever been in. A little place not too big to be unfriendly and not too small to look overcrowded and with green-covered rocks rising so steeply all the way round the bay that every bit of sun is trapped there; to be radiated out again when night falls. Perfect golden sands, wonderful bathing, quite safe yet with the waves breaking large enough for anybody's liking. And in the middle of this beautiful bay is an hotel with its glassed-in restaurant almost touching the sea.'

I have been back since then and even though the rain poured down incessantly, I found that the place retained all of its magic. Its splendid beach would not have changed since the Middle Ages and surely many a footsore pilgrim would have taken a refreshing dip, for nudity in the presence of the other sex did not worry medieval people a bit; it was quite common.

A short walk along the sea front took one to Guetaria, where the pilgrims set eyes upon the island rock called 'El Raton', the Rat, jutting out into the sea with a remarkable likeness to that animal. The church, which is Gothic in style, has been declared a national monument mainly because, in adapting the building to the extraordinary lie of the land, a tunnel leads from inside the church and via the altar down and under the Raton to the fort below. On the quay of this delightful little fishing village is a splendid statue by sculptor Victoria Macho of a native of the place, the great Juan Sebastian Elcano, who, with Magellan, achieved the first circumnavigation of the globe in 1519–22.

Zumaya is another little fishing village of great charm, and the corniche from Zarauz to Zumaya is so picturesque that it has earned itself two stars in the Guide Michelin, which adds that in really bad weather the sea can make it impossible by car. The place was created by Alfonso XI in 1348 to help the pilgrims, and he also gave permission for it to be enclosed by walls.

But the most interesting connection with the pilgrims' route, indeed one of the most important features along all this coast, are the ruins of a former hermitage which the famous painter Ignacio Zuloaga[1] 1897–1945 turned into a splendid museum; it is open to the public and houses a good collection of El Grecos, Goyas and the best of Zuloaga's own works.

At Deva river and town came a parting of the ways and some pilgrims went south to join, via Vitoria, the *Camino Frances* at Burgos, while the rest went slightly inland for a while through Guernica to take the coast road.

The reason I know this town so well is on account of my frequent trips on the pleasant modern drive-on drive-off Swedish Lloyd ship, the *Patricia*, on which I have acted as lecturer on Spain for their five-day mini-cruises. My talks were confined to the ship, but I frequently joined the coach which took passengers from the *Patricia* at Portugalete, some seven miles away from Bilbao, for a tour through the pleasant green countryside, invariably ending up in Guernica, where in the attractive main square of this clean, pleasant town a first-rate lunch was served at the reasonably priced, typically Spanish restaurant, Arien.

But Guernica y Luna, to give this town of 14,000 inhabitants its correct name, has not only one of the largest indoor *pelota* courts in the Basque country but has also a special place in Spanish

---

[1] With his Basque beret and open-neck shirt he is currently depicted on the face of the 500-peseta note, while his superb picture of Toledo is reproduced on the back.

history – more important than the fact that it was bombed in the Civil War.

These tour coaches were always manned by a driver and a very young hostess-commentator whose knowledge of English was almost nil. When we got settled she picked up the microphone and said: 'My name is Carmen!' This was received with roars of applause and hand-clapping.

She then turned her back on her audience and started a never-ending flow of chat to the driver until some hours later when, well out in the countryside and having passed a superb castle and two Romanesque churches, we approached a hideous factory which I thought was a cement works. Carmen languidly turned round and, picking up the microphone, said: 'On our left is the processed milk factory of the region.' Applause!

We then passed on to Guernica, ate a good lunch, stopped at a large bazaar in Bilbao – Carmen's English became much better when she explained what a good shop it was – and home, and I forgot all about it until a month later when Carmen was on the coach again and the pattern repeated itself.

Between visits I had learned something about one of the castles and as we passed I asked – in English – to hear something about it and Carmen shrugged her shoulders and continued her conversation with the driver. So as we approached Guernica I approached the girl and said: 'As you were so late back from the dance last night, you must be feeling tired, and so with your kind permission I will tell the passengers what I am sure you were going to tell them about the interesting history of Guernica.'

The girl's jaw dropped, but before she had time to recover I had the microphone in my hand.

'Ladies and Gentlemen,' I said, 'you are approaching a town which has a special place in Basque and Spanish history. Behind the main square is a charming little museum and in front of it, encircled by iron railings for greater safety, is the most cherished oak tree in Spain, for under it the *fueros* of the Basques were ratified. This word is a most important one in Spain and an understanding of it will help you get a better picture of the Spanish history of the seven-hundred-year reconquest of the land from Arab domination.'

I saw that I had my audience gripped and in the pause needed to take breath I cast a look at Carmen, who had definitely turned a few shades paler: 'As the conquering Christians moved south,'

I continued, 'it was necessary to raise townships, start families, build fortresses and cultivate the land around, and the inducement put forward was the granting to the new citizens of these municipalities a form of charter of rights and privileges called a *fuero*, which they could hand down to their children.'

I went on to explain that as the centuries passed these municipal laws, for such the *fueros* really were, became an impediment to effective government when the country was more or less at peace, but they were cherished by the towns and their peoples even to the extent of forcing succeeding kings to uphold their rights.

When I had finished my talk I turned to Carmen and rapidly gave her a Spanish précis of what I had said.

'You've told me more about Spanish history than I have been told before in all my life,' she commented.

The coach was now drawing up in Guernica's main square and the passengers started to get out. The hostess pointed to the Arien restaurant, but quite a knot of the mini-cruisers had formed a circle around her and were gesticulating with some animation.

'Can I help?' I asked.

'Yes,' said one. 'Tell her that we want to see the oak tree before we go to lunch.'

But it was a hollow triumph, for we arrived at the restaurant so late that my favourite course of grilled red mullet had to be omitted.

The pilgrims next went on through Portugalete to Castro Urdiales, a place of importance in Roman times and the oldest town along the coast, recently declared a place of historical interest; then through Laredo (one of the most important fishing towns of Spain in the Middle Ages) and afterwards to Santona and Santander.

This provincial capital (14,900 inhabitants), is the pride of the whole of this north coast of Spain and has a golden, sandy beach called El Sardinero, with a good collection of hotels (try the Sardinera or the Marie Isabel), which makes San Sebastian's *concha* plage look quite insignificant.

At this point mention should be made of another English writer on Spain whose rollicking prose, in his great book, *The Bible in Spain*, makes instructive reading, but without striving for effect, as Ford constantly does. George Borrow, born at East Dereham, Norfolk, in 1803 was – and for this we must be thankful – a wanderer over the face of Europe. After being articled to a solicitor in Norwich, his urge to be out in the open caused him to set out on a tour of Wales which produced *Wild Wales*. He was then sent to Spain 'by the Bible Society, as its agent for the purpose of printing and circulating the scriptures', as he tells us. He was imprisoned in the country (in Madrid in 1838), for 'sending home a too faithful account of General Quesadas' exploits', says the *Dictionary of National Biography*, whereas Borrow in his book says it was for illegally distributing his gipsy translation of the Bible.

It is said that it was Richard Ford, who recommended John Murray to publish *The Zincali, or an Account of the Gipsies of Spain* and *The Bible in Spain*, and as Santander is such a splendid town it is interesting to see what these two men, who both loved Spain so much, who both can at times say such cruel things about the poverty there and who were both writing their travel books during the same years, Ford in 1840 to 1843 and Borrow in 1839 to 1841, say about the place. Ford starts by saying that the place was called Portus Blendium, that it is well placed on the south tongue of a headland, that the harbour is accessible and good and that the population was 'above' 13,000.

'It is a thriving place having risen at the expense of Bilbao, for during the Civil War the merchants removed their establishments to this less disturbed district. The fine quay and newly built houses of the chief merchants have rather a French than a Spanish look and the shops abound with Parisian colifichets and poor hagiographical engravings.'

He then has a crack at the poorer part of the town, says that the 'hospital and prison do little credit to science and humanity' and, falling over backwards to be witty, points out that the porters' work 'is done by women, if the androgynous, epicene Amazons can so be called'.

Borrow is very enthusiastic about the 'bustle and activity' of the town, which 'is almost the only city in Spain which has not suffered by the Carlist wars'. He estimates that the population is 60,000 souls, and continues:

'Till the close of the eighteenth century, it was little better than an obscure fishing village but it has of late years almost entirely engrossed the commerce of the Spanish transatlantic possessions, especially of the Havannah. The consequence of which has been that whilst Santander has rapidly increased in wealth and magnificence both Corunna and Cadiz have been rapidly hastening to decay. At present it possesses a noble quay on which stands a line of stately edifices far exceeding in splendour the palaces of the aristocracy of Madrid. These are built in the French style and are chiefly occupied by the merchants.'

Which of the two population figures is correct? Ford gives the population of La Coruña (he recommends El Commercio at 3s 4d a day) as 25,000 and Bilbao ('damp and pulmonary diseases are prevalent') as 15,000, and if he is basing his figure on when he was there, say 1832, and not when he started to write ten years later, this would have been about right. Borrow was writing in 1840 within a year of having visited the town, but even then I do not believe the population could have expanded so much in so short a time.

The 'noble' and 'fine' quay to which both authors refer is still animated and splendid; and, most unusually, right on the docks is a huge 180-bedroom, very old, luxury hotel, the Bahia. The place is no longer rated as *de grande luxe* from the price point of view, but it has all the trappings I like so much. I quote from an article I wrote when I stayed there six years ago:

'At the Bahia *de luxe* means that the staff at the reception desk are in immaculate deep black tails, the keys are kept by a key porter in a splendiferous uniform with crossed keys embossed on his lapels at another desk, and at a third one is the department which sells stamps, books, postcards and so on, while small bell hops are continuously rushing around handing you out of cars, pushing revolving doors and pressing the correct buttons of lifts. The bedrooms are immense and airy and the view from the windows is twofold; in one direction is a splendid view along a palm and flower decked avenue with the sea beyond, while to the right are scores of little cargo boats unloading pig iron and cheap tin trays. And more unusual still, the shopping centre and cathedral are only five minutes away.'

It is just as though the Savoy Hotel found itself next door to the London Docks and Bond Street.

Santander was victim of a terrible fire in 1941; a large part of the town having been destroyed, it had to be rebuilt, including the present town hall of magnificent and elegant proportions. Formerly Portus Victoriae, and then Sancti Emerethi, it was Alfonso VIII who repopulated it in 1187 and granted it *fueros* or its own municipal laws.

But Santander was not a particularly important stopping place for the pilgrims and after Laredo (population now 7,000), which was much more important, many of them by-passed it completely. It breaks all the rules in another way; Pamplona, Logroño, Burgos and León were all important halts and have remained important to this day. Sahagún, Carrión and Beldorando and scores more were important and have faded away; Santander is the only one which was relatively unimportant (like say Los Arcos, Castrojeriz Molinaseca) but has grown enormously.

Trudging slowly on, and now in a very mountainous region, the pilgrims went through Carmargo and got to Santillana del Mar which, in spite of its name, is not on the sea but leaves one bereft of superlatives. It is a tawny-walled, medieval village, the whole of which has been declared of historical national interest and is every bit as lovely as Riquewihr in Alsace and Rothenburg ob der Tauber in Germany.

The place was 'discovered' – if that is the right word for a village which has been in existence for a thousand years – by the Spanish Anglophile republican writer Benito Perez Galdos around 1876 and in writing about it he has made the point that it was only by a series of coincidences, 'which could be called happy miracles', that the place had remained so wonderfully intact. Borrow visited it while travelling in the opposite direction from San Vicente de la Barquera to Santander:

'The country at last began to improve and in the neighbourhood of Santillana was both beautiful and fertile. About a league before we reached the country of Gil Blas we passed through an extensive wood in which were rocks and precipices. The wood has an evil name and our guide informed us that robberies were occasionally committed in it. No adventure however befell us and we reached Santillana at about six in the evening.'

The population, he tells us, was about 4,000 and so has not dropped as have others, for it has this population today.

Richard Ford was there, of course, and actually has a good word for it, calling it a 'pretty town', which for him is praise indeed. Ford correctly points out that the name Santillana is the corruption of Santa Juliana. She was a most popular saint in the Middle Ages; she was grievously scourged by her own father and Ford has got it right when he says that the town has for its arms St Juliana holding the Devil in chains, since this Devil, 'transforming himself into an angel of light', tried to get the saint to marry a Roman official, she did not like. Ford then continues: 'The Casa Consistorial in the plaza is a fine building and worthy of a town which really did give birth to the Inigo Jones of Spain, Juan de Herrera.' Writing nearly eight years after his visit and dashing through the countryside far too quickly, Ford should have checked his facts.

The Casa Consistorial (town hall – but now a parador and a lovely hotel to stay in) is magnificent and Juan de Herrera (1530–97) was even more than the Inigo Jones of Spain; his birthplace was at Valladolid, where he designed the cathedral.

I think I know how Ford made the mistake. Many small towns in Spain are made attractive by the coats of arms or blazons, sometimes two feet square, sculpted in stone over the main doors of large houses. These sculptures are mostly in towns in the southwest, where the conquistadores settled after returning with their spoils from America. At that time they were of far from ancient lineage and there was no better way to keep up with the Joneses than by having a nice shield carved over one's gateway. Ciudad Rodrigo is the town most noted for these, but there are many many others and Santillana has more such shields than most.

Now my Santillana book gives the drawing of a couple of dozen coats of arms of various Spanish families, Ceballos, Quevdo, Calderón de la Barca, Estrada, Bustamente, Salazar and so on, including Herrera, and one can only assume that Ford saw somewhere the shield of someone of the same name as the great architect and came to the wrong conclusion.

Although the tourists invade the village by day, when evening comes the place is invaded by returning beasts from the outlying fields. It is incredible that so little can have changed; when I strolled about the place on my last visit in 1970 things had not altered since Muirhead Bone wrote in 1937:

'The farms and the valleys have their centre in Santillana. The chief sounds in the street are those of the farmyard. Cows and asses and mules live in the lower storey of the palaces in the patriarchical way as part of the family. Passing when the doors are open one sees stables as vast and cool as caverns, with the motionless silhouettes of oxen and mules in the dusky interior. Morning and evening the street is full of the soft tramp of cows coming for water. There is the splash of a pail, the call to driven animals, the clatter of a mule; the quick step of a donkey carrying fodder or Indian corn. The voices which linger are those of women about the fountain.'

Two long and parallel narrow streets, with houses of tawny sandstone, each with wrought-iron balconies from which tumbles a profusion of flowers, lead to the jewel of this perfect little townlet: the twelfth-century Romanesque collegiate church with a cloister as exquisite as any to be seen along the Way.

An entire book has been written about Santillana in which it is claimed that the town has had more poems in its praise than any other comparable place in Spain.

Only a little more than a mile from Santillana are the Altimira Caves, a 'must' for any traveller in this region. The pilgrims, of course, never saw them or their magnificent prehistoric paintings. These are about 25,000 years old and are of the usual animals, bison, boar, horses, and so on, and are in an oblong chamber between two shelves of rock and in a 'room' which it is thought was intended to be used for some other purpose than domestic life. The colourings are earth pigments and so are limited to red, orange and deepest black, probably made from soot, and they were mixed with animal fat to make them adhere to the rock surface, which some experts think had been chiselled to give the drawings a sort of sculptural effect.

Returning to Santillana for a moment: it is also the birthplace of that fifteenth-century rogue and valet, Gil Blas, around whom the French author Le Sage wrote the famous novel which appeared between 1715 and 1735. Most people now assert that the whole story was borrowed from a Spanish author.

The *Jacquaires* next plodded on through Cobreces and Comillas until they came back to the sea and arrived at San Vicente de la Barquera, or Barqueria, at present a town of 10,000 inhabitants, of great antiquity, with a splendid modern beach. I was pleasantly delayed here for a day as I received a surprise invitation from the two girls who had borrowed my car jack at Fromista. The huge quayside and main square are all one, and I parked my car there and set off on foot to see what the pilgrims would have seen when they passed through.

One tourist brochure has called the harbour the 'Scapa Flow of olden Spain', for there is not one harbour here but, though now thoroughly silted up, five harbours with an entrance so narrow that no enemy could be blamed for failing to sight it. It was into this harbour that the intemporate and gluttonous monarch Charles V sailed one day to take formal possession of Spain. To celebrate the event the noblemen laid on for him his first bull fight; they were then fought not by paid toreadors but by *hidalgos*[1] of the Court to prove their mettle.

The church is Romanesque, with the extra interest and beauty of having been a fortified place like the glorious cathedral at Tuy. Inside is the tomb of Inquisitor Corro, Archbishop of Seville in the days of Queen Isabel; he had it made in Genoa but came back to the family town to be buried.

When I returned to the quayside there was a mini parked beside mine and in my own was a note: 'Are we forgiven? We are staying at the Miramar; we have found a nice restaurant called the Maruja and we would like to invite you to dinner.' It was a very good eating place; I had an omelette with fresh prawns into which I persuaded them to put some diced fried potatoes to prevent it from being too rich, which reminded me of an amusing incident recounted by Alexandre Dumas (*pére*) in his travel book *From Paris to Cadiz*.

He was at Vitoria when, coming down for breakfast, he saw the breakfast tariff on the wall. He asked for the first item, which was two boiled eggs. The girl understood Dumas' Spanish but puzzled him by, 'Asking me whether I would like a monk's couple or a layman's'.

' "Surely a couple of eggs means simply a couple of eggs," I said. I learned that the former consists of three eggs but "a couple of eggs for a layman" meant only two. It seems that the monks enjoyed wide privileges before the revolution drove them from Spain, privileges only remembered in such catch phrases as this.'

Dumas, who wrote his lively diary in the form of letters to a lady – no one yet knows who this lady was – left Paris suddenly in 1846, at the height of his fame, to attend the wedding of the Spanish Infanta in Madrid; he only passed through one pilgrim

[1] Derived from *hijo de algo*, son of something, i.e. one of the lesser nobility.

town, Burgos: 'If ever you go to Burgos, Madame, you must visit the immense cathedral with its bas reliefs showing Our Lord's entry into Jerusalem, its wonderful ironwork choir-screen, its dome like a Florentine jewel, its priceless art treasurers.'

After San Vicente the pilgrims continued along the seashore through Llanes till they got to Ribadesella; then they went on to Oviedo, where a number would have decided to turn inland and take the mountainous route via Lugo. We must leave them in this wild region of deep ravines and torrents and mention only that on their way they had to traverse the Seven Bellotas (Acorns) Mountains, so-called because of their shape; they had an evil reputation. Then they had to cross a rickety structure made of tree-trunks called 'The Bridge which Trembles'. This frightened the pilgrims so much, especially because of the raging torrents below, that *Le pont qui tremble* went into one of the many pilgrim songs[1] which abounded in the early seventeenth century:

> 'When we saw the trembling bridge
> Thirty of us were together,
> As many Waloons as Germans,
> And we said, "If you please
> Friend, you go first!" '

The other poem talks of the 'waves of the sea in their fury; the shock made us tremble and fear for our lives'.

But mostly the pilgrims went by the sea road and it was on the borders of the Asturias and Galicia, at the mining town of Ribadeo, that the pilgrims at last left the coast and turned inwards. The charm of Ribadeo has scarcely been affected by the mining industry on which it lives. They had come along what is still the least spoilt part of all Spain's coast line, a series of enchanting little fishing villages nestling at the foot of verdant hills. What preserves the charm is that you cannot get from one tiny place to the next by motoring along the coast but have to motor back to the main road and dip down again. And at every one of these villages fishing is still a livelihood and at one end of the bay will always be a small quay from which the little boats sail and on which the catch is landed.

Before getting to Ribadeo the pilgrims arrived at Castropol on the other side of a huge *ria*, the Spanish equivalent of a fjord. This

[1] Printed in Valenciennes in 1616.

was so wide that it was necessary to hire a boat to cross and there are many references to how dangerous the pilgrims thought the boat was and how dangerous they thought the boatmen, too.

I have already mentioned the severe measures taken by the state against vagabonds pretending to be pilgrims and I am tempted to believe that Ribadeo was a place where spot checks by the police were particularly severe, as evidenced by part of a sixteenth-century pilgrim song:[1]

> *'Quand nous fumes dans la Galice à Rivedieu*
> *On voulait nous mettre aux galeres jeunes et viex*
> *Mais nous nous some défendus de notre langue*
> *Avons dit qu'étions Espagnols et nous sommes de France'*

The pilgrims had a number of places to stay in this seaside town and the modern traveller has an admirable twenty-five double-bedroomed luxury albergue, run by the State, which has a lovely view over the ria and the mountains.

Mountains are now everywhere. First Villanueva de Lorenzana with its famous monastery founded by Count Osoric, and then a stiff climb to a high range leads – and what a superb view there is of the town below – to the pretty little village of Mondoñedo. Here is the least visited cathedral of Galicia and probably all Spain, and in relation to the smallness of the town itself the façade appears to be immense. Anyway, it is the cathedral architect's dream. It was started in the thirteenth century and now is mainly Gothic but with profuse Renaissance decorations. It is the front which is so striking, for it has towers outside the aisles, in between which is a superb and enormous rose window.

Inside the great attraction for later English pilgrims was a very large standing figure of the Virgin and Child with six seraphims carved in wood and called 'La Inglesa' because it is said to have been brought by one John Ilton from Old St Pauls in the mid-sixteenth century to escape iconoclastic Protestants.

A big climb follows to the pass of La Xesta at 1,788 feet, then a gradual descent through meadows, fields and lovely groups of trees in long straight lines and with avenues of birches via the

---

[1] 'When we were in Galicia at Rivedieu
They wanted to put in the galleys both young and old,
But we stuck up for ourselves in our language,
They having said we were Spanish though we are from France.'

village of Abadin (the marble quarries are famous) to Villalba of 20,000 persons. The place has fifteenth-century ramparts and the remains of a castle so big that one tower alone has sufficed to be turned into a magnificent State-run parador. The countryside now, with its grey granite, its green vegetation and its roadsides lined with apple trees, is strongly reminiscent of Brittany.

Next, on the main road from Lugo to La Coruña, is Bahamonde with its Romanesque church and granite calvary. As this is spelled Baamonde by both Baedeker and the Firestone map, I wonder if there are two spellings. The former is General Franco's surname and he was acually born near here at El Ferrol.

A little farther on is Sobrado. Even at a distance it is possible to see what an enormous place it was and still is. At the end of the tenth or beginning of the eleventh century Sobrado had two monasteries, but since both were dilapidated and deserted by the twelfth century, Alfonso VII asked St Bernard for his help. The saint sent two monks, Peter and Giles, and after 1142 the pilgrims were again received, thanks to the monks in white. The church is mighty; it is the work of Juan de Herrera and is considered the most beautiful Renaissance work in Galicia.

From Sobrado the pilgrims trundled down to Arzua (the last town on the main road before Santiago) where they met the main route.

Chapter 15

SANTIAGO DE COMPOSTELA

Now they were well and truly near the end. With amusing accuracy the Spanish Tourist Office's splendid Santiago Guide gives the distance to the shrine from the Franco-Spanish frontier at Somport-Canfranc, via Jaco, as 736·560 kilometres or 451 miles, so that at Arzua the pilgrims had covered all but one-nineteenth of their journey and had only twenty-four miles more to walk.

From Arzua they went on to Ferreiros and then Duas Casas, after which they reached a stream, the significance of which can hardly be overstressed. They were now only a mile and a half from a hallowed spot where they would get their first glimpse of the towers of the Apostle's cathedral. For that moment the pilgrims wished to be clean in mind and body; so at Lavacolla they took off their clothes and washed themselves all over.

Aimery Picaud, in a chapter entitled 'The Rivers Good and Bad which are encountered along the Road to St James', calls the river and place Lavamentula, which I translate as the washing of the private parts, though the actual Latin is far less polite. He says that the spot was a wooded one, two miles from Santiago, and that they actually did wash themselves all over, and for love of the Apostle.

Lavacolla is always prominently marked on modern maps because the city's airfield is there. I wonder how many air passengers know that the place they land at has a verbal connection with washing tail ends?

If your name is King, or in French Le-Roy or Leroi, it is quite likely that one of your ancestors trod the Way. How it started is not known but a practice grew up that when a group were travelling together he who first saw the spires of the cathedral was entitled to be called 'King' of the party and the appellation was taken as a surname thereafter.

The spot where this first glimpse was obtained was a little hillock reached after passing through the hamlet of San Marcos, and it was so important that the early fifteenth-century English poet *Purchas His Pilgrim* tells us:

> 'Then to Saint James that holy place,
> Where you will find all fair grace
> And two miles this side of the town
> To a chapel shall you go
> Upon a stony hill on high;
> Where Saint James you first shall see
> At Mount Joie, there are many stones
> Also four stately large stone pillars.
> Here you will get four days of Pardon
> At this chapel that is; should you wish it.'

There is also a charming seventeenth-century song about the place:

> 'When we got within a mile
> Near to the famous Town
> Of Mister Saint James the Greater
> I felt much stronger
> For walking than heretofore.'

The hallowed spot, now approached by a tiny, winding minor road away from the huge motorway, has great charm. It has had a number of different names according to period and place. In the Middle Ages it was Mons Gaudius, or Monxoi. The Spaniards now call it Monte del Gozo (joy, gladness). The French call it Mont Joie, Montjoie or Monjoie; the Italians call it Monte Gaudi or Gaudeo; and the English call it Mountjoy. And now I add a name myself, which I have so far not seen, but which is accurate and very English: Gaudy Mountain.

The mounted pilgrims, when they got to Monxoi, got down from their horses and went the rest of the way on foot; all of them bared their heads. Words cannot often describe strong emotions but on this truly momentous occasion Domenicio Laffi, the seventeenth-century Italian priest, does convey the poignancy of things:

'We got to the summit of a little mountain called Monte Gaudio and there only half a league away was our first sight of the long-desired Santiago. We fell down upon our knees and as we did so we started to cry. Then we started to sing the *Te Deum*, but the floods of tears welled up so much that we could only manage two or three verses and we had to stop. Then when our weeping had abated we continued singing all the way down the mountain until we got to the very outskirts of the city.'

It was very late in the afternoon and cloudy when I got to Monte del Gozo, but it would have had to have been much later, darker and cloudier not to have been able to see clearly, through the pine trees, the spires of the cathedral.

In winter it is a desolate spot with the wind blowing over the gorse, and through the little cluster of stunted oaks below which, about fifty yards down from where I reckon the pilgrims' cross used to stand, is the tiny chapel hermitage of San Marcos, built in 1105 and then called the Church of the Holy Cross, though at this time it was on ground nearly a mile closer to the city. The reason that the chapel was later named after St Mark is that the great Bishop Gelmirez organised a solemn procession out from Santiago cathedral to Monxoi on the day of the saint's nativity.

As for the cross, it was mentioned in a document concerning the cathedral's property in 1228 and also by the late fifteenth-century German traveller, Kunig von Vach. More interesting is the fact that there is a picture of it still extant, showing this same cross, on the retable in the cathedral at León.

From the Gaudy Mountain the descent is fairly steep and so, passing the hamlet of San Lazaro and singing all the way, the pilgrims with lightened tread entered the longed-for city.

Aimery Picaud says that the town was full of delights and that, because it guarded the precious body of St James, it was the most agreeable and noble of all the towns in Spain. I feel that he is right to this day, and this was in part due to someone who, though not of Royal blood, was the creator of the city's splendour.

After the saint's body had been found in Galicia the news was transmitted to Alfonso II, the Chaste, at his court in the Asturias. Having satisfied himself that the facts were true, Alfonso ordered the construction of a basilica of stones and baked earth at the place where the corpse had been found. King Alfonso III, the Great, demolished this edifice in order to replace it with a larger church of three naves, constructed of precious materials from many different parts of Spain and Portugal. The church was finished in 886 and was consecrated three years later with great solemnity.

The news of the miracles which now began to be attributed to St James was soon bruited abroad, so widely that a vast concourse of men and women, of all social strata and from all places, started to converge on north-west Spain. This movement was accelerated when the great long-reigning Pope Leo III (795–810) officially issued a charter which solemnly gave papal credence to the miracles.

From this time onwards the road to St James was also called the Milky Way, or more euphoniously the Lacteous Circle, and donations poured in to the great prosperity of the cathedral. But the real wealth of the town came from the gift of a tax which later caused bitter quarrels lasting about eight hundred years. This Vow of St James was imposed on the whole country – at least, that part of it which lay in Christian lands – by King Ramiro I because he attributed his success to the presence of the Apostle who on a white charger turned the tide of battle of Clavijo. The tax payable was a percentage of corn and wine on every plot (about seventy acres) of land worked. From this time onwards and within the short space of fifty years the town passed from obscurity to one of the most important crossroads in Christendom.

Perhaps the most extraordinary aspect of the city's growth is the way it has managed through the centuries to rise again after pillage, and especially after that greatest devastation of all, its destruction by Almanzor on 10 August 997. But from the ruins and the ashes a new agglomeration rapidly arose, thanks to the energies of Bishop Pedro de Mezonzo, a man of energy and austerity who started a dynamic rebuilding of the city and its cathedral.

Later came Cresconio, who was an even greater driving force. The new cathedral, made this time of granite from surrounding quarries, was started in 1074 and such was the enthusiasm of the masons that it was possible only thirty-one years later, in 1105, to consecrate the High Altar. The efforts of these two worthies pale into insignificance, however, when we consider the life of one who is generally considered, as I have said above, to have done more for the cult of St James and his city than anyone else in the Middle Ages.

Don Diego Gelmirez, at first a student in Paris, was a protégé of the mighty Abbot of Cluny and this was of inestimable value eventually to the town of Santiago. Don Diego was a man for all seasons and with a breadth of interests unequalled in his own or any other century. He was a great patron of literature and the sciences; he took an active interest in national politics, and to help finance the huge cost of building the Episcopal Palace, and innumerable hospitals and churches both in the town and along the pilgrim route, Don Diego Gelmirez even obtained the right to mint his own coinage.

But the Architect of Santiago, as Gelmirez was called, did a great deal more than that; twice he made the long journey to Rome to show his obedience to the Pope. The first time was before he was made a bishop. When Gelmirez began his second trip to the Eternal City he passed by Cluny, where its most famous abbot, St Hugo, came out to meet him and gave the Spaniard some useful advice on how to approach the sovereign pontiffs more tactfully for the benefits he, Gelmirez, was proposing to ask. 'Get your priests to do the asking,' said Hugo. 'The Court of Rome is on its guard against the prelates of Santiago.'

Finally all was well, and though Don Diego did have to travel through parts of northern Italy in disguise he arrived in Rome on 21 October 1104 and presented himself to Pascual II, who warmly welcomed the first visit ever from a bishop of Santiago.

After a few days of austere celebrations, Gelmirez and his priestly entourage got down to a certain amount of hard bargaining and the Spaniards did not do at all badly. In the first place Don Diego received the pallium from the Pope 'as a proof of the Holy See's admiration and affection for the church of St James'. Formerly called the pall, this was a woollen vestment with short lapels hanging down before and behind and ornamented with crosses, worn by the Pope but conferred by him on certain archbishops.

It was Gelmirez's priests who asked this favour for their bishops. Don Diego himself asked, and it was granted, that the archbishopric be transferred to Santiago from Augusta Emerita – now Merida – an infinitely more important place at that time than Santiago, as it was personally founded by Emperor Augustus for the retirement of his soldier veterans who had served him in the Cantabrian War.

It is perhaps revealing to know that Pope Calixtus II was the fifth son of Guy, Count of Burgundy, and that as Archbishop of Vienne and before he had been raised to the papal chair had made a visit to Santiago to call on his older brother Raymond who, having married Dona Urraca, was governing Galicia.

There is little doubt that if Calixtus II, who was one of the finer popes of the Middle Ages, had not died suddenly in December 1124, Toledo would have lost the primacy to the town of Spain's patron saint. But Honorious III, an aged man of humble origin, followed and he had heard things about Gelmirez that he did not like. The saintly old man disapproved of the vestments that were worn and of the haughty manner in which the offerings of the pilgrims were received. Anyway Santiago lost for ever its bid for the Spanish primacy.

The events which took place between Rome and Spain in the five years of Pope Calixtus II's reign were historically interesting but have had almost no effect on the material lives of people living today. Not so with something else. The papacy had given its blessing to the pilgrimage by agreeing that miracles in fact took place at the tomb of the Apostle, but Gelmirez and Calixtus II now discussed and set in motion a Holy Year. This occurs when St James' Day, the day of his martyrdom, falls on a Sunday and this has a recurring incidence of 11, 6, 5, 6 and 11 years and so on. There will be fourteen in the twentieth century and the more recent ones and those soon to come, are 1954, 1965, 1971, 1976, 1982, 1993 and 1999. The Hotels Reyes Cátalicos and San Marcos were expressly rebuilt for the Holy Years 1954 and 1965.

Although the Holy Year was initiated by Pope Calixtus II, it seems that it was necessary that succeeding popes should continue to grant the honour, but eventually it was granted in perpetuity by Alexander III, who issued the papel bull dated 25 June 1179 at Viterbo.

Reverting to Don Diego, he has a final claim to being the Great Man of Compostela for causing a work entitled *Registrum Venerabilis Compostellane* to be written which was soon and for ever after known as the *Historia Compostelane*.

Santiago de Compostela is in the province of La Coruna; it has a population of 70,000, a large and exceptionally active university and a main square. This square, at least until 1885, was called the Plaza del Hospital; in 1965 it was named the Plaza del Obradorio and is now also called the Plaza de España. There is nothing to compare with it anywhere in Spain.

It is a rectangle bounded by the five most beautiful buildings in the town and perhaps in all Spain. To the north, facing south, is the hotel with its magnificent carved front; to the east, facing west, are the Archbishop's Palace and the superb Cathedral façade; to the south, facing north, is the College of St Jerome, also called the College of Artists; and finally to the west, facing east, the Palace of Archbishop Rajoy. In this Plaza there is no roadway as such in that there are no pavements or kerbstones, though cars dash silently and frighteningly through. It is about 110 yards long by 70 wide, and if you stand in the middle not one commercial sign, not one neon light, not one poster will you be able to see; you will not descry a roof tile missing or anything out of place.

Another of the great architects of Santiago was Archbishop Fonseca de Acebedo and it was he who founded in 1501 the College of St Jerome. This abuts upon another of Fonseca's gifts to the city, the College of Fonseca, whose history is to be found in an inscription chiselled in sandstone along all the four sides of the cloister.

Though I have called the superb building on the west side of the square by its more official name, the Palace of Rajoy is generally known as the Ayuntamiento or the Municipal Hall. The local worthies had proposed to build a palace on the spot but Archbishop Don Bartholomeo Rajoy offered to pay for the entire construction on condition that a part of the building should be set aside for a school to instruct priests attached to the cathedral. Construction began in the 1770s and the building was ready for occupation about a decade later. The length is about a hundred yards, and it has such a striking likeness to the Capitole in Toulouse[1] that I feel the latter must have served as a model. If there could be a façade more beautiful than that of the Hostal in the same square and the San Marcos Hotel at León then it must be this splendid Renaissance building. The front is of three floors harmoniously broken by groups of slender pillars, the whole surmounted by a flamboyant equestrian statue of St James, below which are sculpted scenes of the semi-legendary battle of Clavijo whose castle is near Logroño.

So much has been written about the Cathedral of Santiago that I hardly know where to begin. Perhaps to fulminate against guide

[1] Built and finished 1750–60.

books which tell you that you 'need four hours' to 'do' it. I cannot make it the 'mostest' in any single way. With a length of 348 feet it is nothing like the longest, since Toledo is 446 feet long, Granada 416, Palencia and Salamanca 407 and Seville 454. It is 233 feet wide, but Vallodolid is 236 and Zaragoza is 253. Its south tower is 262 feet high, but the towers of Murcia and Salamanca cathedrals are respectively 312 and 361 feet, which makes this last even taller than the Giralda in Seville.

So Santiago Cathedral would not get into any book of church records, but it was the first of the great medieval cathedrals of Spain and it is particularly fortunate that we should have from a contemporary source a record of the methods of organisation which produced such a marvellous building. What must be borne in mind though is that the clerics, who had charge of large funds and of the administration of the works, left the design and building to individual persons who were sufficiently talented for them to have their names recorded for posterity. And the credit for the architectural character of the building is fairly and squarely given to one Bernard, called 'the Old' to distinguish him from the Canon Bernardo Gutierrez who later in the cathedral's building took charge of the administrative side of the operation. Working with Bernard – who was called the Marvellous Master – was Robert and he was either the joint architect or more likely nearly equal to Bernard, but foreman of the working masons.

Now these two Christian names were typically French and this is of some moment as it gives us a little more information concerning the controversy which raged for many years over the nationality of the design of the cathedral. There are close French affiliations and a remarkable similarity to St Sernin at Toulouse, and to a lesser degree St Martin at Tours, St Martial at Limoges (now vanished) and St Foy of Conques. The main similarity, new to Spanish churches, was the ambulatory which was devised as a passageway permitting the crowds of pilgrims to circulate round the saint's tomb; it was not a novelty in France, where several churches already had relics to display.

The next builder after Bernard (probably a Benedictine from Cluny) was Esteban; then came the great Maestro Mateo, probably a bridge builder before he came to Santiago on the invitation of King Ferdinand of León, who granted him a salary for life. Thus secure for his bread and wine, he started to build his gate or Portico de la Gloria, which faces the Plaza de España and is one of the glories of the cathedral world. The sculptings here are the richest in Spain. Of course, they include all the saints, and the great law-givers such as Samuel, David and Moses, but the most lovely scene is that of the four and twenty ancients all playing different musical instruments: the citola, the sinfonia or zanfona or hurdy-gurdy, the zither, harp and an ancient oriental instrument called the *saltero* or psaltery, rather like a dulcimer.

In the centre of this amazingly rich profusion of carving and beneath a fine Christ is what is considered the finest sculpture of St James along the route; he is shown seated as if to imply that his journey is finished.

Naturally, all these carvings face outwards, overlooking the square; but placed at the bottom of the huge central pillar supporting the statue of St James there is on the reverse and therefore facing straight down the nave to the high altar, a stone carving of a curly headed youth kneeling and holding a scroll. This is a youthful effigy of the artist Master Matthew who received royal permission to 'sign his name' on his imperishable work, which was begun incidentally in 1168. And over the centuries it has become the tradition for students before their exams to bump their heads against the granite forehead of Mateu in the hope that some of his wisdom will be transferred to them. Hence he is called 'the Saint of the Bumps'.

The cathedral gives the impression of being larger than it is because it is surrounded by no less than four squares, with one of which – the one to the west – I have already dealt in detail. The northern plaza, which makes the corner of the Episcopal Palace, is called La Azabacheria because it was here that the workers in jet carved their little lignite figures which they sold to the pilgrims, along with little statues worked in tin or lead. The large square to the east is the least colourful, the Plaza de los Literarios; here the cathedral is entered by the Puerta Santa, the Holy Door which is only opened during the Holy Year. Finally, to the south there is the oldest façade of the cathedral, that of the Platerias or silver-smiths, which is also the name of the square where from the early days of the pilgrimage, and still today, merchants have had their souvenir shops to sell silver trinkets.

The cathedral interior is as beautiful as many and more beautiful than most; it is packed with chapels, paintings, altars and sculptings in a profusion which is explained by the wealth which poured into the town from the Conquistadores returning from Peru. The high altar is a marvel; it dates from 1672 and is constructed of jasper, silver and alabaster in the rich Churrigueresque style. This altar encloses a heavily painted wooden statue of St James which could possibly date from the twelfth century. In 1765 it was given a sumptuous silver cape, set with diamonds and other precious stones, almost covering the body. Behind the statue is a flight of stairs across which pilgrims can pass and, in accordance with an old established custom, embrace the Saint.

In the principal nave there hangs an enormous lustre measuring over three yards square; a sort of giant chandelier with over three thousand pieces of gleaming glass, made in Germany for showing at the Paris Exposition of 1855 and then offered to the cathedral.

But no description of the cathedral's interior would be complete without mentioning the enormous publicity-provoking censer which the Spaniards have nicknamed the Botafumeiro. It is almost certain that they have swung some incense-bearing monster in the cathedral since the fourteenth century; the last of them but one was six feet high and made of solid silver, so it is no wonder that Napoleon's troops looted it in 1801. The present censer is slightly smaller and made of some white base metal and dates from 1851. I saw it in a corner of the museum that stands beside Bishop Gelmirez' palace; I assume it is kept there save on the rare days when it is swung in the cathedral; there was a small placard beside the Botafumeiro saying which days they were.

The relatively few who have both seen and described this swinging thurible have all left vivid impressions of what must be an awesome and rather frightening sight. Seven acolytes dressed in scarlet and black pull down a huge hook nicknamed the *alcachofa* (artichoke) and by a pulley and rope lift the huge censer, which will now have been lit, off the ground. Then it is pushed to and fro. It goes very slowly at first; then it gathers momentum while flames and incense-scented smoke are to be seen coming from what one writer describes as a flaming meteor, which seems to swoop – and it is this which has been described as so frightening – within inches of the pilgrims' heads.

The night life of the city, however, does not take place in the squares surrounding the cathedral. The Plaza de Epaña is dead at night and so are all the others. In Santiago the *paseo*, or night walk-about, takes place in three nearly parallel streets – the Rúa

Nueva, Rúa del Villar and Calle del Franco, which lead off from the tiny Plaza de las Platerias and meet at Plazas Toral and Vigo. These squares lead directly to the Paseo de la Herradura, a very pretty wooded park sloping gently up away from the town and exactly the shape of a horseshoe, as its name implies. In the middle of these gardens is the very old but seldom visited church of Santa Susana.

For a city of only 70,000 inhabitants the number of really old places which should be visited is astonishing.

In the Rúa Nueva, rather curiously placed, stands the fifteenth-century church of Santa-Marie-Salomé, with its splendid twelfth-century door; it has an unusual roof, too, with a lamb and cross motif. There are a further seven churches and three chapels, besides a number of convents with churches, and convents without. Finally there are monasteries, of which the two most important are those of St Augustin, which also has a huge seventeenth-century church, and the monastery of San Martin Pinario, one of the most important Benedictine establishments in Spain.

On the outskirts of the town is the monastery and royal collegiate church of Santa Maria del Sar, which should not be visited merely because of the structural freakishness of the interior, for in 1134 Muno Alfonso, Bishop of Mondoñedo, chose this site as a place for himself and several canons attached to St James' church to 'get away from it all' and meditate. Such was his piety that after his death Gelmirez founded here a monastery of Augustine monks. It has an exceptionally beautiful cloister, but inside the church the columns which support the arches incline outwards; they give one a mildly sea-sick feeling. This part of the church is about eight hundred years old. Is the inclination of its walls due to a deformation of the sub-soil or did the master mason build in this fashion intentionally – perhaps, as one writer has suggested, to carry the eyes of the worshipper up to the heavens? Anyway I have joined in the past the scores of people who have written it up as a mystery, but I have now decided that it was done deliberately.

Twelve miles due south is the place where it all started. About eleven miles from the Atlantic coast, on the river Sar and near its confluence with the swift flowing river Ulla, is the town of Padrón, with 8,000 inhabitants, known and important in Roman times as Iria Flavia. It is a charming, untidy, multi-styled town which was of such moment to the pilgrims that there grew up the saying:

'*Quien vay a Santiago e non va al Padrón
O faz Romaria o no.*'[1]

It was St James the Greater who caused the change of name, for
when his disciples brought his body to Iria Flavia the boat was
moored to a stone pillar or *pedrón* which was part of the Roman
altar that can still be seen and venerated under the high altar of
the parish church.

I have wandered around the town so many times that I think I
really have the feel of the place. By the main square is a lovely,
old pilgrims' cross and near by the Carmen fountain with a modern
though excellent representation of St James in the little boat that
brought him to Galicia; on the other side of the Sar, which has a
long tree-lined esplanade beside the river, is the seventeenth-
century Convent of El Carmen.

On my way back to Santiago, and on the outskirts of the town,
I once again went to look at the façade of the former collegiate
church of Santa Maria which was of great importance until
Almanzor destroyed it. 'During the pontificate of Pope Theodore,
Padrón began to cede its spiritual leadership to Santiago' says one
Spanish writer, though this Theodore – the Second – was only on
the papal throne for twenty days. Next to this charming little
church, with its Romanesque portal and its sixteenth-century
towers in the form of pagodas, is a large cemetery, usually quite
empty, but this time, at about dusk, I noted a score of people,
mostly women, with mops, brushes, buckets of water and packets
of detergents, all scrubbing away the lichen from the tombstones.
'It's All Saints' Day tomorrow,' said one onlooker, noting my
bewilderment. Behind the church is a lane; it is muddy, narrow,
decrepit and ugly, but it is supposed to be the way the pilgrims
trudged to Padrón. So to my eyes the little path has charm.

I said earlier that no writing or signs could be descried from
the Plaza del Obradoiro or 'Workshop Square' as I translate it,
but this is not wholly true, for if you were to stand in the centre
your eyes might just be able to see in quite small letters on two
glass-plate swing doors: 'Hostal de los Reyes Cátolicos.' And when
you read on you will agree that Isabel and Ferdinand more deserve
that their names should be perpetuated in this Hotel of the Catho-

[1]   'He who goes to Santiago and not to Padrón
         Either does the pilgrimage or does not.'

lic Monarchs than any other personage of history who has given his name to a majestic building.

The noblemen of Galicia did not take kindly to Isabel being proclaimed Queen of Castile in 1474, so they revolted; but after Don Pedro de Cela was by her order hanged in the main square of Mondoñedo, the revolt collapsed, thanks in part to the help of Archbishop don Alonso de Fonseca and the townsfolk of Santiago, fervently loyal to the monarchy.

But with the Galician nobles dead, disbanded or disgraced the province went into a steep spiritual decline and this at a period when the *Camino Frances* or French road to Santiago was at the height of its popularity in Europe.

Almost certainly Ferdinand and Isabella felt that one of the best ways of continuing the unification of Spain was to see that the Way to the Apostles' shrine was made safe, that the province in Spain where it was situated became less barbaric, and that foreigners should be encouraged to make the journey in safety. Thus it was that in 1478, from Seville, they confirmed all the privileges, mercy donations and graces that the Santiago enjoyed, that in 1479 they published an order 'to all Christians in Italy, France, England, Germany, Hungary, the Danube States, Sweden and Norway' guaranteeing a safe passage, protection and freedom to all pilgrims and 'for all they carried with them'. Then seven years later, in 1486, they themselves set out for the shrine.

On their way, one of the places they stopped at was Cebrero and, noting how inadequate was the accommodation there, they gave a generous donation towards improvements and they persuaded Pope Innocent VIII to place it under the control of a monastery nearer to Cebrero so that it could be more efficiently administered.

Then, filled with pious grace but much lighter in pocket, the Catholic Monarchs finally reached Santiago, where they first made the traditional visit to the tomb of the Apostle and then, visiting the old hospital, noted in what a poor condition it was. There can be no doubt that Magnus Fernandus and Grandis Helizabeth, as they were called in Latin, were in a serious dilemma. Here they were full of fervour after their longed-for pilgrimage to the patron saint of Spain; on the other hand their purses were well nigh empty as a result of their wars against the Moors and especially after the siege of Granada. But they reckoned without the forceful personality of the dean, Don Diego de Muros, who rightly has a street named after him in the centre of the town today, for it was he who bullied Ferdinand to make the fateful decision to build a completely new hospital, which by the end of the sixteenth century was reckoned to be one of the finest in the world.

Once Ferdinand, spurred on by Isabella, had made the decision his enthusiasm knew no bounds. As soon as they had won the siege of Granada, they ordained that a generous percentage of the taxes to be levied should go to Santiago, of which a third should be for the solemn commemoration of the feast of the patron saint of the cathedral, a third for the upkeep of the cathedral itself, and the remaining third for the maintenance of the poor in the hospital that the King and Queen had ordered to be built in the city.

Although Ferdinand employed the greatest architect of those times, Enrique de Egas, he was so interested in the project that wherever he was, he and Isabella would send notes to the architect continuously concerning the minutest details. It was an astonishing effort; both of them seem to have pushed important problems of government to one side in order to worry about the quality of stone to be used for the walls, whether labourers should be hired for piecework or whether by the day, the colours of the painting of the carved ceiling of the chapel, and against which wall a fireplace should be placed.

Nor as the months passed did their interest wane. 'Let the roof be covered with limestone and pitch so that the pilgrims be protected against the rainy climate of Santiago . . . Let the house be built in such a way that there are five or six steps up to the patio because this makes the house happier and healthier.'

Ten years were spent on the construction, but let no one imagine that things went smoothly, for after the first enthusiastic rapture every party in the town seems to have had some reason for almost literally damming up the works. The Benedictine monks refused at first to allow their spring to be used for the hospital and when they lost this case they tried to stop the water-pipes from passing beneath their pavement. Eventually Ferdinand himself had to force the monks to 'let the tubes pass'.

At last the multitude of difficulties was overcome and in 1509 the Royal Hospital was ready to take its first sick pilgrims, though all the work was not finished until two years later. This remained a great hospital for the care of the sick for 444 years.

They have been progressively shortening the car waiting times in front of the hotel on my several last visits, and now even those staying at the Reyes Cátolicos have no longer the right to park in front of the hotel. The policeman on duty when I arrived on the last occasion was particularly tough and I unwittingly infuriated him by standing and admiring the fabulous façade of the hotel instead of quickly securing a porter.

To build the hotel, the architect and technicans got the final instructions in November 1953; even if they had possessed at that moment working plans down to the last detail one can only remain astonished (as with San Marcos) that by July 1954 the place was ready enough to sleep visitors in its 157 double rooms, receive General Franco, to 'sign in' and entertain for lunch the future Pope John XXIII.

Though somewhat smaller than the San Marcos palace, the hotel is still enormous, beautiful, in exquisite taste, evocative of the past and easier to get lost in since there are four patios and thus sixteen stairways to negotiate.

Of these courtyards named for Marcos, Lucas, Matero and Juan two have wells in the centre and fountains designed by Enrique de Egas and built (note the extraordinary amount of information handed down) by Jacome Garcia in 1510.

The essential difference between this hotel and the one at León is that the latter had been empty for scores of years before the rebuilding, while the other was in use as a hospital till the very last minute; indeed, when the announcement of its conversion was made, a great number of Santiago townsfolk were most incensed and a wave of resentment swept through the town, which abated when it was revealed that the sick of the hospital were all to be removed to a spacious modern clinic.

Though the hotel has 157 double rooms the official sleeping capacity is ten more than double this number on account of another link with the past; for in the Middle Ages worthy poor and genuine pilgrims were given free lodging. So two charming dormitories have been preserved, though details of when they are available for free are kept rather vague.

When the building was closed as a hospital, the little artistic gem of a chapel was closed to worship, but in 1958 splendid use was found for it by guitarist Andres Segovia, and now with the occasional help of Victoria de los Angeles and José Iturbi the 'Music in Santiago' festival is becoming famous.

I have already mentioned the glorious façade to the hotel, two storeys high, which is a lovely blend of the Gothic and Renaissance and which looks for all the world like an altar piece. Parallel to this front, some five yards away, is a row of weathered stone posts linked by massive iron chains. They are the most remarkable and dramatic link with the past; I thought that this fence was just to keep the tourist public from the exclusive hotel, but it dates back to a bull of Pope Julio II of December 1507 whereby, persuaded by King Ferdinand, he suppressed all the hospitals in Santiago and then fused them again into one and placed them directly under the apostolic chair. And these chains in the plaza are the outward sign that the hospital was free and exempt from all civil and criminal jurisdiction.

Like Bordeaux, happy town of my youth, Santiago has also the reputation of being a veritable chamber-pot, as the French call a place which has continuous rain, but on my last visit there the weather was dry, so that in the evenings I wandered down the Rúa Nueva, across the Plaza Toral, up the Rúa del Villar, over the minute animated Plaza Fonseca, by the south side of the Plaza de Platerias, and then back down the Rúa Nuera again.

At first I would do the round trip three or even four times of an evening, but the crowds of students, clerks and workers was so dense that I had to brush past them; so I soon got accustomed to strolling along at the very leisurely pace that these people used. Moreover, nearly every stop was a wine bar, or wine bar restaurant, or a coffee shop where the new season's white-green sweet-sour fizzy Ribadavia wine was on tap everywhere at almost nothing a glass and up to a point you might imagine you were drinking champagne.

But when I wanted more exercise between periods of writing than I got from wandering round the patios of the hotel or climbing one of its many stairways I would motor out to the hillock at Monte del Gozo, because it haunted me. One afternoon I went to this hallowed spot for a three o'clock picnic lunch and seated myself upon the stone bench and table a few yards from the tiny San Marcos chapel which is surrounded by a low stone wall under shady trees. There are many such shady rest-places for modern travellers by the roadside in Spain; many are indeed medieval resting places for pilgrims and these usually have a fountain where the water is ice cold on the hottest of days.

As my bottle emptied I again mused on my theory that along the Way there must be countless thousands of trinkets, badges, buttons and coins that had been lost on the journey.

With my bottle finished and my cold Spanish omelette eaten, I walked to the tiny knoll which was at the very summit of Monte del Gozo and scratched away at the grass surface with a broken-bladed kitchen knife; and I found something! It was a rectangular stone block some eighteen inches deep and six inches across. It had been wedged into the earth by surrounding stones so that it stood upright. Chiselled into the top face of the stone was a square hole an inch across and three inches deep, obviously made to let in a wooden cross.

A few minutes later a couple of peasants arrived with sickles and cut the gorse for their beasts. They confirmed that the children in the past had taken all the crosses stuck in the ground by travellers. When they had left with their cartload of gorse and I had taken some bearings so that I could find my stone when I returned, I looked afar to the spires of the great cathedral and thought that although I would be back home in minutes, and though they daily covered distances which surprises us, the pilgrims still had quite a walk before them.

I wondered how the sick and infirm would have got on, and this reminded me of that attractive person, William X, Duke of Aquitaine who, although ill at the time, set out for Compostela to get absolution for the outrages he had committed during his skirmishes in Normandy. He must have stood in the year 1137 a few days before Easter within yards of the stone I had uncovered at Monte del Gozo, for on 9 April, Good Friday, just after receiving the holy sacraments the Duke died in front of the altar of the apostle St James. The news of his death swept through Europe and a troubador wrote of it:

> 'Where will you go my pilgrim,
> My pilgrim where will you go?
> On the road to Compostela,
> But I know not if he will arrive.'

And that more or less sums it up for me too.

APPENDIX
AIMERY PICAUD'S GUIDE

There is a manuscript in the archives of the Chapter of Santiago de Compostela, and there was one in the monastery at Ripoll too, which can fairly be described as the first tourist guide of the western world. The whole work is in Latin and is called the *Liber Sancti Jacobi* (The Book of St James), a work dedicated to the glory of the Apostle, St James the Greater. More accurately it is really five different books.

Book One is an anthology of liturgical offerings, hymns and sermons in honour of the saint; it is the longest section of all.

Book Two is The Book of Miracles. This is a recapitulation of miracles worked through the intercession of the saint, especially during the twelfth century.

Book Three is the Book of the Translation, which recounts the evangelisation of Spain by St James; also the martyrdom of the Apostle and the removal of his ashes to the place in Galacia where Compostela was founded.

Book Four is the History of Charlemagne and Roland by Bishop Turpin, the legendary history which is commonly called the pseudo-Turpin. Of the five books this one had the widest circulation.[1]

Book Five. This is the guide book for the use of pilgrims, compiled to give them practical advice when embarking on their pious journey. It was produced especially to tell them of the sanctuaries at which they should halt so that they could venerate the relics of the saint, and finally to show them how to admire in its minutest details the cathedral built to the glory of Apostle.

As I have said, there are two manuscripts in Latin but there is not all that much to say about them. The manuscript at Compostela is designated 'C', and it should be noted that Book Four (Charlemagne)

[1] One translator worked from forty-five manuscripts but knew of a further sixty.

was detached from the whole at the beginning of the seventeenth century and re-bound separately; that is why Book Five (The Pilgrims' Guide) is sometimes called Book Four. The twelfth-century handwriting is clear and tidy and almost entirely without erasures.

The Ripoll manuscript, designated 'R', is actually not at the monastery but in the Ripoll section of the archives of the Crown of Aragon in Barcelona. The whole work comprises eighty-six folios and the handwriting is again of the twelfth century and is quite neat.

When we come to date the work we can be fairly accurate within forty years.

I must explain that the Compostela manuscript of the *Liber Sancti Jacobi* is also more usually referred to by historians as the Codex Calixtinus on account of an apocryphal letter of Pope Calixtus (1124) which serves as a preface; and in this manuscript is a record of the last miracle, around 1139. And it is before 1173 that the year the monk at Ripoll (Notre-Dame-de-Ripoll, by the way, is in Gerona) made the transcription there.

The author of the Fifth Book, the Guide, is possibly (even probably) a devout cleric called Aimery Picaud from Parthenay-le-Vieux near Poitiers; anyway, he was certainly a devout Frenchman from the Saintes or Poitiers region who himself had done the pilgrimage and wanted to share his enthusiasm with the faithful and to help them by passing on his knowledge.

THE PILGRIMS' GUIDE TO ST JAMES OF COMPOSELA

From the Latin text of the twelfth century
from manuscripts at Compostela and Ripoll

Translated and abridged by T. A. Layton

HERE BEGINS THE FOURTH BOOK OF THE APOSTLE ST JAMES
If the well-lettered reader seeks to understand the truth written in this book, if he approaches this book without hesitation or scruple, he is assured of finding herein the said truth. This is because people who are still very much alive will testify that all that has been written is true.

THEME OF THE BLESSED POPE CALIXTUS

Chapter One THE ROADS TO ST JAMES

Four roads lead to St James which all meet at Puente la Reina on Spanish soil. The first goes via St Giles Montpellier, Toulouse and the Somport Pass.

The second is by Notre-Dame du Puy, Ste Foy de Conques and St Pierre de Moissac.

The third goes by Ste-Marie-Madelaine or Vézelay, St Léonard in Limousin and the town of Perigueux.

The fourth by St Martin of Tours, St Hilary of Poitiers, St Jean d'Angely, St Eutropus of Saintes and the town of Bordeaux.

The roads which pass by Ste Foy de Conques, by St Léonard and St Martin meet at Ostabat and, having crossed the Pass at Cize, meet at Puente la Reina those pilgrims who have gone over by Somport Pass and from thence onwards only one road leads to St James.

Chapter Two THE STAGES ON THE ROAD TO ST JAMES

Pope Calixtus[1]

From Somport to Puenta la Reina there are three short, small stages; the first takes the traveller to Borce, a village near the Somport Pass, on the Gascony side, and then to Jaca; the second from Jaca to Monreal; the third from Monreal to Puenta la Reina.

From the pass at Cize (St Jean-pied-de-Port) to St James of Compostela there are thirteen stages; the first goes from St Michel, at the foot of the pass at Cize on the Gascony versant, to Viscarret; and this stage is short.

The second goes from Viscarret to Pamplona and this is a small one.

The third goes from the village of Pamplona to Estella.

The fourth, from Estella to Najera, is done on horseback.

The fifth from Najera to the town of Burgos is also done on horse-back.

The sixth goes from Burgos to Fromista to Sahagún.

The eighth from Sahagún to the town of León.

The ninth from León to Rabanal.

The tenth from Rabanal to Villafranca at the entry to the Valcárcel valley after crossing the Irago pass.

The eleventh goes from Villafranca to Triacastela having passed the summit of the Cebero pass.

The twelfth goes from Triacastela to Palas del Rey.

While the thirteenth goes from Palas del Rey to St James of Compostela. It is a short stage.

---

[1] This is meant to lead the reader to think that the chapter had been written by that Pope.

Chapter Three NAMES OF TOWNS AND LARGER VILLAGES
ALONG THE ROAD ST JAMES

First, at the foot of the mountain on the Gascony side, is Borce. Then, having crossed the summit, one comes to the Hospice of Ste Christine. Then comes Canfranc, then Jaca, then Osturit, Tiermas where there are the royal baths and where the water is always hot; then Monreal; and at last Puenta la Reina.

Alternatively from the pass of Cize are to be found the most important towns and larger villages on the road to St James to the Basilica in Galicia.

First, on the Gascony side is the village of St Michel. Then comes the Hospice of Roland; then the town of Roncevalles. Next is found Viscarret, then Larrasona, then Pamplona. Then Puente la Reina, then Estella where the bread is good, the wine excellent, the meat and fish are abundant and which enjoys all delights. Next comes Arcos, Logroño, Villaroya. Then Najera, Santo Domingo, Redicella, Beldorado, Villafranca, the forest of Oca Atapuerca, the town of Burgos.

Then Tardajos, Hornillos, Casterogeriz, the bridge of Itera, Fromista, Carrión (de los Condes) which is a busy and industrious city rich in bread, wine and meat and all kinds of things. Then comes prosperous Sahagún. Here too is the field where it is said that the shining lances of victorious warriors placed there for the glory of God started to sprout like green shoot.

Then there is Mansilla, and the town of León, residence of the King and the Court and full of all sorts of delights.

Next comes Orbigo, then Astorga, then Rabanal, then Puerto Irago, Molinaseca, then Ponferrada, then Cacabelos, Villa-franca at the mouth of the Valcárcel. Then the camp of the Saracens; Villa Us. Then the top of Mount Cebrero and the hostelry at the top of this mountain.

Then Linares, then Triacastela at the foot of this mountain in Galicia and it was here that the pilgrims received a stone (of lime) which they carried all the way to Castañola[1] to make the lime which was used in the construction of the Apostles' Basilica. Then comes the village of San Miguel, then Barbadelo, then the bridge of the Miño (Portomarin), then Sala Regina, then Palas del Rey, Leboreiro, then St James de Boente, Castañola Villanova, Ferreiros, lastly Compostela, the very excellent town of the Apostle, full of delights, which has the charge of the precious body of St James.

[1] Here was a lime-making works; when the lime was ready it was transported in carts to Compostela.

Chapter Four THE THREE GREAT HOSPICES OF THE WORLD

Three mainstays of the church for looking after the poor have been established by God in this world. The Hospice of Jerusalem, the Hospice of Mont-Joux (Grand St Bernard) and the Hospice of Ste Christine at Somport. These hospices have been built at points where they have been considered necessary.

Those who will have helped in building these holy houses without any doubt whatever will possess the Kingdom of Heaven.

Chapter Five NAMES OF CERTAIN PEOPLE WHO HAVE WORKED FOR THE REBUILDING OF THE ROAD TO ST JAMES

Aimery[1]

Here are the names of certain road builders who, in the time of Diego, Archbishop of Santiago, and Alfonso, Emperor of Spain and Galicia, and Pope Calixtus, have made up the road to St James from between Rabanal until the bridge over the Miño, for the love of God and St James before the year 1120, under the reign of Alfonso (the First) King of Aragon, and Louis the Fat, King of France; André, Roger, Avit, Fortus, Arnauld, Etienne, Pierre, who reconstructed the bridge over the Miño which was demolished by the Queen Urraca.

May the souls of these men repose eternally in peace.

Chapter Six RIVERS, BOTH GOOD AND BAD, WHICH ONE ENCOUNTERS ALONG THE ROAD TO ST JAMES

Pope Calixtus

Here are the rivers which one encounters from the pass of Cize and the Somport until we get to St James. From Somport descends the Aragon which irrigates Spain. From the pass of Cize springs a river which is healthy and which many people call the Runa which crosses Pamplona. At Puente la Reina the rivers Arga and Runa both flow. Be careful not to drink any of the water or to water your horses because these rivers deal death. As we were going to St James we found two

[1] This is to denote that this part of the book was written by Aimery Picaud.

people from Navarre seated beside the banks and sharpening their knives, for they have the habit of taking the skin off the mounts of pilgrims who have drunk this water and have died from it. To our questioning they replied in a lying fashion, saying that this water was good and drinkable. We therefore gave some to our horses and immediately two of them died and these men from Navarre flayed them on the spot.

At Estella runs the river Ega whose waters are soft, healthy and excellent.

At Logroño we come to the great river Ebro, which is healthy and abounds in fish. All the rivers between Estella and Logroño have dangerous waters and fish. If by some chance you eat them and you are not ill, that is because you have more health in you than other people and that you are acclimatised to them by a long stay in this country. All the fish and the meat of beef and pork in Spain and Galicia makes foreigners ill.

The healthy rivers are generally called thus: La Pisuerga, which passes the bridge of Itera de Castrillo; Le Carrión, which waters Carrión de los Condes; the Cea which passes Sahagún; the Esla at Mansilla; the Porma, which crosses the big bridge between Mansilla and León; the Torreo, which runs at León underneath the Field of the Jews; the Bernesga, which passes by the same town and from the other side. The river Sar which flows between the Mont de la Joie and the village of St James is known for its healthiness. The same goes for the Sarela, which flows from the other side of the town towards the west.

If I have described these rivers it is so that the pilgrims going to St James shall be careful to drink only healthy water and shall not drink unhealthy ones.

Chapter Seven NAMES OF COUNTRIES WHICH THE PILGRIMS' ROAD CROSSES. OF ST JAMES AND THE CHARACTER OF THE INHABITANTS

In travelling to St James by the Toulouse road, after you have first crossed the Garonne you come into Gascony country, and the after Somport you get to the country of Aragón and then Navarre, that is until you get to the bridge on the River Arga, and from thence onward. If you take the road from Cize after the town of Tours you come to the fertile Poitevin country, an excellent part of the world and full of all delights. The Poitevin people are vigorous, good fighters, clever with their bows and arrows and with their lances in war. They are courageous at the battle front, very fast on horseback, elegant in the way they dress themselves, handsome, witty, very generous and kind in their hospitality. Then you get into the Saintonge country. From there, having crossed a strip of sea and the Garonne, you get into the Bordeaux district, where the wine is excellent. The Saintonge people already speak in a rather uncouth way, but those of Bordeaux are even rougher. Then to cross the Landes of Bordeaux you need three days' walk, because people are already tired.

It is a desolate country where everything is missing. There is neither bread, nor wine, nor meat, nor fish; no water and no springs; the villages are few and far between in this sandy country, where, however, there is a fair amount of honey and millet; and there are pigs.

If by hazard you cross the Landes in summer, do be careful to protect your face from enormous flies which abound there, and which are called wasps or gadflies; and if you are not careful with your feet you will find yourself almost up to the knees in a sort of marine sand which invades the place.

After having crossed this country you will find yourself in Gascony.

The Gascons are frivolous, talkative, full of mockery, debauched, drunken, greedy, dressed in rags and they have no money; nevertheless, they have been well taught how to fight and are remarkable in their hospitality towards the poor. Sitting round the fire they have the habit of eating without a table, all drinking from the same cup. They eat an enormous amount, they drink wine without it being watered down and are very badly dressed. They have no sense of shame and the master and mistress lie down along with their servants on a pallet of mouldy straw.

Leaving this country, the road to St James crosses two rivers. It is impossible to cross either of them save by boat. And cursed be their boatmen. In fact, although these rivers are quite narrow, these terrible boatmen have the practice of demanding from each person who goes from one side to the other, whether he is rich or poor, a sum of money and for a horse they extort four pieces by force. Now the boat is small; it is only made of a single tree trunk and can hardly take a horse. Not only that, but after having received money the ferrymen take such a large number of pilgrims that the boat upsets and the pilgrims are drowned and then it is that these boatmen are wickedly happy because they take from the dead all their things.

In this region there are a number of bad toll collectors. These people, frankly, should be consigned ot the devil. They actually go in front of the pilgrims with two or three sticks to extort from them by force unjust fees, and if any traveller refuses to give in to their demands and give them money they hit them with their sticks and take away from them their taxes; and greatly swearing they even rummage into their trousers.

And although they should not extract a tax save for certain salesmen they take it unfairly from pilgrims and all travellers. When the regulation empower them to charge a tax of four or six sous they take eight or eleven.

That is why we urgently demand that all these tax collectors, together with the Kings of Aragón and other rich people to whom they remit money from this tax, should be punished by a sentence of excommunication, published not only in the cathedral seat of their country but also in the cathedral of St James in front of the pilgrims.

One should know that these tax collectors have no right to collect a tribute from the pilgrims and that the ferrymen should ordinarily only ask rich pilgrims an abole for two people and a piece of money for a horse, whereas if they are poor they should ask nothing at all.

Furthermore, the ferrymen should be obliged to have large boats in which men and their mounts can cross in comfort.

In the Basque country, the road to St James crosses a noteworthy mountain called the pass of Cize,[1] first because it is the entry pass into Spain and here also important commodities are transported from one country to another. To cross over there are eight miles to ascend and then eight miles to descend.

Then, descending from the top of the pass, comes the country of Navarre. These people wear clothes which are black and short and which end at the knees in the mode of the Scots; they wear shoes which they call *lavarcas*,[2] made of untanned leather with the hairs of the beast still on them, which they attach to their feet with thongs, but which only cover the soles of their feet leaving the upper part bare. They wear wool cloaks of a dark colour which come down as far as the elbow. These people are badly dressed and they eat and drink badly; with the people of Navarre the entire household, servant and master, maid and mistress, all eat from the same cauldron in which all the food has been thrown. They eat with their hands without using spoons and all drink from the same goblet. When one watches them eating one is reminded of dogs or pigs gulping gluttonously; and listening to them talk sounds like dogs barking.

Their language is quite barbaric; they call God – *Urcia*; the Mother of God – *Andrea-Maria*; bread – *orguip*; wine – *ardum*; meat – *aragui*; fish – *araign*; the house – *echea*; the priest – *elicera*; barley – *gari*; water – *uric*; the King – *Ereguia*; St James – *Jaona Domne Jacue*.

They are a barbarous race, different from most others and by their customs and race full of wickedness, black in colour, with ugly faces, debauched, perverse, perfidious, disloyal, corrupt, drunkards, expert in all deeds of violence, fierce and savage, dishonest and false, impious and rude, cruel and quarrelsome, incapable of any decent sentiment and used to every vice and iniquity. Nonetheless, they are good on the battlefield but bad at attacking fortresses; they are regular in the pay-

---

[1] Now St Jean-pied-de-Fort.

[2] A Castilian word *Abarca* from the Catalan word *Avarca*.

ment of tithes and accustomed to making their offerings at the altar; in fact, every day when he goes to church the man of Navarre will make an offering to God of bread, wine, barley or other things.

It is currently recounted that the Basques come from the same race as the Scots. It is said that Julius Caesar sent three races into Spain, the Nubians, the Scots and the tailed[1] people of Cornwall, to wage war there as the Spaniards refused to pay their tributes; Caesar gave orders to put to the sword all the male inhabitants and to save only the women. The peoples, having arrived by sea, landed in the country and after breaking their vessels devastated the land from Barcelona to Zaragossa. They could get no further because the Castillians united to chase them out of their country. Having thus fled they reached the Marins mountains, which are between Najera, Pamplona and Bayonne and by the sea in the region of Biscay and Alava, where they built a number of fortresses and then massacred the males. They then took away their wives by force and gave them children who were then called Navarrais; but this is a false name because they had not come from a pure race, a legitimate source.

After this country one crosses the forest of Oca and the lands of Spain to continue towards Burgos; that is Castille and the countryside.

Then one comes to Galicia; that is, after one has crossed the country of León and the summit of the mountains Irago and Cebrero. Here the countryside is wooded, carpeted with flowers, abounding in prairies and green roadsides. The fruits here are good and the springs clear, but there are very few villages, towns or cultivated fields. Bread of wheat flour and wine are scarce, but there is plenty of rye bread and cider as well as cattle, horses, silk and honey; there are plenty of fish from the sea, both large and small. As for gold and silver and tissues and furs of forest animals and other riches, all is here as well as the sumptuous treasures of the Saracens.

The people of Galicia are, above all the other uncultured races of Spain, those who are closest to our French race in their customs; but they are, it is said, inclined to anger and chicanery.

Chapter Eight HOLY REMAINS WHICH LIE ON THE ROAD ST JAMES AND WHICH PILGRIMS SHOULD TO VISIT

In the first place those who journey to St James by the St Gilles Road[2] should go to Arles to see the body of the blessed Trophime the Confessor. His Saint Day is 29 December.

And in the cemetery of the same town the pilgrim should look for the relics of the Bishop of St Honorat. His Holy Day is celebrated on

[1] The English in the Middle Ages were reputed to have tails.
[2] Near Montpellier.

16 January, and it is also in this venerable and magnificent basilica that the body of the most holy martyr, Genês, lies.

There is a suburb near Arles called Trinquetaille, where is to be seen a magnificent column of marble. There it is said that the wicked populace tied up the blessed Genês before beheading him and even today one can see purple traces of his red blood. As for the Saint, he took his own head in his hands as soon as it was severed and threw it[1] into the Rhone; his body was carried by the river as far as the basilica of Saint Honorat, where it was given a very honourable sepulchre. As for the head, it descended the Rhone right to the sea and, carried by an angel, reached Cartagena in Spain.

From there one must pay a visit near Arles to the cemetery in a place called Aliscamps; the cemetery is over a mile long. Nowhere can you see in a cemetery so many large marble tombs spread out on the ground. They are all worked in different ways, carrying ancient inscriptions chiselled out in Latin letters, but the meaning is obscure. As far as the eye can see there are these rows of sarcophagi. In the cemetery are seven churches.

Also a visit should be paid to St Giles, pious confessor and abbot. For St Giles should be venerated by everyone and loved by all. Oh, how wonderful and worthwhile to visit his tomb! The very day one has really prayed with all one's heart one will be exorcised without any doubt. Who, then, will not want to pass much of his time in his presence? Who will not wish to kiss his tomb again and again? Who will not wish to embrace his altar and tell the story of his most holy life? A sick man puts on his tunic and is cured. By his inexhaustible virtue a man bitten by a serpent is cured. Another man possessed by a demon is delivered; a tempest on the sea is calmed. I think I shall be dead before I shall have time to recount all these marvellous happenings; there are so many which are so important.

A large shrine in gold lies behind his altar and above are the sculptured images of the six apostles, with on the same level a likeness cleverly sculptured of the Virgin Mary.

On another side of the shrine at the back there is a representation of the Ascension. In the first niche are the six apostles. In the second niche are the other six apostles in the same stance, but each one is separated by a column of gold. In the third niche Jesus is standing on a golden throne. Such is the tomb of the blessed St Giles, confessor, in which his venerable body reposes with honour.

And so may the Hungarians[2] flush with shame when they pretend that they have his body; may the monks of Chamelières feel sorely troubled when they allow their imagination to believe that they have the whole

---

[1] The column was still there in 1806; hence the church was called St Genês of the Column.

[2] He was especially popular in that country.

of his body; may the monks of St Sequanais be confounded who boast of having their chief; and in the same way may the Normans of Cotentin be troubled with fear when they brag that they have his body in its entirety; for under no circumstances can these holy bones – as all will witness – have been taken away from this spot. Some while ago certain persons did try fraudently to take the holy arm[1] of the blessed confessor from the precincts of the church and away to foreign climes; but they were quite unable to achieve it.

Those who go to St James by the Toulouse route should visit the body of the blessed Guillaume, the most holy standard bearer. Guillaume was a count in the entourage of King Charlemagne and a very brave soldier, most experienced in the art of war.

On the same route a visit should be paid to the bodies of the blessed martyrs Tiberius, Modeste and Florence, who in the reign of Diocletian suffered various tortures for the Christian faith. They lie on the banks of the Herault.

On the same road one should venerate the very holy remains of the blessed Sernin, bishop and martyr who, held by pagans on the capitol[2] of the town of Toulouse, was tied to a number of angry and untamed bulls and was then flung from the very height of the capitol down a mile-long flight of stone steps. He was enshrined in a splendid place near the town of Toulouse and a basilica was then built by his faithful followers in his honour.

Finally, the most precious body of the blessed Foy, virgin and martyr, was entombed by Christians in a valley commonly called Conques. Above was built a very fine basilica, and many blessings are bestowed on both the fit and the sick; in front of the portals of the basilica there runs an excellent spring, of which the virtues are even more admirable than one can express. Her Saint Day is celebrated on 6 October.

A visit must also be paid to the holy remains of the blessed Léonard, confessor, who came from a very noble Frankish family. He led for a long time a hermit's life at Noblat[3] in Limousin. Finally, in the region which belonged to him, he rests after a holy death and his holy remains have not left these parts.

So may the monks of Corbigny blush with shame when they pretend that they have the body of Saint Léonard, when, as we have seen above, not even the smallest of his bones or his ashes could have been taken away. The monks of Corbigny enjoy his benefits and miracles but they are deprived of the presence of his body. Not having his body they venerate as though it was *his* body the corpse of a certain Léonard who they say was brought to them from Anjou in a silver shrine. Thus it is

---

[1] Nonetheless, at the church of the Holy Sepulchre at Cambrias the relics of his arm were at one time venerated.

[2] Literally a citadel on the top of a hill.

[3] Now St Leonard de Noblat (Haute Vienne).

that those people of Corbigny are capable of a double crime, for they do not even show gratitude to him who has generously favoured them with miracles and they do not even celebrate his Saint Day but in their confusion render homage to another in his place.

After St Léonard the pilgrims should pay a visit to the town of Perigueux to the body of the blessed Front, bishop and confessor, who was consecrated bishop at Rome by the apostle St Peter and was dispatched to preach in this town with a priest named Georges.

They left together but, Georges dying *en route*, the blessed Front returned to the Apostle and announced his companion's death. St Peter therefore gave him back his stick saying, 'When you have placed your own stick on the body of your companion you will say "In virtue of the mission which you have received from the Apostle arise in the name of Christ and accomplish it".' Thus did it come to pass. His holy day is celebrated on 25 October.

Turning back somewhat we exhort those who go to St James by the Tours route to go and see at Orléans the wood of the Holy Cross and the chalice of St Euverte, bishop and confessor, of the Church of Ste Croix.

One day when St Euverte was saying Mass the hand of God appeared in the air above the altar with every appearance of being human and visible even to the assistants; and everything that the Bishop did the divine hand did also. From this we know that wherever a priest sings a Mass Christ sings it too. That is why St Isidor expressed himself in these terms: 'It is not on account of the holiness of a holy priest that a Mass is less good; neither is it less good on account of the wickedness of a bad priest.'

Also, the pilgrim who goes along this particular route should pay a visit along the banks of the river Loire to the greatly venerated body of St Martin,[1] bishop and confessor. It was he who gloriously resuscitated the dead and who gave back their health to those who wished it.

After this the pilgrim should visit the very holy body of the blessed Hilaire, bishop and confessor, in the town of Poitiers. There by his divine power he chased away a great number of serpents; it was he who at Poitiers gave back to a mother in tears her infant who had been stricken by a double death.[2] His Saint Day is 13 January.

Pilgrims should also go and see the venerable head of St John the Baptist, which was carried by monks from Jerusalem to a place called Angély in the Poitiers region. There a splendid basilica was magnifi-

---

[1] This, of course, is the great St Martin of Tours. We get our phrase 'A Martinmas Summer' (a very late one) from the legend that when St Martin's body was being carried along the Loire for final burial at Tours the summer flowers started to spring up along the route.

[2] The infant dying before being baptised had lost both the life of its soul and of its body.

cently constructed under his patronage; the very holy chief is venerated there night and day by a choir of a hundred monks and his presence is attested by innumerable miracles. On the sea he caused many tempests to become calm and gave back life to several dead people.

On the road to St James at Saintes the pilgrims should pay a visit to the body of the blessed Eutropus, bishop and martyr. His most holy passion has been told in Greek by his companion, St Denis, Bishop of Paris, who sent the story through the Pope St Clemen to his parents in Greece, who were already converted to Christ.

Then at Blaye, which is by the seashore, the pilgrims should ask for the protection of St Romain. In his basilica reposes the saintly body of Roland.[1] He was a martyr, that issue of a noble family, a count in the entourage of Charlemagne. He was one of the twelve companions in arms who, spurred on by the seal of his faith, went to Spain to repulse the infidels. His strength was so great that at Roncevalles, so it is recounted, he cleaved a rock in half with only three blows of his sword. It is also recorded that in sounding his horn[1] the power of his lungs split it down the middle and this ivory horn, thus rent, is to be seen at Bordeaux in the basilica[2] of St Seurin[3]; and on the rock at Roncevalles a church has been built.

[1] The body of Roland was indeed here as is recorded in 'The Song of Roland'. This is the relevant verse from Dorothy L. Sayers' translation (1957):

> 'So the King brings his nephew back to Blaye
> With his companion Oliver the Great,
> And the Archbishop that was so wise and grave.
> All in white tombs these noble men are laid;
> There they lie still good lords, in St Romayne's.'

Thousands of pilgrims visited this particular tomb and Francois I visited it in 1526, had it opened and contemplated the remains. Both an abbey and a church were built at Blaye; the former was destroyed by the English in 1441 and the latter demolished by Louis XIV in 1676.

Roland was buried at Blaye because it was the first place returning from Spain that was in Aquitaine, which province in the eleventh century (probably around the time 'The Song of Roland' was written; the battle at Roncevaux took place in the eighth century AD) recognised the authority of France, whereas Gascony, on the other side of the River Gironde, then recognised no authority save 'the grace of God and the sword of the Count.'

[1] Dorothy L. Sayers' again:

> Roland has set Oliphant to his lips,
> Firmly he holds and blows it with a will;
> High are the mountains, the blast is long and shrill;
> Thirty leagues the sound went echoing.'

The *Oxford Dictionary* says that Oliphant is an obsolete form of elephant and retained by historical writers to signify a horn or trumpet of ivory. Aimery Picaud may have got things muddled here, since the second time Roland blows his horn so hard he blows his brains out.

[2] Built on the site of a Gallo-Roman cemetery.
[3] Severinus, Bishop of Bordeaux, AD 410–20.

Then at Bordeaux a visit should be paid to the corpse of this blessed St Sevrin, bishop and confessor, whose day is 23 October.

Then in the region of the Landes of Bordeaux, in the little town of Belin, a visit must be paid to the bodies of the very holy martyrs Oliver,[1] Condebaun, King of Friesland, Ogier, King of Denmark, Arastain, King of Brittany, Gavin, Duke of Lorraine, and many other companions in arms of Charlemagne, who, having conquered the pagan armies, were massacred in Spain for their love of Christ.

They all lie at Belin in the same tomb and from it a very sweet-smelling perfume emanates which cures the sick.

Farther on in Spain one should visit the corpse of the blessed Dominique, who built the paved road between Najera and Redecilla, where he is buried.[2]

A visit should also be paid to the Sts Facundus and Primitif at the basilica,[3] which was built by Charlemagne. Near to their town there are fields planted with trees which it is said were originally the tips of lances stuck into the ground by the warriors, which then sprouted. Their Saint Day is 27 November.

From there one should go to León to visit the blessed Isidore, bishop and confessor and doctor, who instituted for his clergymen a very pious order.

Finally, it is the blessed James in the town of Compostela that one should visit with great devotion.

And may all these and other saints of God help us with their prayers to our Lord Jesus Christ, who lives with God in the eternity of centuries. Thus let it be.

Chapter Nine CHARACTERS OF THE TOWN AND THE CATHEDRAL OF THE APOSTLE ST JAMES IN GALACIA

Between the two rivers Sar and Sarela stands the town of Compostela. The Sar is to the east, between Mount Joy[4] and the town; the Sarela is to the west. The town has seven gateways or entrances. The first gateway is called the Gate of France.[5] The second is the Peño.[6] The

---

[1] The 'Song of Roland' had him buried at Blaye with Roland.

[2] The present town, Santo Domingo de la Calzada, is just half-way between these two places.

[3] At Sahagún.

[4] Or the Monte Gaudi, so called because of the joy evoked by the pilgrims when from this spot they first saw the spires of the church at Compostela. It is today called Monte del Gozo.

[5] Now called Puerte del Camino (Gateway of the Road), to the north-east of the town, and leading to the road used by pilgrims from France.

[6] Rocky, craggy.

third is the gateway beneath the home of the monks.[1] The fourth the Holy Pilgrim gateway.[2] The fifth the Fougeraies.[3] The sixth the Susannis.[4] The seventh the Macerelli[5] through which the precious liquor of Bacchus entered the town.

1 The Churches of the Town

In this town there are ten churches, of which the first is that of the glorious Apostle James.

The second built in the honour of the blessed Apostle is St Peter;[6] the third is St Michael; the fourth is St Martin; the fifth the Holy Trinity; the sixth Ste Susan;[7] the seventh St Felix; the eighth St Benedict; the ninth St Pelago; and the tenth the Virgin Mary.

2 Dimensions of the Cathedral

The basilica of St James measures in length fifty-three times the height of a man. In width it is forty times less one from the gate of France to the south gate; as for the inside height this is fourteen times the height of a man; but no one can measure what is the exterior length and height of the edifice.

In this church there is no fault; it is admirably constructed, large, spacious, light, with harmonious dimensions, well proportioned as to length, width and height; it is more splendid than words can express. It is even built on two floors,[8] like a royal palace.

Anyone who walks around the upper parts and who started off unhappy would leave happy and contented after having contemplated the perfect beauty of this church.

3 The Windows

The windows to be found in this church, all with stained glass, are sixty-three in number.

4 The Principal Doors

The church has three portals[9] and seven smaller ones.

5 The Fountain of Saint James

When we people from France wish to enter the basilica of the Apostle we go in from the north side. In front of the door by the side of the

[1] Now the St Martin gateway.
[2] Now Trinidad.
[3] Now Fajera, gateway to the west. The French word *fougeraie* means a fern patch. Fern in Spanish incidentally is Helecho or Polipodio.
[4] But now the Mamoa.
[5] Now the Mercado gateway.
[6] San Pedro d'Afora.
[7] This tiny Romanesque church can still be seen in the Pasco de Hernadura (horseshoe-shaped) on the outskirts of the town.
[8] At this period few houses had a second floor.
[9] Described in detail farther on.

road stands the alms house of the poorer pilgrims to St James and beyond extends a square reached by descending nine steps. At the end of the steps of this parvis[1] is to be found an admirable fountain which has no equal in all the world. It stands on a pedestal supporting a very beautiful basin in stone so large that fifteen men, I should think, could bathe in it with ease. At the top are four lions with four jets of water flowing from their mouths for the use of pilgrims and inhabitants. This water falls immediately into the basin beneath and from thence flows through a hole in the conch and is lost in the soil. Thus one cannot tell from whence comes the water and whence it goes; but furthermore this water is soft, fortifying, healthy, clear, excellent, hot in winter and fresh in summer.

6   The Parvis of the Town

After the fountain comes the parvis; its pavement is of stone and it is here that the pilgrims were sold the little scallop shells which are the insignia of St James. Also they sell leather bottles of wine, rope-soled shoes, scrips made of the skins of stags, straps, belts and all sorts of medieval herbs and other drugs and all kinds of other things. On the French road one meets money changers, inn-keepers and various merchants.

The dimensions of the parvis are as broad and as long as that of a stone's throw.

7   The North Door

After this parvis comes the north door,[2] called the Door of France; the two entrances have six columns each, some of marble and some of stone.

Above the column Our Lord is seated in His Majesty, giving benediction with the right hand and holding a book in his left. On the right are sculptures representing Adam and Eve sinning and to the left they are seen being chased from Paradise.[3]

Furthermore, there is sculpting all around of figures of saints, beasts, men, angels, flowers and other things too numerous to mention.

8   The Meridional Doorway

The southern[4] doorway of the apostles' basilica has two doors and four small inner doors. Above the right door the betrayal of Christ

[1] A square enclosing a church.

[2] This door has disappeared and was placed by the existing one – the Azabacheria – finished in the middle of the eighteenth century. Some of the old bas reliefs were re-used.

[3] This bas relief has been transported to the south side above the left door of the Doorway of the Silversmiths (*platerias*).

[4] Now the Doorway of the *Platerias* or Silversmiths.

has been sculptured in a remarkable way. On the jambs of this same door, seeming as though to guard the entrance, are two apostles.[1]

Then there are the wicked angels resembling monsters who show Christ stones and challenge Him to turn them into bread.

9   The Western Door

The west[2] door, with its two entrances, surpasses in beauty and work-manship of its decoration all the other doorways. It is flanked by columns of different kinds of marble and decorated with figures and various ornaments which are so rich and varied that we cannot describe them in detail.

10   The Towers of the Basilica

There are nine towers in the church; two above the door of the fountain[3] and two above the south door; two above the west door and two above the spiral staircase, and the largest surmounts the transept in the middle of the basilica.

11   The Altars of the Basilica

The altars of the basilica are: the altars of St Nicholas of the Holy Cross,[4] of St Foy,[5] of St Jean; then the altar of the Holy Saviour. Then there are altars of St Peter, St Andrew and St Martin;[6] then the altar of St John the Baptist.

12   The Body and Altar of St James

Up to now we have discussed the characteristics of the church; now we must deal with the venerable altar of the Apostle. In his holy basilica there reposes, according to tradition, the revered body of St James below the chief altar splendidly erected in his honour; it is enclosed in a marble tomb of excellent workmanship.

It is certain that his body is there and never to be moved, that is if one believes the witness of St Theodomir, bishop of this town, who dis-covered it formerly, and it has never been moved since.

May, then, those rivals beyond the mountains who pretend to have certain fragments of his body or keep relics of this saint be confounded.

To tell the truth, the body of the Apostle is here in its entirety; this

---

[1] All these bas reliefs, of which some are terribly mutilated, are still in place.

[2] This door, as described by the Guide, has entirely disappeared, being re-placed in the last third of the twelfth century by the Portal de la Gloria which still exists behind the actual façade.

[3] Now the north door.

[4] Almost certainly because a small piece of the true cross was venerated there.

[5] Whose tomb was at St Foy de Conques, France.

[6] The Sanctuary of the great French bishop St Martin of Tours was one of the stopping places on the Pilgrim's Road.

body divinely lit by paradisial carbuncles,[1] unceasingly favoured by soft perfumes, adorned with celestial torches and carefully watched by zealous angels.

Above his sepulchre is a modest altar which, so it is said, was erected by his disciples; no one for this reason has wished to destroy it.

And above there is another altar which is large and admirable, five palms high, twelve palms long and seven palms wide.

These at least are the measurements taken by my very own hands. And anyone who would, out of devotion to St James, send an altar cover or cloth to cover the altar of the Apostle should allow in dimension twenty-one palms long and nine palms wide, but if one wanted to offer for the love of God and the Apostle an adornment to cover the front of the altar one should see that it measures thirteen palms long and seven palms wide.

13 *The Front of the Silver Altar*[2]
The adornment on the front of the altar is a magnificent work in gold and silver.

14 *The Three Lamps*
In front of the altar of St James are three lamps of silver which are suspended in honour of Christ and the Apostles.

May the soul of King Alfonso of Aragon who, it is said, made this gift to St James, repose eternally in peace.

15 *Of the High Rank of the Church of St James and of its Canons*
At the altar of St James no one celebrates mass unless he is a bishop, archbishop, pope or a cardinal of that church.[3] In fact there are seven cardinals who celebrate the divine office at this altar and their privileges have been recognised by several pontifs, and in particular they have been confirmed by Pope Calixtus. And these rights are held by the church of St James and no one should, out of respect for the Apostle, try to take them away.

16 *The Lapicides*[4] *of the church. The Starting Date and Finishing Date in the Construction of the Church*
The stone masons who undertook the construction of the church were Master Bernard the Elder[5] – an inspired craftsman – and Robert, with

---

[1] In ancient times carbuncles were red or fiery precious stones such as sapphires, garnets, rubies and the like, but in the Middle Ages the word – as meant above – was also applied to a mythical gem which could emit light in the dark.

[2] This altar front has disappeared; it is thought that it was melted down at the end of the seventeenth century when the one that exists today was erected.

[3] The title 'cardinal' in this instance was purely an honorary one and carried none of the privileges of a cardinal of the Roman church.

[4] Stone-cutters; we would probably say masons.

[5] These two names indicate that they were of French origin.

the assistance of about another fifty lapicides[1] who all worked actively under the direction of Don Wicart, Master of the Chapter of Segeredo, and the abbot Don Gundesindo, in the reign of Alfonso, King of Spain, and of Diego I 'a valiant cavalier and generous man.

The church was started in 1078 and from the date when construction started until the date of the death of Alfonso, the valient and illustrious King of Aragón, there is a span of fifty-nine years; and until the murder of Henry, King of England, there are sixty-two years; and until the decease of Louis the Fat, King of France, there are sixty-three; and from the year when the first stone of its foundations was laid there are forty-four years.

17   The Rank of the Church of St James

One should not forget that the Blessed Pope Calixtus of worthy and saintly memory transferred to the basilica of St James and to the town the archipiscopal[2] rank formerly attached to the see of Merida.

Chapter Ten   THE NUMBER OF CANONS AT ST JAMES

According to tradition sixty-two canons are attached to this church. They follow the rules set by the blessed St Isidor of Spain, doctor. Each week they divide up the offerings made at the altar at St James; to the premier canon all the oblations are given during the first week; to the second canon all in the second week and so on down to the last.

Each Sunday tradition decrees that the offerings be divided into three parts; the first part to be given to the hebdomadary[3] for his work; the second towards building the church, and the third to the archbishop.

The oblations which come in during the week from Palm Sunday to Easter are allotted by right to those poorer pilgrims who are lodged at the hospice. But over and above this, one should at all times give to the poor who arrive at the hospice a tenth part of the offerings made at the altar of St James. In fact all poor pilgrims should from the very first night following the day of their arrival, and for love of the Apostle, be given free and complete hospitality.[4] The sick should be charitably cared for until they are cured, as is done at St Leónard.

[1] Aimery Picaud calls Bernard and Robert, as well as the fifty others, all paicides. Now, one supposes, they would be the architect, the master mason and the stone masons.

[2] This enactment by which Calixtus II conferred this rank on Santiago de Compostela in 1200 is conserved in the cartulary (a place where the records of a monastery are kept) of the Chapter House.

[3] A word special to the Roman Catholic church; a member of a chapter who took his (or her) weekly turn in the performance of the sacred rites of the church

[4] This is a cunning paragraph. Aimery Picaud was of course writing a guide book, but this makes one feel that he wanted as many people as possible to undertake the pilgrimage. He has pointed out some of the dangers of the journey, but here he redresses the balance by stressing the free welcome at the end.

Every pauper who arrives there receives his pittance. Furthermore, customs ordains that such offerings as are placed on the altar from the early hours of the morning until tierce[1] on every Sunday be given to the lepers of the town. And if any priest of this church committed any fraud in this matter or if he changed the destinations of these offerings which we have indicated, he would have to explain his sin before God.

Chapter Eleven THE RECEPTION OF PILGRIMS OF ST JAMES

Those pilgrims, be they poor or rich, who are returning from St James or who are on their way there should be received with respect and out of charity by everyone. For anyone who has received any pilgrims and lodged them in a friendly way will have St James also as host. Indeed, there are many people who have incurred the wrath of God in not wishing to receive pilgrims.

At Nantua, between Geneva and Lyon, a weaver once refused to give bread to a pilgrim who asked for it; he suddenly saw his cloth fall to the ground, it being cut in half.

Then at Villeneuve a poor pilgrim of St James went up to a woman who was watching over a loaf of bread which was under the hot cinders and asked for a crust for the love of St James. The woman replied that she had none to spare. As he left the pilgrim exclaimed 'May it please heaven to turn your bread into stone!' And the pilgrim walked on. When he was at a considerable distance from the house, the wicked woman approached the cinders to take out her bread and found only a round stone. With a contrite heart the woman now went to seek the pilgrim but could not find him.

That is why, whether they be rich or poor, the pilgrims of St James have the right to hospitality and a warm welcome.

Here ends the fourth book of the Apostle St James.
Glory to him who wrote it; glory also to him who reads it.

It is the church of Rome which was the first to welcome this book warmly. It can in fact be found in many places; for example at Rome, in the vicinity of Jerusalem, in France, in Italy, in Friesland and above all at Cluny.

[1] In ecclesiastical terms: the third hour of the canonical day ending at 9 a.m.

Bibliography

SPANISH TEXT

Arrondo, Eusebio Goicoechea, *El Camino de Santiago* (Editorial Everest, León, 1971).

Deben, Carmen, *El Hostal de los Reyes Catolicos en la Historia de Santiago* (Editorial Everest, León, 1968).

Deben, Carmen, *El Hostal de San Marcos* (Editorial Everest, León, 1972).

Eleizegui, Luis Maiz, *El Apostal Santiago y El Arte Jacobeo* (A. Torre, Madrid, 1953).

Ferrart, Enrique Lafuente, *El Libro de Santillana* (Diputaction Provincial Santander, Santander, 1955).

La Orden Miracle, Ernesto, *Santiago en America y en Inglaterra y Escocia* (Publicaciones Españolas, Madrid, 1970).

Lomax, Derek W., *La Orden de Santiago* (Consejo Superior de Investigaciones Cientificas, Madrid, 1965).

Lopez, G. Paz, *Portomarin* (Consejo Superior de Investigaciones Cientificas, Imp. Librera san Miguel, Madrid, 1961).

Martinez, Vicente, *El Camino de Santiago* (Publicaciones Españolas, (1965).

Michelin Guide, *España–Portugal* (Services de Tourisme, Paris, 1973).

Parga de, Luis Vazquez, Lacarra, Jose, M., and Rui, Juan Uria, *La Peregrinaciones a Santiago de Compostela* (Consejo Superior de Investigaciones Cientificas, Madrid, 1948).

Rodrigues, Manuel Vidal, *La Tumba de Apostol Santiago* (Tipografia del Seminano, Santiago, 1924).

Sampedro, Elias Valina, *El Camino de Santiago* (Consejo Superior de Investigaciones Cientificas, Madrid, 1971).

Sanchez, D. Jose M. Fernandez, *Guia de Santiago* (Tipografia del Seminano, Santiago, 1885).

Valina, Elias, *Caminos a Compostel* (Eliasvalina, 1971).

Vallejo de, Elena Garcia-Soto, *El Camino de Santiago y Miranda de Ebro* (A. Torre, Madrid, 1971).

Also various accurate and informative maps, guides, plans and leaflets on the Pilgrims' Road, published by the Direccion General de Promocion del Turismo.

ENGLISH TEXT

Atkinson, William C., *A History of Spain and Portugal* (Penguin Books, Harmondsworth, 1960).

Attwater, Donald, *A Dictionary of the Popes* (Burns Oates & Washbourne, London, 1939).

Baedeker, *Touring Guide – Spain and Portugal* (George Allen & Unwin, London, 1959).

Bone, Gertrude, *Days in Old Spain* (Macmillan & Co. Ltd., London, 1939).

Borrow, George, *The Bible in Spain* (John Murray, London, 1907).

Borrow, George, *The Zincalia* (John Murray, London, 1905).

Flower, Wickham, *Aquitaine* (Chapman & Hall London, 1897).

Ford, Richard, *A Handbook for Travellers in Spain* (Centaur Press Ltd, London, 1966).

Jessopp, The Rev. Augustus, *The Coming of the Friars* (Ernest Benn Ltd, London, 1885).

Keller, John Esten, *Alfonso X, El Sabio* (Twayne Publishers, New York, 1967).

Kendrick T. D., *St James in Spain* (Methuen & Co. Ltd, London, 1960).

King, Georgina Goddard, *The Way of St James* (Dutton, New York, 1920).

Lane-Poole, S., *The Story of the Nations: the Moors in Spain* (T. Fisher Unwin, London, 1887).

Layton, T. A., *Wines and Castle of Spain* (Michael Joseph, London, 1959).

Livermore, Harold, *The Origins of Spain and Portugal* (George Allen & Unwin, London, 1971).

Sayers, Dorothy L., *The Song of Roland* (Penguin Books, Harmandsworth, 1957).

Starkie, Walter, *The Road to Santiago* (John Murray, London, 1957).

Stone, J. S., *The Cult of Santiago* (London, 1927).

Thompson, E. A., *The Goths in Spain* (Clarendon Press, Oxford, 1969).

Thurston, Herbert S. J. and Attwater, Donald, *Butlers' Lives of the Saints* (Burns & Oates, London, 1956).

Watts, H. E., *The Story of the Nations: Spain* (T. Fisher Unwin, London, 1897).

Wiseman, F. J., *Roman Spain* (G. Bell & Sons Ltd, London, 1956).

FRENCH TEXT

Bottineau, Yves, *Les Chemis de Saint-Jacques* (Arthaud, Paris, 1960).

Ducrot, Janine, *Vers Compostelle* (Nouvelles Editions Latines, Paris, 1962).

Lopez, Roman Lopez Y, *Guide Officiel* (Saint-Jacques-de-Compostella, Paris, 1958).

Secret, Jean, *Saint Jacques et les Chemins de Compostelle* (Horizons de France, Paris, 1955).

Index